ROUTLEDGE LIBRARY EDITIONS: THE LABOUR MOVEMENT

Volume 42

LABOUR'S BATTLE IN THE U.S.A.

LABOUR'S BATTLE IN THE U.S.A.
The Fight for Industrial Unionism

J. RAYMOND WALSH

LONDON AND NEW YORK

First published in 1938 by George Allen & Unwin Ltd

This edition first published in 2019
by Routledge
2 Park Square, Milton Park, Abingdon, Oxon OX14 4RN

and by Routledge
711 Third Avenue, New York, NY 10017

Routledge is an imprint of the Taylor & Francis Group, an informa business

© 1938 J. Raymond Walsh

All rights reserved. No part of this book may be reprinted or reproduced or utilised in any form or by any electronic, mechanical, or other means, now known or hereafter invented, including photocopying and recording, or in any information storage or retrieval system, without permission in writing from the publishers.

Trademark notice: Product or corporate names may be trademarks or registered trademarks, and are used only for identification and explanation without intent to infringe.

British Library Cataloguing in Publication Data
A catalogue record for this book is available from the British Library

ISBN: 978-1-138-32435-0 (Set)
ISBN: 978-0-429-43443-3 (Set) (ebk)
ISBN: 978-1-138-32936-2 (Volume 42) (hbk)
ISBN: 978-1-138-32940-9 (Volume 42) (pbk)
ISBN: 978-0-429-44821-8 (Volume 42) (ebk)

Publisher's Note

The publisher has gone to great lengths to ensure the quality of this reprint but points out that some imperfections in the original copies may be apparent.

Disclaimer

The publisher has made every effort to trace copyright holders and would welcome correspondence from those they have been unable to trace.

LABOUR'S BATTLE IN THE U.S.A.

The Fight for Industrial Unionism

J. RAYMOND WALSH
HARVARD UNIVERSITY

LONDON: GEORGE ALLEN & UNWIN, LTD.

Published in the U.S.A. by
W. W. NORTON & COMPANY, INC.
under the title
C.I.O., INDUSTRIAL UNIONISM
IN ACTION

First published in Great Britain 1938

Printed in the U. S. A.

To my Mother and Father

PREFACE

WRITING this book had to be telescoped into a few short weeks. Yet its preparation was a grateful task: in part because the subject throbs with life; no less because it required scores of interviews with leaders and members of labor unions, unorganized workers, business men, and persons in positions of public responsibility. Preoccupied though they were with immediate and heavy obligations, their typical response was quick and cordial. Often the discussion broke away from the superficial to touch freely and deeply upon questions of sober import to Americans. The number of these people precludes other than a general, hearty acknowledgment of generous assistance given.

More specifically I wish to thank Mr. Joseph Broderick, a student of mine at Harvard, for much tedious reading of newspapers and for many suggestions about labor leaders and the steel strike; Mr. Lawrence McHugh, a colleague in the Department of Economics, with whom I discussed at length certain portions of Chapter VIII; Mr. Milton Wright, Jr., who assisted in gathering material and scrutinized most of the book with a careful and critical eye; and particularly Mr. Beverly M. Bowie, who has walked with me every step of the way. Without his generous and skillful assistance, this book would not have been completed at all. A kindly company, whose names may here remain untold, were friends indeed, when typing and correction were the order of the final days. To them my gratitude.

Needless to say, errors of fact and mistakes of judgment in this book are my own.

J. Raymond Walsh.

Cambridge, Massachusetts,
October 1937.

CONTENTS

	PAGE
Preface	7
CHAPTER	
I. Introduction	11
II. The Background of a Crisis	16
III. C. I. O. in Steel	48
IV. C. I. O. in Automobiles	96
V. Other Fields to Conquer	139
VI. C. I. O. Tactics	166
VII. The Employer Fights Back	196
VIII. The Economics of the C. I. O.	229
IX. The Politics of the C. I. O.	248
X. Problems Ahead	272
Notes on Sources	283
Index	287

I. INTRODUCTION

IN May, 1937, the Republic Steel Corporation refused to enter into any written agreement with the Steel Workers' Organizing Committee. The union called its members on strike to protest what it considered a patent violation of the law and a denial of their rights. Maintaining its refusal, the corporation continued to operate its plants with what forces it could muster. On Memorial Day a union meeting was held near the South Chicago shops—a meeting touched with holiday, and attended by women and children as well as several hundred men. The question was an important one: how could the workers who were still on the job be brought to see the seriousness of the issue and the need for full support of the union's protest against the company's stand? A mass demonstration was decided upon. Fifteen hundred strong they would march to the plant, past the gates, and establish a picket line with slogan bearers. The union speakers assured the crowd of their right to do this, their right to picket. The President had said so, the Wagner Act had said so. More important, the Chicago Corporation Counsel and the mayor had said that "peaceful picketing is legal." The police commissioner had supplemented this assurance with the opinion that the number of pickets need not be limited, as long as they were peaceful.

The crowd turned away from the meeting, and began its half-festive walk across the junk-strewn flats between it and Republic.

Before the plant, a large assignment of police, ostensibly there to protect property and strikers' rights, stretched like a blue coast line. The police were reached by the marchers. The leaders began earnestly to explain what they intended to do. To make their intentions clear they pointed to the slogans on their banners. No physical encounter occurred, except at one point where the men in front may have been pushed into the policemen's ranks by those behind.

Then, to the amazement of watchers and participants, of strikers and police who were later unable to explain it, tear gas was fired at the crowd. Events followed with bewildering rapidity. The crowd began to retreat before the gas had actually exploded. Isolated objects were thrown from the rear ranks of the strikers. A tree branch sailed through the air. A patrolman fired three revolver shots over the crowd. Only then came the "shower of missiles" about which police were subsequently to make so much. Simultaneously police revolvers barked twenty, fifty, a hundred, two hundred times, sending scores of bullets into the crowd, now in panic and making every effort to escape from the scene. No shots came from the strikers.

The marchers in front, attempting flight, were blocked by "the mass of tangled bodies of those already shot or fallen in their haste to flee." The police advanced in full line swinging their clubs and shooting, striking laggards to the ground, and clubbing the fallen where they lay. Within a minute or two those who could had got away. But ten lay dead or mortally injured; forty bore gunshot wounds, most of them in their backs; over a hundred, one a lad of eight years, were less seriously hurt. None of the twenty-two injured policemen was critically wounded. Not one had been shot.

For the injured strikers there was no police first-aid, no classification of the wounded, no rapid hospitaliza-

Introduction 13

tion. Union aid was not permitted. "Gratuitous clubbing," "deliberate brutality," "callous indifference to human life" are phrases which mark the pages of the U. S. Senate Committee inquiry.

Responsibility was clearly not that of the strikers, according to this report. Nor was it, in a simple sense, that of the policemen on duty. They were stationed in a highly charged atmosphere. But their superiors had failed to prepare them for it. They were equipped with tear gas. They had not been taught how or when to use it. They had been given hatchet handles instead of the customary nightsticks. They were not instructed what to do with them. Presumably they were assigned to guard plant and strikers alike. One of the rights of the strikers was peaceful picketing. Yet they were given no instructions as to what constitutes such picketing. They were not taught the law as it relates to civil liberties. The responsibility was clearly that of their superiors who displayed little regard for the difficulties involved. The fact that the tear gas and the hatchet handles were furnished by Republic raises a sober suspicion of criminal collusion against the strikers.

The defense of the police—that the crowd was armed, that it was in wild disorder, that it was organized like an army, that it was planning an attack on the plant and the police—was completely rejected by the Senate Committee. Too palpably it was an effort to escape the blame for what has accurately been reported as a "massacre."

One of the policemen on duty described the crowd as under the influence of a drug which made them chant as they came, "C. I. O.—C. I. O." So he and his fellows, unprepared to act intelligently, yet terrifyingly armed, drowned that chant in the explosion of tear-gas shells, the bark of revolvers, and thuds of flailing batons.

The chant of the marching men was silenced. But

14   C. I. O. Industrial Unionism in Action

the echoes rumbled out to forty-eight states and they did not die for a long time. For behind the crowd that was stampeded in Chicago on Memorial Day, stood and still stands the C. I. O.

And the C. I. O. is not so likely to be stampeded. In it now are thirty-two national and international unions, with a membership reaching toward four millions. The C. I. O.'s regional and sub-regional offices cover the country. The C. I. O.'s organizers are now established in every major industry. The C. I. O.'s national headquarters in Washington are the focal point of the organized labor movement in the United States and the nub of the largest political bloc in the country.

The C. I. O. is something new under the American sun. It has set out to do what the A. F. of L. had been either unwilling or unable to do—to organize the unorganized, to tackle the mass-production industries, not with the diversive craft union, but with a bigger cudgel —industrial unionism.

It is a new thing, because in the long, haphazard history of American unionism, these industrial areas have lain across the labor map as immense, sterile, openshop deserts, never organized and all but untouched. And, inside two scant years, the C. I. O. has enrolled five hundred thousand steel workers, three hundred and fifty thousand auto workers, seventy-five thousand rubber workers, four hundred thousand textile men, and ninety thousand transport workers. It has corralled one hundred thousand lumber workers, one hundred thousand cannery and agricultural workers, sixty thousand maritime men, forty thousand state and local employees, and invaded successfully a dozen different and contested fields. Within thirty days the C. I. O. defeated two of the proudest recalcitrant open-shoppers in the economy—General Motors and the United States Steel, their contracts covering a combined four hundred and fifty thousand men.

Today the C. I. O. overshadows the American economic and political scene. And the shadow stretches forward. Applications for charters from new groups of workers continue to flood C. I. O. headquarters; five hundred local industrial charters have been granted—but six hundred more have been asked for. The textile, maritime, state and federal, aluminum, agricultural, and transport industry drives have begun. Add to this the fact that the C. I. O. has projected a political agenda that threatens the disruption of the old parties, and one arrives at some notion of its potentiality.

To the industrialist, the emergence of this genie from the A. F. of L.'s old bottle may well seem the release of irresponsible and bolshevistic elements. To the liberal middle class, it may appear inevitable, possibly commendable, but latent with dangerous implications of social disruption and flouting of legal processes. To the worker it may look like a pretty good bet for his money.

But to all groups, no matter how disparate in viewpoint, the American labor movement has assumed a new maturity, a new significance. The American labor movement is now a fact. The C. I. O. is a fact. Where it will go from here, no one can reckon with easy accuracy. But that it holds important possibilities for the nation—of that there can be no smallest doubt.

II. THE BACKGROUND OF A CRISIS

1.

FOR ninety minutes by the convention hall clock William Green belabored his point before the United Mine Workers. They were threatening to secede from the American Federation of Labor, he said, along with the other seven unions which had formed the Committee for Industrial Organization. This "would be the greatest mistake ever made by a labor body," he warned them. There was room in the A. F. of L. for both types of unionism—craft and industrial. Why withdraw?

Why withdraw, he asked, mopping his brow, when the national A. F. of L. Convention decided by a majority of eighteen thousand to ten thousand not to organize the mass-production areas on industrial lines? Was the minority to force the majority? Was there to be a rift in the great family of labor? Was there to be a rift? ...

Mr. Green, president of the A. F. of L., sat down at last, damp, hoarse, exhausted. He had done what he could, he had given his best, and he wanted peace. He had been president for twelve years and nothing like this—this mutiny, this rebellion—had ever occurred before. Things had been peaceful, going along all right. The membership had dropped a good deal, it was still not very large, not over three and a half millions out of the nation's forty million eligibles; but what of that? They were doing their best. And now these hotheads, these impatient. ...

The Background of a Crisis

He watched John L. Lewis rise slowly and step forward on the rostrum. Lewis, stormy-browed, shaggy, looked out over the miners from Nanty Glo, from Wheeling, from Herrin, from Youngstown. How many, he asked them, how many delegates had changed their minds about the C. I. O., after having heard Mr. Green's speech?

Two men stood up.

How many believed he should dissolve the C. I. O.?

One delegate got up.

Then—"let those who believe the policies of this convention should be carried out, ARISE—"

With a shout the Convention came to its feet, stamping, clapping, whistling, yelling, seventeen hundred unanimous delegates. Smiling, John Lewis turned to Green: "You have received the answer of the United Mine Workers to your ultimatum!"

In the hubbub that followed, Mr. Green could be discerned shaking his finger under Lewis's nose and shouting that his remarks had been "unfairly" termed an "ultimatum." But the show was over. The miners had followed Lewis on that day, February 3, 1936, and the other unions of the C. I. O. came trooping after. There was a rift in Mr. Green's family of labor.

2.

That rift had been a long time in coming. The C. I. O.'s spectacular championing of the cause of industrial unionism has given the public to believe that this issue is something brave and new, and even some students of the labor movement think its appearance due to the post-war era's mass production and assembly-belts. But technological conditions called for industrial unionism many years ago when the Industrial Revolution, given a final impetus by the Civil War's stimulus to manufacturing, completed its transformation of the nation from an agricultural into a commercial economy, and created its own army of unskilled laborers to do its work.

What, then, has so retarded the coming of the C. I. O.? First, the American's dream of a steadily rising standard of living, given substance by our twentieth-century exploitation of inventions and the rich resources of a continent—a dream which has engendered individualism in employer and employee alike, causing the one to join with his fellow-industrialists to fight unionism, and the other to ignore it altogether in his rush to get ahead by himself. That dream, broken only in occasional slumps, persisted well into the Great Depression of 1929. It might have ended sooner had there been a labor movement to educate the common worker, leading him to an awareness of his actual and not his imaginary status.

But the American Federation of Labor was ill-conditioned to undertake such a task. It had come into being as an antidote to the immaturity and the extravagances of earlier movements, and it reacted as violently away from mass unionism as it could well manage. The Federation's foremost leaders were brought up on an ascetic creed of craft unionism, taught to confess contempt for their "quixotic" predecessors, schooled in the philosophy of Samuel Gompers, forty years president, who built upon the aristocracy, not the unskilled mass of labor.

Possibly even the old-line captains, however, might have turned apostate if unionism had ever been able to capture a key position where the industrial form of organization was inherently logical. Steel, in no merely figurative sense, set the pattern of the whole economy; once organized by the crafts, the nature of this industry would almost inevitably have forced an amalgamation

The Background of a Crisis

of the separate unions. The industrial unionists would then have had a pivotal point from which to apply their formula to textiles, farm machinery, clothing, machine tools, structural steel, foundries. But they never got the chance. The steel industry was smart and smashed the Amalgamated at Homestead in 1892, and finished the job of extinction in the "Marne" of 1901.

Federation leaders, guided by Gompers, stuck to their craft unionism for one good reason: within its limits, it worked. The craft unions survived, and that was a rare trait in the American labor movement. They charged high dues, paid good benefits, depended for their strength on the consciousness of a brotherhood of skill, of mutual if exclusive interest. They acted as a monopoly of labor to the degree that it was possible. They did not take in many members; but relative to workers in other organizations, these stuck.

It was this capacity to hold members that gave the crafts their soundest talking point. Perhaps some believed it possible to organize the unskilled; but they were convinced it was impossible to hold them. Such labor being easily replaceable, employers could find non-union substitutes if they were determined to prevent organization among the men. Again, since the unskilled workers' wages were small, their dues would have to be small, and their union insurance benefits non-existent; and often benefits are a union's strongest bond.

3.

In 1901 the U. S. Steel Corporation was formed, employing chiefly unskilled men. Even if there were craft lines still faintly discernible in this rationalized industry, could separate little groups of skilled workers even exist in the palm of giants such as this? As far back as 1877, there had been intimations that craft structure

20   C. I. O. Industrial Unionism in Action

was too frail a reed. For five grim years the depression of 1873 had ground its course, bringing in its wake a period of flaming, strident revolt.

It began with the "Molly Maguires." They took over the miners' strike of 1874-75, wrecked it from the inside, and with a fine impartiality exploited both the employers and strikers. It did not end with the hanging of ten Mollies and jailing of fourteen in 1876. The next year a strike on the Pennsylvania and the Baltimore and Ohio Railroads provoked general insurrection in a dozen cities. Mobs attacked and in many places routed police, militia, and the regular army. In Baltimore two companies of the 6th Regiment were nearly annihilated. When the local militia capitulated in Pittsburgh, national guardsmen imported from Philadelphia were besieged in the railroad roundhouses and machine shops —promptly fired by the crowd. Property damage reached about five million dollars.

Into this strange, unplanned, undisciplined upheaval was born the organization most often compared to the C. I. O.—the Knights of Labor. The child of America's industrial revolution, the Knights built upon a conviction that the worker's status had been fundamentally and irrevocably changed. He was now an anonymous worker, increasingly unskilled; he was a class. And he now confronted a powerful, distant, owning group, controlling larger and larger aggregates of capital and setting increasingly the pattern of political life.

The Knights of Labor stood for a united-we-stand policy. Their solidarity was only partly motivated by economics; the rest was religion. Industrial unionism was expressed in the most haphazard fashion. The Order comprised both mixed and trade assemblies in about equal proportions. The mixed assemblies were often simply a geographical conglomeration of unrelated trade union locals—much like the A. F. of L.'s city centrals. Only where the assembly happened to be located in an area dominated by one industry was it in any sense an industrial union. The trade assemblies, of course, were mostly gatherings of locals of but one craft. Moreover, the Knights contained some of the largest national craft unions in the country, such as the glassworkers and the shoemakers.

The Knights, then, were industrial unionists only in that they contained a few industrial and semi-industrial assemblies, and practiced a catholicity of membership which excluded only doctors, lawyers, bankers, and bartenders. But there the matter ended, for the Knights never really made up their minds as to what kind of unionists they were, and even suffered at times from doubts as to whether their main interest was unionism anyway. Frequently they seemed to think co-operation, agrarianism, prohibition, or third parties more vital. Like Stephen Leacock's energetic character, the Order was wont to leap upon its horse and dash madly off in all directions.

Moreover, there was always some difficulty in determining what the Knights thought about anything, because of an ideological gap between the leaders and the led. The executives wanted reformism; the rank-and-file did not know whether it did or not. The executives denounced and repudiated strikes; the locals conducted some of the most hair-raising and successful strikes of the century. The executives preached centralization; the local units practiced autonomy. The executives decried the narrowness and divisive nature of the craft unions; the trade locals continued to appear and flourish.

The Knights rose spectacularly; they declined as suddenly. Reaching 729,677 members in 1886, they were practically extinct four years later. Before the impact of the collapse of the Southwest railway strike and their

22 C. I. O. Industrial Unionism in Action

implication in the Haymarket bombing, the Knights' flimsy structure founded on ill-assimilated idealism and low dues faded abruptly.

It was the national craft unions, however, that delivered the fatal blow. Led by the printers, the iron and steel workers, and Samuel Gompers among other leaders of the cigar-makers, these unions set up the American Federation of Labor in 1886. To their ranks they later added the carpenters, cigar-makers, shoe and leather workers, the brewers, and the miners.

The essence of the split between the unions and the Knights is less a matter of irreconcilability of principle than of clarification. Certain elements in the Knights were, to be sure, opposed to the unions. But there would have been room enough for both parties had there not been as well a deep-rooted intent on the part of the unions to get clear of the Knights' fuzzy political radicalism and its concern with everything at once and with nothing in particular.

The national unions, in short, were at last ready for some tough-minded business unionism, with a strong and exclusive emphasis upon tight internal organization, craft autonomy, and collective bargaining. This last is important. The Knights had struck often enough, and sometimes won concessions. But such action was customarily regarded as extracurricular activity, and any long-term bargaining as a compromise with capitalism. For the Knights had not yet made their peace with the wage-system. In the back of their minds was still the confused hope of becoming their own masters again, and from this desire sprang their interest in cooperatives and their religious belief in the solidarity of labor.

The A. F. of L., however, was now prepared to come to terms with the industrialists and to haggle over the spoils of exploiting a continent. From the Knights'

The Background of a Crisis

motto of "An injury to one is the concern of all," it turned to its own banner of *"Sauve qui peut,"* and under the aggressive leadership of Gompers the Federation proceeded slowly and with sureness to build up highly centralized national unions and highly decentralized federal authority.

The lines which were then laid down have scarcely been shifted since. The Executive Board of the A. F. of L., with the exception of its president, is nothing more than a rough council of equal captains, heads of the nationals, each being far more intimately responsible to his union than to the organized labor movement at large. For membership in the A. F. of L. is not direct but by membership in an affiliated body, and the carpenter, Joe Doakes, has no more control over the machinist, Vice-President Wharton, than he has over Admiral Byrd.

Consequently the possibility of effective unified national action is quite ephemeral. The Executive Board, having practically no power independent of its constituent unions, can undertake little independent organizing activity. It can afford no sufficient body of organizers, for one thing; in addition, it has not the requisite authority. Because of this, most of the organizing of new territories must be conducted by any union who claims jurisdiction there; and if the union doesn't care, or is unable, to press its jurisdiction, or if no unions have clear jurisdiction in the field, then that area will likely go unorganized.

4.

No one will care to underestimate the sensible qualities of the A. F. of L., nor to play down its record. It took the American labor movement back to the fundamentals of union activity, and what is conspicuous in

24   C. I. O. Industrial Unionism in Action

the broken line of trade union development it kept alive. Other organizations before it had not managed even to survive. If it was exclusive, if it maintained only an "aristocracy of labor," yet that was more than any other body had been able to maintain at all. If its aims were limited, its execution was dogged.

Though this be true, yet those limitations were bound to provoke recurrent attempts from outside the A. F. of L. to do the job it refused to do in the unorganized areas. The first attempt at industrial unionism came with Daniel De Leon's Socialist Trades and Labor Alliance which, however, foundered in its preliminary task of razing the old craft unions before building bigger ones.

Closely succeeding it came the Western Federation of Miners, in 1895, which comprised pick and-shovel workers, smeltermen, millmen and engineers. Originally it had been under the wing of the A. F. of L. But it broke away soon—and for reasons which composed a vital criticism of the A. F. of L. The W. F. M. asked for Council aid in its strike at Leadville, Colorado, and didn't get it. The A. F. of L. simply couldn't give it, as William Z. Foster was to find in 1919. And the W. F. M. got no more assistance from those quarters in the years up to and especially including 1904 when the Mine Owners Association was crushing out the mine unions with vigilantes, deputies, company police, militia, federal troops, and subservient courts. In all those bloody years in Salt Lake, Coeur d'Alene, Telluride, Idaho Springs, and Cripple Creek, no effective word or action came from the A. F. of L. while the most powerful union in the West was being outlawed and broken.

The fragments, however, gathered in Chicago with the American Labor Union, brewery men, and railroad men to form the Industrial Workers of the World in 1905, and to give the labor movement its most dramatic

The Background of a Crisis

presentation of the idea of "one big union." By 1907, however, the machinists and the W. F. M. had withdrawn, and in 1908 the brewery men retreated into the A. F. of L. This left the I. W. W. as an organization of "wobblies"—casual laborers, lumber-jacks, dock workers and hoboes.

All told, the I. W. W. sponsored about a hundred and fifty strikes, the most spectacular being those in Goldfield, Nevada (1906-7); in Lawrence, Massachusetts (1912), among the textile workers; in Louisiana the same year among lumber workers; in Paterson, New Jersey, with the silk workers; and among the miners of the Mesabi Range in 1916. The I. W. W.'s membership never rose much over sixty thousand, it never created a stable organization or achieved much of tangible value, its forces and temper being strongly psychotic and its philosophy anarchistic. But in the intangibles its contribution was considerable, for it kept alive and articulate the issues into which the C. I. O. at long last has breathed new life.

The World War and its accompanying criminal syndicalism laws destroyed the I. W. W., 166 of the leaders being indicted, and 93 convicted; some of them, including Bill Haywood, receiving twenty years. But the "opposition" spirit of the I. W. W. lived on in the postwar Communist party and in the progressive wings of the regular unions.

Within the A. F. of L. itself, meanwhile, the issue of industrial unionism cropped up recurrently. The Convention of 1900 approved the principle of amalgamating related crafts, but the Convention of the following year adopted the "Autonomy Resolution" upholding the strict thesis of craft separatism. In 1903 Samuel Gompers declared that "the attempt to force the trade unions into what has been termed industrial organization is perversive to the history of the labor movement."

26 C. I. O. Industrial Unionism in Action

But whether or not Mr. Gompers approved, the drift was against him. The central problem of craft organization—jurisdictional disputes—was coming to be exceedingly conspicuous. The A. F. of L. had contented itself with organizing a rather small "family of labor," as they were fond of terming it; but if peace could not be kept even within the bosom of this intimate group, the labor movement was in a bad way. So a compromise movement toward amalgamation commenced. By 1905 the Building Trades Alliance had been formed, to be supplanted by the institution of a Building Trades Department within the A. F. of L. In 1908 a Metal Trades Department was set up. Neither of these departments came within hailing distance of solving their problems, since they were given the problems but not the authority to enforce their decisions. In every major instance, the Executive Council of the A. F. of L. backed up the recalcitrant national union which flouted the decree of the arbitrators.

The slow movement of amalgamation kept on, however. By 1915 only 28 of about 133 national unions could still be considered as run on strictly craft lines. The brewers and the miners were out-and-out industrial unions, and the Amalgamated Iron, Steel, and Tin Workers Association was at any rate industrial in theory.

As early as 1912 it had become apparent, nevertheless, that amalgamation was not enough. To the Convention of that year the miners brought a resolution to revamp the Federation's structure along industrial lines and saw it voted down, 10,934 to 5,929.

But industrial unionism had found supporters. Mr. William Green, himself, was one of them. In 1917 he published a quite succinct defense of it:

"The organization of men by industry rather than by crafts brings about a more perfect organization, closer cooperation, and tends to develop the highest forms of organi-

The Background of a Crisis 27

zation. The causes of jurisdictional disputes are considerably decreased, and in many industries can be eliminated altogether...

"When men are organized by industries they can concentrate their economic power more advantageously than when organized into craft unions... By this process the interest of the unskilled worker is given as much attention as that of the skilled worker. It is indeed... a policy of all for each and each for all...

"The advantage of such a form of organization is so obvious that one can scarcely conceive of any opposition thereto. ... Much complaint has been directed against craft organizations because little regard has been given to the problems of the unskilled workers. It is becoming more and more evident that if unskilled workers are forced to work long hours at low wages, the interests and welfare of the skilled worker are constantly menaced.

"In the development of industry and organization the tendency is toward concentration and perfection.... Hence the reason why organized labor is gradually passing from craft organization to the more effective industrial forms of organization...."

Mr. Green's emphatic words lent a wry note to the disastrous campaign to organize the steel industry in 1919. A. F. of L. membership was booming in those war years, rising from 1,996,004 in 1913 to 3,260,068 in 1919, which meant that the percentage of organized to unorganized labor in the United States had risen from about 8 per cent to the grandiose figure of about 16 per cent.

Yet the energy released by these successes spilled over into a movement to invade no-man's-land—steel. Since 1909 the Amalgamated Iron, Steel, and Tin Workers Association had been nearly dead, having been routed at Homestead in 1892 and variously defeated in 1901, 1902, and 1909. But now, with the Wilson government proclaiming labor's right to organize and bargain

28 C. I. O. Industrial Unionism in Action

collectively, a national committee of the A. F. of L., headed by William Z. Foster, pumped life into the old Amalgamated.

To say that the handling of this strike by the A. F. of L. was significant is to reveal the inadequacy of language. In the chill clammy light of a great failure, two points lay pitilessly exposed: the inertia and weakness of the Executive Council; and the folly of craft structure in a tremendous mass-production industry.

From 1919 there stretches a long arid period in which the A. F. of L. forgot structural problems in its fight to hang onto wartime gains. Occasional resolutions raking the crafts came before the conventions—to be shelved or killed. And the two industrial unions in the Federation had their own difficulties. The brewers were sunk in the depths of Prohibition, and the miners, in a sick industry, were struggling with internal dissension. The Federation's own rolls dropped from the 1920 high of 4,078,740 to the 1929 figure of 2,933,545; while the miners' muster fell from its customary 400,000 to 220,000.

The depression added insult to considerable injury. The Federation shrank by another eight hundred thousand, and the soft-coal miners were extinguished altogether. In these hand-to-mouth days self-preservation was necessarily the only issue. Industrial unionism had to wait upon the coming of the N. R. A.

5.

On June 16, 1933, Section 7A of the National Recovery Act became effective, providing that "employees shall have the right to organize and bargain collectively through representatives of their own choosing, and shall be free from the interference, restraint, or coercion of employers of labor, or of their agents, in the designation

The Background of a Crisis 29

of such representatives or in self-organization or in other concerted activities for the purpose of collective bargaining or other mutual aid or protection."

As it turned out, this law meant little enough as a guarantee of those rights. For the government, worried about the constitutionality of the whole Act, was unwilling to go to the courts to uphold these specific provisions. This became so apparent, in fact, that regional directors of the Labor Board began unofficially to warn would-be strikers to stay on their jobs because there was no assurance whatever of Washington's backing them up.

But if Section 7A proved a dud in this respect, the shell looked sufficiently explosive from a distance to have a remarkably invigorating effect on the labor movement. The A. F. of L. jumped to nearly four million members in eighteen months. For the workers, interpreting the Act as the perennial Magna Charta and eager to retrieve their depression wage cuts, took it enthusiastically at its face value and flocked into the unions, confident that the national administration was now behind them.

It was interesting to note where the largest increases centered. Membership in three industrial unions of the Federation—the United Mine Workers, the International Ladies Garment Workers, the Amalgamated Clothing Workers, rose 132 per cent between 1933 and '35; while the craft unions gained 13 per cent. And in the new service unions, organized on a semi-industrial basis, the rise in membership was about 94 per cent.

In fairness to the crafts, it must be said that the industrials were the ones which had dropped most to begin with, and much of their accruals made up old losses. In the coal areas, John L. Lewis plastered the mines with the thesis: "The President Wants You to Join." It worked. It was exceedingly important that it should have worked, for it was from the U. M. W.'s surplus energy that the C. I. O. drive was to stem; and until the miners had assured their own security, they could do little for anyone else.

Organization did not confine itself to the old molds. Attempts were now begun again to unionize the steel and auto industries, which had been all but untouched since the War. In steel the "drive" fell nominally under the leadership of Mike Tighe, president of the Amalgamated; Mr. Tighe was anything but ardent, and the push was taken over by the rank-and-file unions which mushroomed all over the steel territories. These rebellious lodges pulled a number of strong strikes, repeatedly sabotaged either by the administration, which wanted to avoid all possible friction with the industrialists it was trying to tame in the codes, or by Mr. Tighe and Mr. Green, who simply wanted no trouble of any kind. The upshot was collapse. It was becoming customary under the Amalgamated.

In autos, the Mechanics Educational Society, the Associated Automobile Workers, and the Automobile Industrial Workers Association sprouted under the rays of the Recovery Act. All of them were industrials, all of them were independent competitors to the A. F. of L. crafts.

In rubber, likewise, the independent unions took the lead away from the Federation, organized forty thousand workers and applied for federal charters. Promptly the A. F. of L. accepted them—to split them into sixteen jurisdictions. And as promptly the unions atrophied.

6.

It was this situation, duplicated a dozen times over in other sectors of the economy, which faced the delegates in San Francisco that October in 1934. The Convention

The Background of a Crisis 31

resolved that: "The executive council shall at the earliest practicable date inaugurate, manage, promote, and conduct a campaign of organization in the iron and steel industry." That was specific. But more generally, a resolution was pushed through the Convention which directed that the principle of vertical unionism be applied to all the basic industries. Further, it directed the Executive Council to grant industrial charters to the auto, rubber, and cement workers.

To the jubilant "industrial" bloc at the Convention it seemed all over but the shouting; they had won, hands down. But what man had proposed, the Executive Council disposed. They gave the auto and rubber workers charters considerably limiting their scope, and utilized to the full the "rider" which had been tacked onto the resolution—"and to protect the rights of existing craft unions." They sanctioned craft unions in carrying out membership raids on the new unions as they had done on the old federal locals. The customary formula was carried through to the customary conclusion: the federal locals corralled the members; the crafts raided them, split them a dozen different ways; and the organizing movement broke up.

Nor did the Executive Council carry out the spirit of the steel resolution. They did not lay down industrial unionism as the structure. Rebellious lodges which tried to organize their areas along these lines were booted out of the Amalgamated, and President Tighe relapsed into inactivity, nursing a membership of less than nine thousand in an industry of four hundred and fifty thousand.

The paper victory and practical defeat of the industrial unionists at San Francisco brought them to the 1935 Atlantic City convention in a more realistic temper. Behind them was a year of frustration, retreat, and disillusionment. They were in no mood to be stalled off.

32   C. I. O. Industrial Unionism in Action

With some bitterness, Mr. Lewis sighed: "Well, a year ago at San Francisco I was a year younger and naturally I had more faith in the Executive Council. ... At San Francisco they seduced me with fair words. Now ... I am enraged and I am ready to rend my seducers limb from limb, including Delegate Woll."

The main gale blew up when the Resolutions Committee brought back its majority report.

This, framed by Matthew Woll and John Frey, secretary of the Metal Trades Department (which had just broken a strike of the semi-industrial union, the International Mine, Mill, and Smelter Workers), urged that the pro-craft San Francisco declaration be reaffirmed, and that all the industrial resolutions be non-concurred with. In short, that craft structure was adequate, and industrial unionism unnecessary. There seemed to be no suspicion on the part of the majority signers that they might be affixing their names to the death-warrant of the A. F. of L.

The minority report, submitted by C. P. Howard of the Typographical Union, John L. Lewis of the United Mine Workers, David Dubinsky of the Garment Workers, Frank Powers, A. A. Myrup, and J. C. Lewis, was forthright:

"The fact that after fifty-five years of activity and effort we have enrolled under the banner of the American Federation of Labor approximately 3,500,000 of the 39,000,000 organizable workers is a condition that speaks for itself."

It instructed the A. F. of L. to "recognize the right of these workers to organize into industrial unions and be granted unrestricted charters which guarantee the right to accept into membership all workers employed in the industry or establishment without fear of being compelled to destroy unity of action through recognition of jurisdictional claims made by National or International unions."

The Background of a Crisis

Labor oratory is turgid but frequently powerful. In the debate which succeeded the submission of these reports, the big guns of both camps boomed. Swinging into action in his best baroque style, John Lewis cut loose:

"Their (the crafts') unions are already jeopardized and their membership is already jeopardized because unless the A. F. of L. may be successful in organizing these unorganized workers, it is extremely doubtful whether many of these organizations, now so perfect, now so efficient, will long be permitted to endure... There are forces at work in this country that would wipe out, if they could, the labor movement of America, just as it was wiped out in Germany, or just as it was wiped out in Italy. There are those of us who believe that the best security against that menace and against that trend and against that tendency is a more comprehensive and more powerful labor movement....

"Methinks that upon this decision of this Convention may rest the future of the A. F. of L."

Replying to Lewis, John Frey (for some reason he is known as Dr. Frey, the intellectual of the Federation) argued that industrial unionism would provoke its own jurisdictional difficulties. The auto industry has companies which operate their own steel mills and coal mines—shall these men belong to the auto or the steel and mine unions?

No excessive importance was attached by his hearers to this point, but they did give attention when Dr. Frey said he had heard that Lewis was planning to secede from the Federation if the Convention did not meet his demands. This, Frey believed, was most likely a bluff. However—"if we should for a moment yield to those who come into our convention with the threat of secession if they fail to secure their purpose, if we yield, we surrender every drop of independent blood that ever flowed through our veins."

Murray of the Mine Workers felt a little of the same blood heating his own veins. He was annoyed by the craft unions' plea that industrials would invade their jurisdiction. He called it disingenuous since, in the areas to be organized, the crafts had no members and had shown no capacity to acquire them by any other technique than raiding the federal—that is, industrial—locals.

In Aliquippa and Ambridge, Pennsylvania, the steel workers had formed an independent union, asking to be admitted into the A. F. of L. on an industrial basis. They had enrolled sixty-five hundred out of eight thousand men in an area which ranks second only to Harlan County, Kentucky, in coercion and intimidation of unions. And then with their usual alacrity the A. F. of L. crafts answered the call of the union by sending in their men, siphoning off those under their nominal jurisdiction, and decimated the union. Now, said Murray, "they have no organization, they have no charter, they have no independent union, they have no craft union, they have nothing. They are today where they were before they started their campaign of organization 18 months ago...."

A crude test of strength now cut across the war of words and the battle of hyperboles. The motion to adopt the minority "industrial" report was put to a question. And lost, by 18,024 to 10,933.

7.

The defeat came as no surprise. The margin did. No one expected the industrialists could corral so many votes. Their actual strength lay largely in the new federals, in the city centrals and state federations; and none

The Background of a Crisis

of these groups has any voting power, the federals possessing no votes at all, the centrals and federations only one each—while such a craft union as the Brotherhood of Carpenters can itself swing two thousand votes.

The Convention had settled the issue, but the sniping continued. If the "industrialists" could not carry the day, they could at least fill it up with statements of their position. In the discussion which broke out over the petition of the auto workers for an industrial charter, the firing was turned over to newer members of the Federation.

Delegate Shipley's story was not untypical: "I work in the (auto) plant every day. Then I work half the night trying to keep my organization together, with the help of other men who are working during the day. What do the workers say? Some of them don't belong yet. They say—'When you can come back and tell us that we all belong in your organization, we will belong.' What will they tell you further? And this isn't a threat, but they tell us this: 'Well, if you want to segregate us and break us up, to hell with all of you!'"

Mortimer of the auto workers, however, fired the most forceful broadside of the debate. He warned the Federation against further craft raids upon the federal locals: "We are determined upon one thing, whether you like it or not—we don't intend to give them up without a battle."

When the craftsmen had digested that, they heard some more:

"Make no mistake about it, gentlemen, the automobile industry is going to be organized, if not by us, then by somebody else, because the economic pressure in the industry is so great, it is so terrific, it is inexorably driving all the workers into the organization. They will not go into craft organizations because they believe—and I believe they are right—that craft unionism means confusion in the industry...

"How are you possibly going to achieve unity—and unity we must have—unless you change your methods? The automobile manufacturers have achieved that unity. They are a unit in their opposition to labor... They are all agreed, and unless we are able to achieve this unity in the auto industry, we won't have a Chinaman's chance. We know the only way to achieve this unity is through industrial organization. There is no other way..."

Mortimer (since become vice-president of the C. I. O. auto union, three hundred and fifty thousand strong) leaned forward and in words that many delegates were to remember a long while pegged out the plea of the auto workers:

"If you want us to organize this great basic industry, then, for God's sake, let us solve the problem in our own way!

"You men may have had years of experience in the labor movement. That is the trouble—your experience goes back too far. We are working in the industries; we know the industries; we understand the workers' psychology, which you have forgotten long ago, and *it is a significant fact that every dual movement in the automobile industry today is based upon industrial unionism,* and we certainly cannot organize that industry unless you give us that same right."

They were not, of course, given "that same right." The motion to tender the auto workers an industrial charter was lost, 104 to 125. The auto workers could not vote for what they wanted; the votes were in the hands of the national crafts. The cards were stacked in advance.

8.

The blow that Mr. Lewis was to give the Federation was not long in coming. The day after the Convention broke up, the industrial bloc set a date on which to confer, and on November 9, 1935, they set up the Committee for Industrial Organization in Washington. At that time this committee was functioning and hoped to continue to function within the A. F. of L. It was to be the Executive Council and not the C. I. O. which insisted upon its interpretation as a rival and dual organization.

Composed of eight international unions, the C. I. O. had as its director John Brophy; chairman, John L. Lewis; and secretary, C. P. Howard. The original unions were: the United Mine Workers; the Amalgamated Clothing Workers (pres., Sidney Hillman); the International Ladies Garment Workers (pres., David Dubinsky); the International Typographical Union (pres., C. P. Howard); the Oil Field, Gas, Well, and Refinery Workers (pres., Harvey C. Fremming); the United Textile Workers (pres., Thomas F. McMahon); the United Hatters, Cap, Millinery Workers (pres., Max Zaritsky); the International Mine, Mill, and Smelter Workers (pres., Thomas Brown). These men announced the purpose of the committee:

"To encourage and promote organization of the workers in the mass production and unorganized industries of the nation and affiliated with the A. F. of L. Its functions will be educational and advisory, and the committee and its representatives will co-operate for the recognition and acceptance of modern collective bargaining in such industries."

Two weeks later Lewis wrote Green: "Dear sir and brother: Effective this date, I resign as a vice-president of the American Federation of Labor." This was his reply to a letter Green had circulated to all the heads of the C. I. O. unions, warning them of setting up an organization within an organization and provoking dual unionism. "There is no danger to the American Federation of Labor," Green smiled as he prepared to send

38 C. I. O. Industrial Unionism in Action

Lewis's resignation to the Executive Council at Miami. "It has lasted half a century. All I want to do is maintain solidarity and warn of the dangers."

Countering, the C. I. O. mailed copies of its minority Convention report to local union bodies all over the country, while on the radio Lewis declared: "We do not believe any craft union, as is now the case in the American Federation of Labor, should be permitted to interfere, through paper jurisdictional claims or otherwise, with the organization of the great majority of American wage and salary workers in our basic manufacturing and mining industries."

Lewis sounded the first real notes of conflict on December 5: "I do not know if the representatives of the craft organizations may lash themselves into such a mental state as to believe that policies of reprisal are justified. If they do, may I warn them that they stand to injure themselves more than their fancied adversaries."

He followed it up with a public letter to Green that stung:

"It is bruited about that your private sympathies are and individual inclinations lie with the group espousing the industrial type of organization, while your official actions and public utterances will be in support of their adversaries. Such a policy is vulnerable to criticism and will hardly suffice to protect you against advocates of the craft philosophy. They may feel rightfully that more is due them than perfunctory support.

"Why not return to your father's house? You will be welcome. If you care to dissociate yourself from your present position, the Committee for Industrial Organization will be happy to make you its chairman in my stead. The honorarium will be equal to that you now receive. The position would be as permanent as the one you occupy."

The suggestion that the proffered position "would be

The Background of a Crisis 39

as permanent as the one you occupy," may have deserved more attention than Mr. Green at that stage was willing to give it. At any rate, he declined the offer peremptorily.

9.

Ten days later Dr. John Frey laid down the ideological lines of the A. F. of L.'s defense. He shunted aside the question of industrial unionism and declared the sole issue to be that "a minority of international unions have organized for the purpose of setting aside these decisions (by the 1934 and '35 Conventions) and of imposing their will upon the majority in ruthless disregard of the long established trade union policy of reaching decisions on policy and methods by the expressed desire of the majority." He added that the new movement was "also giving encouragement and satisfaction to the Communist party."

The C. I. O. was not worried very much, one way or another, as to whether or not Mr. Browder felt encouraged. And as to the will of the majority, they were beginning to feel that unity can be bought at too great a price. But nominally, as Philip Murray told the Convention of the radio workers, "no hint or threat of leaving the A. F. of L. has been made."

January saw the Executive Council of the Federation meet in Miami. On the twenty-second it condemned the C. I. O. by a vote of eleven to six—which was more unanimous than it looked: five of the six nays simply objected because the censure was not stronger, and because a committee of three was appointed to confer and compromise with Lewis.

The Miami meeting did not break up until it had dispensed a few neat strokes: it refused an industrial charter to the radio workers, it decided to organize the auto industry on craft lines, and it gave Mr. Wharton's machinists the right to raid the auto workers' federal locals for all men employed in parts plants.

Repercussions from the Council's dissolution decree came quickly. In convention at Washington the United Mine Workers voted with considerable noise to withhold forty-eight thousand dollars dues from the Federation, while Lewis bellowed that if the Convention approved his actions "all the members of the Executive Council will be wearing asbestos suits in hell" before they would make him back down; and Murray said that if the Federation continued to carp at the C. I. O., "I say to you as an officer of the United Mine Workers of America, the sooner we get to hell away from there the better off we will be."

The implications of the Mine Workers' adopting the C. I. O. platform, with its promise of A. F. of L. reprisal, were made plain enough by Lewis. "Are you willing to assume that responsibility?" he asked the assembled miners. They roared affirmation. "If you are, I am," he yelled back. "If you do, it will mean a vote for more enlarged and progressive unions—*with* the A. F. of L. if it will, and *without* it if it prefers."

Two days later came Green's intrepid personal appeal to the U. M. W. convention, and the miners' stormy answer.

Events followed thick and fast. The radio workers in February rejected the A. F. of L.'s demand that they dissolve into the Brotherhood of Electrical Workers. The National Executive Board of the American Flat Glass Workers approved the Lewis plan for expansion in their field on an industrial basis. On the twentieth Green dispatched a note to 1,354 local and federal unions, 49 state federations of labor, and 730 city centrals, warning them against any act of affiliation with the C. I. O. or any act of assistance whatsoever.

Next day the C. I. O. responded with its official an-

The Background of a Crisis 41

swer to accusation of dualism. Giving a number of specific replies to specific charges, it concluded more generally that "we wish to emphasize again that we are trying to remove the roots of dualism by making it possible for the millions of mass-production workers now outside the American Federation of Labor to enter on the only basis they will accept—industrial unions."

The C. I. O.'s first stage had passed. From "education" it now passed to the preliminaries of organization. On Washington's Birthday Lewis proposed to the A. F. of L. that a fund of one million five hundred thousand dollars be gathered with which to organize the steel industry—the C. I. O. to give five hundred thousand dollars on the understanding (a) that organization would be on industrial lines; (b) that "a responsible, energetic person" would be chosen to co-operate with an advisory committee of the unions supporting the drive. The provision concerning the "responsible, energetic person" was not too opaquely designed to eliminate Mike Tighe, ancient head of the Amalgamated.

Jammed into a corner by this offer, Mr. Green stalled for time, postponing action until the Executive Council met again in May, and hinting that he would at that time ask the C. I. O. unions individually to contribute to a drive organized on his own lines, a drive he was still mulling over.

A fortnight later he broached it. He wanted a fund of seven hundred and fifty thousand dollars and an approved A. F. of L. man to head the drive; he made no mention of an industrial basis.

The C. I. O. did not wait for him to remember it. On April 20 Lewis wrote Tighe offering the Amalgamated five hundred thousand dollars—if the C I. O. had "the assurance that all steel workers will have the right to remain united in one industrial union." Further— "we propose that a joint committee be established on which the Amalgamated Association will be represented, as well as the C. I. O., and other unions willing to contribute to a joint campaign. This joint committee would select a reliable and energetic person . . . to direct the actual organizing work."

Three days later David Dubinsky baptized the drive with one hundred thousand dollars in the name of the International Ladies Garment Workers. Somewhat tardily, Green on May 8 offered Tighe the assistance of the A. F. of L., but only if "free from interference on the part of any group or groups either within or outside the jurisdiction of the A. F. of L."

Lewis was annoyed. Shouting in Tighe's other ear, he told him that Green's policy "would immediately fill your industry with a horde of organizers attached to craft unions fiercely competing with each other for the few members who might be organized and for the few dollars which might be taken in as initiation fees and dues collections...."

Dickering for a bargain, Tighe sent a committee to Washington to interview both camps. What they learned was apparently reflected in the Convention vote of May 13 at Canonsburg, Pennsylvania, in which the Amalgamated decided, fifty-three to thirty-one, to organize steel on industrial lines. Jealously Tighe clung to his independence, however: "We will manage our own organization. If the American Federation of Labor wants to co-operate, they can do so; and if the Lewis Committee for Industrial Organization wants to help, the door is open to them, too. But under no condition will we waive our rights."

Mr. Tighe was seemingly under the gentle illusion that he was to have his cake and eat it too. He reckoned without Mr. Lewis on the other side of the bargain table.

Wrangling over the Amalgamated was stopped for a

The Background of a Crisis 43

time by more immediate matters: Green announced on the twenty-sixth that the Executive Council of the Federation had written the C. I. O., giving them two weeks in which to dissolve. The ultimatum would expire June 3. Lewis brushed Green aside: "I fear his threats about as much as I respect his promises." And of the possibility of the A. F. of L. suspending the C. I. O. unions, he shrugged his shoulders: "Whom the Gods would destroy—"

Then he turned back to Tighe, whose men wanted to confer with him. On the first of June he put on pressure: "May I suggest that it will be a complete waste of time for all concerned for your committee to attend this meeting unless you are prepared to carry out the instructions imposed upon your officers by the recent Canonsburg convention. The policy of fluttering procrastination followed by your board is already responsible for the loss of some weeks of time and must be abandoned. . . .

"If you do not yet know your own mind, please stay at home. If you are prepared to accept the help of the Committee for Industrial Organization, which is the only agency which can or will aid your organization and the workers in the steel industry, you will be made welcome."

Two days later the committee hustled to Washington. Lewis was relentless. He told their spokesmen they could either snap up the C. I. O.'s offer by the next night, or it would be withdrawn.

The Amalgamated gave in. Mr. Tighe was to have his cake but he was not to be allowed to eat it too. The eating was to be done by the Steel Workers Organizing Committee, formed by the C. I. O. The Amalgamated was to affiliate with the C. I. O., but the campaign and the funds of five hundred thousand dollars were to be handled by the S. W. O. C.

44 C. I. O. Industrial Unionism in Action

It was a little hard on Mr. Green. He contented himself with the thought that members of the Council were even then drawing up suspension drafts for the C. I. O. unions, and with the incontrovertible statement that the C. I. O. had "thwarted" his plans. Lewis's drive he dismissed as an "adventure."

The C. I. O. plunged ahead. Dubinsky of the I. L. G. W. and Howard of the printers reiterated their refusal to disband. On the fourteenth, Lewis appointed Philip Murray as director of the Steel Workers Organizing Committee, David MacDonald as secretary, Clinton Golden as regional director for Pittsburgh, Van A. Bittner as regional director for the Chicago area, and Vincent Sweeney as press relations director. Three days later the S. W. O. C. rented the entire thirty-sixth floor of Pittsburgh's most modern skyscraper. The C. I. O.'s steel drive had begun.

The Executive Council was not folding up without a fight, however. On June 30 it called all ten C. I. O. unions (the original eight having been joined by the Amalgamated Association and the Flat Glass Workers) to appear on July 7 to answer charges of dualism. The comment of the New York *Times* correspondent, Mr. Louis Stark, was pertinent: the Council, he wrote, is "somewhat apprehensive lest a measure of success in the steel organizing campaign may so strengthen the C. I. O. unions that by November at the next annual convention, they will be powerful enough to defy any attempt to discipline them. They therefore feel impelled to 'act now.' "

The C. I. O. did not obey the summons. Its meeting of July 7 decided to ignore the Council, allowing the individual unions to make their own replies as they saw fit. The answer of the Cap and Millinery Workers Union was representative; it voted five thousand dollars to the S. W. O. C.

The Background of a Crisis 45

The deadline passed. Dr. Frey rose at the Executive Council of the A. F. of L. and officially requested the suspension of the C. I. O. But there were no prisoners in the dock. The C. I. O. continued to ignore the court's summonses. So the Council tried again; it cited the C. I. O. unions—now twelve with the Auto and Rubber Workers—to appear for trial on August 3.

This also fell on deaf ears. The C. I. O. unanimously refused to appear and wrote the Council that its proposed suspension was illegal, since to suspend would have the force of expulsion and to expel without a two-thirds vote of the Convention is unconstitutional.

At this point two olive branches were waved. One by William Green, who offered to resign if that would heal the breach. No one thought it would. The Wisconsin Federation of Labor then put forward its own compromise formula: (1) all charges and plans of dismissal, suspension, etc., of the C. I. O. were to be dropped; (2) the A. F. of L. was to co-operate heartily with the C. I. O. in the industrial drive in steel and rubber; (3) the C. I. O. was to confine its industrial organization to steel and rubber until the A. F. of L. took further action on the issue; (4) Green was to appoint a special committee to study all phases of organizational set-up in the labor movement—the committee to include two craft men, two "industrialists," three representatives of state federations, three from the city centrals, and two from the federal locals.

This plan went by the boards as did the offers of a Protestant-Catholic-Jewish group of ministers to mediate the conflict.

The heresy trial started on August 3. Dr. Frey intoned: "There can be no doubt as to what the decision on the facts must be. The C. I. O. members are heading a dual movement and have organized an insurrection."

Next day the Council took Frey at his word. By a

vote of thirteen to one, Dubinsky in the negative, it suspended ten C. I. O. unions. "An act of incredible and crass stupidity," commented Lewis, "dictated by personal selfishness and frantic fear."

The suspension served only to stiffen the C. I. O.'s recalcitrance. The Amalgamated Clothing Workers turned over one hundred thousand dollars to the warchest, and Lewis announced the C. I. O. drive would continue as before.

Meanwhile the controversy seeped down into the lower regions of the labor movement, with local union bodies taking votes and dispatching fervid telegrams of censure or support. The C. I. O. claimed the confidence of three internationals, four state federations, thirty city centrals, and locals "too numerous to list," all of which asked the A. F. of L. to rescind its suspension order.

This order was to go into effect on September 5. On the fourth reporters questioned Mr. Lewis about possibilities of last-minute compromise. "I think we are going out," he said. Someone asked: "What is the zero hour?" Lewis looked at the clock's time at that moment. "Twenty to four, as far as I'm concerned. I don't know how Mr. Green feels about it."

Apparently Mr. Green felt much the same about it. September 5 passed, and the C. I. O. had been suspended from the American Federation of Labor. The coming rump Convention at Tampa was to approve the Council's action and threatened "a more drastic procedure" against the C. I. O. if the suspended unions "make the present relationship beyond bearing." But even now, without actual expulsion, the fractious minority was put beyond the pale. Willy-nilly it constituted a rival organization. As Mr. Lewis explained with his customary simplicity: "If people are driven out of a town and the gates are locked, they have to band to-

The Background of a Crisis 47

gether against the beasts of the night and other nocturnal marauders."

10.

It had taken the American labor movement a long while to reach this juncture. It had traversed a good number of bypaths since its first emergence in the journeymen's societies, led off into the mazes of reform by the Knights of Labor, and down the narrow, well-to-do streets of craft unionism by the Federation, where it had plodded on, wooed and sometimes won by the reiterant siren cries of "One Big Union." Now it was turning its back on those comfortable streets and setting out to explore the vaster sectors.

Old Samuel Gompers would have viewed the expedition with some anxiety; it was not the compass direction set by his twenty-eight years of presidency. He would have been even more perturbed to learn that his own cigar-makers' local, on September 21st, voted by an impressive majority to affiliate with the C. I. O. . . .

III. C. I. O. IN STEEL

1.

IN the early morning of July 6, 1892, barge-loads of blue-clad Pinkerton detectives moved slowly up the Monongahela River. They were on their way to Homestead, Pennsylvania, to break the strike waged against the Carnegie steel companies by the Amalgamated Association of Iron, Steel, and Tin Workers. The strike had been called when Carnegie summarily refused to renew his contracts with the union; it was a strike for recognition, for the right to bargain collectively with the management through representatives of the men's own choosing.

Someone saw the barges approaching Homestead through the river mists. The union sirens screamed. Men tumbled out of bed, grabbed their guns, and stumbled down to the waterfront. The Pinkertons, abandoning attempts to disembark, took cover behind the deck-rails and cabin windows, and began shooting as rifle fire peppered the barges from both sides of the river. Even a makeshift cannon was mounted on a wharf and trained on the boats.

When the smoke cleared away from the Battle of Homestead, the Pinkertons had surrendered in a body, and the casualties stood at three detectives and seven workers killed, and sixty men wounded. The Amalgamated ruled Homestead for six days—until eight thousand national guardsmen arrived and did the work of the Pinkertons. The strike collapsed on November 21.

Andrew Carnegie was in Europe at the time. Jubilantly Henry Frick cabled him: "Our victory is now complete and most gratifying. Do not think we will ever have any serious labor trouble again.... We had to teach our employees a lesson and we have taught them one that they will never forget."

Carnegie replied: "Life worth living again.... Surprising how pretty Italia—congratulate all around."

2.

July 5, forty-four years later at Homestead, Pennsylvania, two thousand steel workers and miners stood with bowed heads while burly Patrick Fagan, district president of the Mine Workers, spoke: "Let the blood of those labor pioneers who were massacred here be the seed of this new organization in 1936, and may the souls of the martyrs rest in peace."

That was a trifle theatric. In reality it was not so dramatic as the speech which followed it. The Lieutenant-Governor of the State of Pennsylvania, Thomas Kennedy—a miner and secretary-treasurer of the U. M. W.—told that crowd, and through it steel workers all over the state: "This is a peaceful, organized drive, and we do not seek any strikes or trouble, but if the steel magnates throw you out, you are entitled to and will receive State relief."

It is impossible to overestimate the significance of those words to his listeners. The machinery of the state was no longer to be used to harass them but to encourage them. To the steel worker the state had signified the coal and iron police, the batons of the state troopers, the courts bought up, the mayors bought up, and the sheriffs bought up. Administration of the state had come to seem interchangeable with the administration of the steel companies. Now it appeared to the puddler that everything was upside down. Behind Kennedy he saw Governor Earle, a friend to laboring men. Behind Earle stood Guffey and Wagner in the Senate. And behind them all was the man in the White House. Things had changed.

3.

They were slow in changing. Over the span of those forty-four years from Homestead in '92 to Homestead in '36 stretched as bleak a period as any union ever survived. Frick's optimism proved justified.

The tangible fruits of victory were no less sweet. From 1892 to 1901, a period of nine years, Carnegie Steel reaped profits of one hundred and six million dollars as contrasted with the pittance of twenty-seven million dollars over the previous period of seventeen years. The historian Bridges remarks that "it is believed by the Carnegie officials, and with some show of reason, that this magnificent record was to a great extent made possible by the company's victory at Homestead."

How it was "made possible" was demonstrated in part by the researches of John A. Fitch, who returned to Homestead in 1907 to discover that over the fifteen years elapsed the common labor rate had risen from fifteen to sixteen and one-half cents an hour, while the cost of living had jumped 22 per cent. The eight-hour day had given way to the twelve-hour shift. Sixty per cent of the men received less than two dollars a day, while earnings for the skilled workers had dropped anywhere from 5 per cent to 40 per cent.

Union attempts to stage a comeback were pathetic. A strike in 1901 began with high hopes. It ended with the Amalgamated swallowing a humiliating and suicidal clause: "non-union mills shall be represented as such, no attempts made to organize, nor charters issued." In

C. I. O. in Steel

short, the Amalgamated politely agreed to cease functioning in the greatest part of its legitimate territory. It was not even to be permitted to retain its isolated backwashes. In 1909 the American Sheet and Tin Plate Company snuffed out the last Amalgamated local within the subsidiaries of the U. S. Steel Corporation. From then on the steel valleys were run according to the formula devised by one of the executives: "If a workman sticks up his head, hit it!"

The Amalgamated stuck by its pledge, forbore organizing any of the open-shop areas. By 1919 it had shrunk to ten thousand men scattered among demoralized lodges in unimportant mills.

Then came William Z. Foster. An organizer on Samuel Gompers' staff, he asked the A. F. of L. for two hundred and fifty thousand dollars and a batch of organizers to tackle steel. He got two thousand four hundred dollars and a few helpers, and went into Calumet, Gary, Indiana Harbor and Joliet as a start. Workers swarmed into the union. If the Amalgamated had any doubts about the effect of the new drive, they were dispelled when U. S. Steel quickly announced the "basic eight-hour day," which meant that the twelve-hour shifts would be kept, but the men would get time-and-a-half pay for the four extra hours.

Organization went forward, but only against the most inflexible opposition. The situation in Allegheny County was representative. The sheriff was a brother of a superintendent of the American Sheet and Tin Plate Company. The president of the Homestead Borough Council was chief of the mill's mechanical department. The burgess of Clairton was a mill official; the burgess of Munhall was a department superintendent.

It was Mayor Crawford of Duquesne who classically defined the nature of civil liberties in steel: "Jesus

Christ himself couldn't speak in Duquesne for the A. F. of L." He would have experienced the same difficulty in Clairton, Homestead, and McKeesport, where all union meetings were forbidden. Literally hundreds of men were fired. Labor spies checked union meetings, spread rumors that the leaders were corrupt, that foreign-born workers were to be deported, that Sam Gompers would oppose any strike.

Foster dissipated valuable energy in an incessant effort to keep his organizers and volunteers out of jail, and to gain some measure of free speech and assembly. But the impetus of the drive carried it surging along past all the artificial barriers thrown in its way—too fast for Mike Tighe, president of the Amalgamated. On the fifteenth of May he wrote Judge Gary, chairman of the Steel Corporation, proposing a peace conference before the "tide of unrest" (which Tighe implicitly deplored) rose any higher.

It was something of a shock to Mr. Tighe—whom Gary had once referred to as "a very estimable gentleman"—when the Judge contemptuously declined his incredible offer, on grounds that the Corporation did not recognize, deal with, or combat labor unions as such.

That was enough for the Amalgamated. By a 98 per cent majority the new one hundred thousand members voted for a strike. The response of steel workers to this challenge to Goliath pleased Foster—another one hundred thousand signed up. Enthusiasm quickened all through the grimy, sprawling steel towns of Pennsylvania, Ohio, West Virginia, Illinois, Indiana. The strike was set for September 22.

Throughout, the workers counted heavily on the national government. President Wilson had said some nice things about labor; Gompers had been seen a number of times at the White House. The Railway Labor Board had been set up and the men's pay boosted. Moreover, the steelmasters stood in ill repute; the public was inclined to scout the patriotism of men who had garnered war profits which equaled the pay of two million American soldiers—an excess profit of six hundred and sixty-one million dollars. And this was the U. S. Steel Corporation alone.

But Wilson, whose intentions were probably of the best, knew very little of strike strategy. Calling in the union leaders he tried to persuade them to postpone action until he should call an industrial conference on October 6. Gompers, lukewarm to the steel campaign from the beginning and increasingly fond of playing partners with men of power, backed Wilson. The local organizers knew they couldn't wait. Steel was already preparing for a scrap; to give them additional weeks to undermine the union would be madness.

Reluctantly, Gompers agreed to strike. The sheriff of Allegheny County mobilized five thousand deputies. Troopers were concentrated all through the Pennsylvania valleys. In the Monongahela Valley alone, Foster estimated there were twenty-five thousand armed men.

On the twenty-second, sixty thousand men walked out in the Pittsburgh district. Next day Foster could claim that three hundred thousand were out; by October 1, three hundred and sixty-five thousand. The strike was at least 90 per cent effective, with Youngstown, Johnstown, Cleveland, Wheeling, and Chicago shut down tight as a tomb.

The breaking of the strike followed familiar lines. The nation's press labeled the union men as aliens, emphasizing the "radicalism" and "foreign" nature of these "agitators." Locally, citizens were assured by the papers and the steelmasters that this was a strike of "hunkies." Excerpts from a sermon preached by the Rev. P. Molyneux of St. Brendan's Roman Catholic

Church in Braddock, Pennsylvania, a steel center, were widely reprinted:

"This strike is not being brought about by intelligent or English-speaking workmen, but by men who have no interest in the community, are not an element of our community, and who do not have the welfare of our men at heart.

"But—you can't reason with these people any more than you can with a cow or a horse.... And that's the only way you can reason with these people; knock them down!...

"Let the women keep off the streets with their children, and give the men a clear field, and we will show these hoodlums what we are."

Governor Sproul of Pennsylvania wrote the Rev. Molyneux: "I wish to compliment you for the very good judgment expressed.... I heartily agree with your analysis of the present situation."

Big Steel asserted in full-page newspaper ads: "There is a strong possibility that the Huns had a hand in fomenting the strike, hoping to retard industrial progress in America."

Even the Senate Committee on Education and Labor joined the pack in full cry: "Behind this strike there is massed a considerable element of I. W. W.'s, anarchists, revolutionists, and Russian soviets." What the "Russian soviets" were doing so far from home when there was a revolution and civil war proceeding in their own country was not explained.

Later the Interchurch World Movements' Investigating Commission found that, "during the strike, violations of personal rights and personal liberty were wholesale; men were arrested without warrants, imprisoned without charges, their homes invaded without legal process, magistrates' verdicts were rendered frankly on the basis of whether the striker would go back to work or not."

C. I. O. in Steel

The companies hired two large labor-detective agencies—the Corporations Auxiliary, and the Sherman Service—"to stir up as much bad feeling as you possibly can between the Serbians and Italians." The companies further contributed to racial hatred by importing carloads of Negroes from the South as strike-breakers: this at a time when race-riots were rife throughout the country.

The press did its bit. As the number of strikers mounted to the hundred thousands, the headlines boomed: WORKERS FLOCK BACK TO JOBS, REPORT LABORERS GOING BACK ALL THROUGH DISTRICT. October 1—the high-water mark for the number of strikers out—the Pittsburgh *Chronicle-Telegraph* capped the climax: STRIKE CRUMBLING—STEEL MEN SAY.

To counteract this barrage of wishful thinking, the strikers had one weekly bulletin.

Credit for the eventual collapse of the strike, however, cannot be surrendered wholly to the steel companies and their allies. A good part of it must be retained by the craft unions themselves. "This organization," said one unionist of the National Committee of craft unions conducting the strike, "has as much cohesiveness as a load of furniture." The Steam and Operating Engineers tangled with the Brotherhood of Steamshovel and Dredgemen over the control of cranemen, while Amalgamated, and the Hod Carriers, Building, and Common Laborers Union quarreled over the common laborers. The trainmen and switchmen couldn't get together for a joint strike in the Chicago area, while the militant railroad locals around Pittsburgh received no backing from the Brotherhoods.

On November 27 the National Committee asked the Interchurch Commission to mediate the strike. The unionists promised to return to work if Steel would agree to accept the award of the arbitrators. Gary sensed that such an offer meant he had the unions on the run. He refused mediation pointblank, on grounds that the strikers desired "the closed shop, Soviets, and the forcible distribution of property."

The strikers surrendered unconditionally January 8, 1920. The hundred thousand who were still out marched back into the plants—those who were not blacklisted. As the Interchurch Commission Report summed it up: "The United States Steel Corporation was too big to be beaten by 300,000 working men. It had too large a cash surplus, too many allies among other businesses, too much support from government officers, local and national, too strong influence with social institutions such as the press and the pulpit, it spread over too much of the earth—still retaining absolutely centralized control to be defeated by widely scattered workers of many minds, many fears, varying states of pocketbook and under a comparatively improvised leadership."

The Amalgamated, after its brief recrudescence, was laid away in mothballs again. Foster was barred from the next Convention. What was left of the steel workers' dues Tighe invested in Pittsburgh real estate.

4.

Throughout the boom years, there were few whispers of unionism to disturb the serene rustle of accumulating profits. The year 1929 found Steel at the apex of its power.

Some indication of the size and ramifications of the industry can be gleaned from a glance at one of its units, U. S. Steel, which represents 40 per cent of national capacity.

In 1929, U. S. Steel alone poured more ingots than all the mills of Germany, and more than the mills of

C. I. O. in Steel 57

Great Britain and France combined. Even in 1934, when its mills were running at a little over one-third of capacity, Big Steel mined 10,000,000 tons of iron ore, 12,000,000 tons of coal and 6,000,000 tons of limestone; produced 5,000,000 tons of coke, 5,500,000 tons of pig-iron, and 6,000,000 tons of steel products. In the way of by-products it sloughed off 4,000 tons of sulphate of iron, 92,000 tons of ammonia, 84 tons of benzol products, 34,000 tons of gypsum, and 7,000,000 barrels of cement.

In 1934 U. S. Steel meant: 131 iron and steel works; 101 blast furnaces; 375 open-hearth furnaces; 89 mines around Lake Superior; 13 mines in the South; one of the world's richest manganese deposits in Brazil; 109 ore boats; 487 Mississippi barges; 4,000 miles of railway trackage; 1,189 locomotives; 50,000 freight cars; 82 coal mines; 2,531 beehive coke ovens; 3,629 by-product ovens.

Control of U. S. Steel, centered in Wall Street, extends out over the industrial life of the country; for on Big Steel's board are representatives of the American Telephone and Telegraph, the Pennsylvania Railroad, General Motors, International Nickel, and, indirectly, all the clients of the House of Morgan. As Mr. Harvey O'Connor quotes a Wall Street reporter: "Big Steel's board and its included finance committee are as completely and neatly separated from the steel business itself as a man from his hat."

The "steel business itself" has not done badly for the man under the hat, particularly considering his original gross overcapitalization. Over a period of thirty-four years the Corporation has grossed $32,000,000,000, and netted $3,909,000,000. Of this, bondholders got $892,000,000, and stockholders $1,965,000,000. Its assets in 1934 were valued at $2,084,000,000, with current assets of $420,000,000 and an earned surplus of $528,000,000.

U. S. Steel was formed to accomplish a monopoly. But the steel business is monopolistic by nature. It constitutes what economists term an oligopoly: which means a situation in which competition has been materially eased by the reduction of the number of competitors. In practical terms in steel, the few major competitors left in the field don't dare to compete because it would be suicidal. Moreover, the alternative of "co-operating" in the fixing of prices is quite pleasant.

This does not mean that steel is an uncompetitive industry; it is extremely competitive in every field but one—prices. Producers will fight tooth and nail for contracts, but they won't wield the two-edged sword of price reduction. There are only a certain number of contracts to go around; these are usually very large, very lucrative, and frequently drawn up for periods of five years or more. The scuffle for these prizes is sharp; but very few cases occur of "unethical" attempts at price-slashing.

The industry is one of very high overhead costs, which continue as fixed charges whether one ingot is being produced or one million. Consequently, if a producer slashes his prices, others will retaliate because fixed costs demand continued revenue, and the whole industry will be dragged down into an ultimately disastrous price war. The pressure of fear is all in the direction of common prices mutually maintained.

It was this industry that the steel worker faced when he made his next attempt to straighten his shoulders in 1933. He has never exhibited a very passionate interest in the economics of Steel; but these facts, whether he liked it or not, concerned him closely. They were facts which inescapably drew separate parts of the industry into collaboration; and when unionism threatened the industry it was inclined to work together in happy unison.

5.

The depression hit steel hard. By 1932 steel production shot down to a new bottom for the twentieth century. By '33, blast-furnace activity reached the lowest ever recorded. Steel had not produced so few rails since 1865; nor shipped as little iron ore since 1885. America's share of the world market dropped from one-half to one-third. U. S. Steel cut its common stock dividend to one-half of one per cent in 1932, and then quit trying. Its market value in 1932 stood at $370,000,000—the shadow of a concern originally capitalized at $1,399,000,000.

Times were hard for the stockholder. They were a trifle harder for the steel worker, perhaps because he had had little opportunity to roll up a back-log.

In 1923, his average annual earnings stood at $1,650, when a minimum health and decency budget for his average family of five required $1,990, and a "frugal comfort budget" $3,180. In 1929, presumably rolling in the fat of the land, he was getting $1,740, with a minimum budget of $2,000 and the comfort budget at $3,200. He was, meanwhile, working well over fifty hours a week.

What the worker was getting in nominal pay was in some ways of less interest to him than the manner in which he had to earn it. He lived in shack-towns crouched near the soot-belching mills, spent his money or scrip at high-priced company stores. The company dominated his politics, his church, and even his recreation. Within the shop he had nothing resembling economic democracy; as an individual without a union to protect him against discrimination he stood at the mercy of the straw-boss. He had, in his own phrase, to like it or lump it.

One of the things he found it hardest to lump were his hours. In 1924, 5 per cent of the blast-furnacemen were working eighty-four hours a week, while another 9 per cent worked seventy-two hours. From 1922 to 1924 the percentage of men working seven days a week rose from 30 to 50 per cent, while the average week ran sixty hours. Even in 1929, 8 per cent of the men were still working the old twelve-hour day, while 28 per cent had ten-hour shifts. To cap it, one-third of the working force spent seven days a week in the mills without any concession in hours—a higher proportion than in 1920 or '22.

If the worker felt he was not too well off during this boom period, he was later to look back on it as the halcyon days. On October 1, 1931, U. S. Steel and Bethlehem cut wages 10 per cent. Weirton Steel slashed payrolls five times in eleven months. May 15, 1932, Steel and Bethlehem again lowered rates 15 per cent. Once started, wages dropped to the bottom, and the worker was once again holding the bag.

In 1929 his weekly pay had averaged $32.60. In 1932— if he was employed at all—he was getting $13.20. A study of fifty-three thousand steel workers by the Department of Labor showed average weekly earnings for the unskilled of $11.71. The average base rate had been 40 cents an hour; it fell to 30.5 cents. In addition to the drop in hourly rates, hours worked declined from fifty-five a week in 1929 to thirty-one in 1933. Not from motives of regard for leisure; it was the simple resultant of the slump in steel production from 88.5 per cent to 19.5 per cent.

The result in terms of annual earnings is staggering. The average worked out to under $600. To compare this again with the minimum budget of health and decency,

C. I. O. in Steel

adjusted to lower costs of living, the steel worker had $560 as against the $1,500 required, and as against the $2,400 set for a frugal comfort standard.

Among seven comparable industries Steel's $560 rated lowest, far surpassed by chemicals, automobiles, electrical equipment, rubber tires and tubes, foundries and machine shops, and agricultural implements, in that order.

These wages applied to those who were working. But 1932 found 210,600 employed, out of a normal half million. Two years later, even with some recovery, a federal census of four major steel towns revealed:

	Employable	Unemployed	Part-time	% Employed	% Part-time
Braddock	5,313	2,244	1,756	42.2	33.2
Duquesne	6,211	1,457	3,482	23.5	56.0
Homestead ...	5,754	1,815	2,682	31.5	46.6
Rankin	2,146	947	778	44.1	36.3

The pangs of the depression must also have been felt by executives in steel; but if so, the pain was of a predominantly spiritual nature. Joe Doakes in the mills might be getting his $560, or sporadic relief; but the Securities Commission in 1934 reported the salaries of steelmasters as follows: E. R. Crawford of McKeesport Tin Plate ($173,750); E. T. Weir of National Steel ($53,671); Tom Girdler of Republic Steel ($129,372); George Crawford, president of Jones and Laughlin ($100,000 plus a bonus of $150,000); Charles Schwab of Bethlehem ($250,000); Eugene M. Grace of Bethlehem ($180,000). With the exception of Mr. Crawford's, no mention is made in this list of any additional bonuses the executives may have gratefully received or as gratefully voted themselves. But it is known that Grace alone voted himself $4,000,000 worth during the depression.

62   C. I. O. Industrial Unionism in Action

With Big Steel employing only eighteen thousand on full-time, with starvation an encroaching reality for thousands of workers, and the company spending an average of ten cents a week per person for relief, Chairman Myron Taylor reported to his stockholders: "There has been no brighter page in the history of any corporation than the treatment of U. S. Steel employees during the depression. So far as I know, no employee of the Steel Corporation has been in want."

The most delightful feature of company relief: the worker, to preserve his moral integrity, must turn it back as soon as he got work again, and to make sure he did, the paymaster docked his wages. "It is a standing rule of our Corporation (U. S. Steel) that none of the employees is to apply for relief of any charitable organization." Consideration for this rule broke down among the workers in the face of somewhat more stringent pressure, and soon private charities were doing what they could to help out. They were, however, reproved by Chairman Taylor, who saw quite plainly the futility and almost the immorality of helping such people. As he told the St. Nicholas Society in New York: "No doubt much of the want that is so willingly ministered to by the public as a whole at the present time is due to the lack of thrift by large numbers of unskilled laborers."

6.

In 1932 steel workers listened to speeches like that of Mrs. Walter L. Riggs: "There is not a chance of our mills resuming capacity operation as long as you cast your votes for Democratic candidates. As long as you are willing to sacrifice your own prosperity for a will-of-the-wisp called the New Deal, you will live on charity and raise your children in poverty."

The idea that they had any prosperity to sacrifice

C. I. O. in Steel 63

must have appealed to Steel's thousands; but wholesale election frauds as in Rankin, Homestead, East Pittsburgh, Wilmerding, McKees Rocks, and Sharpsburg, Pennsylvania, obscured their reply. However they voted, what they got was N. R. A.

The N. R. A. Steel Code, signed August 19, 1933, was not drawn up for them. It was an inter-company price-fixing pact and little more. Labor had no representation whatever. On the Code Authority sat President Irvin of U. S. Steel, Grace of Bethlehem, Girdler of Republic, Block of Inland, Morrow of Sloss Sheffield, and Weir of National. Filbert of Big Steel led the statistics committee, Irvin headed the administrative committee, and two of his vice-presidents shepherded the commercial or price-fixing committee.

Each company in the industry signed an individual contract with the treasurer of the Iron and Steel Institute, which provided for a fine of ten dollars a ton for any infringement of the price structure. It was an exceedingly pleasant arrangement from the viewpoint of the Institute. In former days it had had to depend on the less certain methods of price leadership, and indirect persuasion and pressure. Now the government would police the whole deal and enforce monopoly.

Under such a scheme the results were foreordained. The steel composite price jumped from $28.12 in 1933 to $32.42 by the end of the year. The finished composite price rose from $45 to $51.

And these were the minimum, base prices. On top of these more or less theoretical figures were heaped surcharges of all sorts which shocked even initiates in the business.

Extension of the basing-point system was under the Code another means of profit. It meant that when General Motors bought sheet steel from the Youngstown Sheet and Tube Company at Youngstown, Ohio, it had to pay freight charges based on a mythical haul from Pittsburgh to Detroit. It meant that a Pacific Coast consumer had to pay freight charges from Pittsburgh on steel that was made near San Francisco. Prices were set which not only protected backward plants but also gave more efficient companies huge spreads between their costs and their prices.

The government had neither hypothetical nor actual control over this situation. The records of the Labor Committee were not even available to the Recovery Administration. The reports of the Consumer's Advisory Board had no sanctions and were completely disregarded in any practical sense. What is more important, the administration betrayed no desire to control price-fixing. The steelmasters held all the aces; and trumps in this case was their threat to abandon the Code altogether and sabotage the N. R. A. The administration felt that it could not afford that defection; it bowed meekly whenever the Steel Institute nodded.

Of course something had to be handed the steel workers. The Code set up twenty-one wage districts; for seven of them in the North, the base rate was forty cents an hour; one district thirty-nine cents, two thirty-eight cents, three thirty-five cents; and in the South, twenty-seven cents for the Birmingham area, and twenty-five cents for the rest of the region. This North-South differential was based on a supposed difference in the cost of living which, according to W. P. A. studies, in reality scarcely existed in the cities involved.

The Code also stipulated the forty-hour week except "in case compliance proved impracticable."

As a concession, steelmasters agreed under pressure to omit from the text their anti-union clause, but added the statement: "It should be distinctly understood that the omission of the section does not imply any changes in the attitude of the industry."

Workers took the Code at its word, joined their unions and sought recognition. April 16, 1934, the Amalgamated met in convention. As an observer decided: "The union had the choice of a national strike to force recognition from the hostile magnates, or an inch by inch retreat under the steady drumfire of company unions, discrimination, propaganda, and espionage until its demoralized members abandoned the union. It was the same choice that faced Foster in September, 1919."

But Tighe could not see it. "There is no hope for a large majority of the workers in the steel industry," he figured. "You cannot fight a two billion dollar diversified corporation." Some of the rank-and-filers decided to try. They set up a committee of ten, over Tighe's all but dead body, and on May 21 began visiting steel companies to negotiate. Thwarted, they went to the White House. When Roosevelt told them to go home and await elections in their mills to determine representation, they startled the press and the nation by flatly terming it "just so much bunk." They doubted the ability of the President to arrange elections in the first place, and were certain he had no intention of enforcing collective bargaining even if the union won. It was not polite, but it was common sense.

The delegation failed, however, to get what it wanted —a conference between labor, Roosevelt, and the Institute. Instead they were offered another board. They drooped home discouraged, and called off the strike.

In the meantime the industry was getting a real taste of company unionism. In 1929 employee representation plans, as company unions are generally termed, covered only about 21 per cent of the employees in Steel. By 1932-33, that percentage had dropped to 20 per cent. But with the inauguration of N. R. A. and the threat of a new campaign by Amalgamated rank-and-filers,

66 C. I. O. Industrial Unionism in Action

Steel started a drive of its own. Executives didn't bother to pretend that the plans were coming spontaneously from the workers. Their formula originated with Industrial Relations Councillors, Inc., a Rockefeller-endowed group formed to sponsor company unionism. From Councillors went Arthur Young, to take over the job of vice-president in charge of industrial relations for U. S. Steel. The philosophy behind these plans was epitomized in the statement of one millionaire industrialist: "My people do not know what is good for them. Only I know what is good for them. And I know that a union is not good for them."

Mr. Grace of Bethlehem put it a little differently: "If ninety-five per cent of my men belonged to a union, I would not recognize them as union men or as members of the union. I think that is better for the men."

Conversely, the company union was to foster "that fine spirit of loyalty and co-operation between labor and management so badly needed in these controversial times."

Few would be disposed, perhaps, to quarrel with such purposes. On the other hand, it would be out of place to confuse them with unionism, or to believe that the plans duplicated and eliminated the functions of unions. The latter are interested primarily in certain basic facts of employment: hours, wages, conditions of work; plans, when they were used at all, aimed primarily at the adjustment of petty grievances.

By 1934 the industry could boast that 90 to 95 per cent of the mills were under company union plans. This meant next to nothing as far as the worker's sentiment was concerned, since in most cases he had no choice in the matter. Even when managers allowed a ballot on a plan's adoption, favorable majority and recalcitrant minority alike became members. Personnel managers announced that thousands supported the plan—merely

C. I. O. in Steel 67

because they voted in its elections for representatives. But the number of ballots "Mickey Mouse," "Mae West" and "Hitler" cast grew astonishingly.

Elections supervised by an impartial agency could speedily have cleared up a great deal of this hocus-pocus. However, the Steel Labor Relations Board and the National Labor Board, because of their lack of subpoena power, the obstructionist attitude of the companies, and delay in appellate procedure, were able to hold only six elections in the whole troubled industry. Of these, company unions lost five and captured one. A strong union and an administration that was willing to enforce the laws it made would have greatly strengthened the work of both these boards. But the Amalgamated was doddering and disrupted, and Washington proved exceedingly shy of antagonizing the industrialists.

7.

The Amalgamated slumbered. Meanwhile company union representatives were opening their eyes. On May 15, 1935, the N. R. A. died under the impact of the Schecter case. On May 21, company union representatives in Braddock, Pennsylvania, decided to call Arthur Young's bluff; brashly they demanded a general 10 per cent wage increase, vacations with pay, and a representative on the board of U. S. Steel. Their committee was put out of the office when it tried to interview the plant superintendent, Mr. Slick.

Before long, however, other company unionists took up the idea. In Youngstown and Chicago, employee representatives banded together to push similar demands, receive refusals, and grow in wisdom.

It was at this point that the C. I. O. began angling for control of Tighe's union. On June 4, 1936, they attained it, signed a formal treaty of annexation, Mike

68   C. I. O. Industrial Unionism in Action

Tighe was eased out of the picture, and the Steel Workers Organizing Committee took charge under Director Philip Murray. At once the S. W. O. C. decided to win over the company union representatives instead of attacking them as "betrayers of the working class." It would have been easy to fall into the error of antagonizing them; it was sagacious to understand that these men were not anti-union but simply experimenting with the nearest forms of organization at hand. This policy was to bear fruit.

On the twenty-ninth of June the C. I. O. steel drive had begun; the American Iron and Steel Institute recognized the fact and fired the opening gun of a barrage that grew in intensity throughout the summer. Charging that steel was being invaded by "outsiders," it announced that "the steel industry will oppose any attempt to compel its employees to join a union or to pay tribute for the right to work." In a somewhat more menacing tone it went on to warn the nation that "any interruption of the forward movement (of recovery in the industry) will seriously injure the employees and their families, and all businesses dependent upon the industry, and will endanger the welfare of the country. The announced drive, with its accompanying agitation for industrial strife, threatens such interruption."

But the "drive" went on, swelled by the company unions themselves. In Chicago, sixty employee representatives, speaking for forty-five thousand steel workers, met with the regional S. W. O. C. directors officially to endorse the C. I. O. and its steel campaign.

Executive officers shivered, but maintained a brave front. Spokesmen for National Tube declared: "We have nothing to fear from Mr. Lewis or his organizers." But Barron's financial weekly took a more realistic view: "For the first time in the history of the United States, industrial management is faced with a labor movement which is smart and courageous, wealthy and successful—a movement, moreover, which is winning its battle by applying a shrewd imitation of big business organization and technique."

Homestead, Pennsylvania, cracked wide open for the memorial meeting on the fifth of July; but such towns as Aliquippa (known in Steel as Little Siberia, or "the place where you never see a smile") continued to be "tough" to organize. Jones and Laughlin distributed a circular, warning the populace that "the $30,000,000 plant now being erected in Pittsburgh was lost to Aliquippa through labor agitation and the value of every dwelling dropped thirty cents on the dollar. . . . Business districts never recover from strikes. . . . Have someone estimate what the value of your property or business would be if Jones and Laughlin Steel Corporation closed their plants. And the plant will close if the union and communistic agitation continues in our community."

Despite such pressure, the S. W. O. C. pushed out into no-man's-land, sending organizers to Allentown, Reading, Coatesville, Pottstown, and Steelton. When union headquarters appeared in Bethlehem, the company added eighteen to its police force and forbade any outsiders to circularize or talk to the workers.

Talking over the radio, John Lewis quoted some figures to the nation: while hourly rates in steel stood at 65.6 cents, they were 79.3 cents in bituminous coal, 83.2 in anthracite, 77.5 in petroleum, and 79.8 in building construction. Hourly basic rates averaged 47.9 cents, making steel fourteenth out of twenty-one major industries, and twentieth as far as actual weekly earnings were concerned.

A week later S. W. O. C. welcomed the biggest company union west of Pittsburgh into the Amalgamated—three thousand workers in the Carnegie-Illinois plant at

70   C. I. O. Industrial Unionism in Action

South Chicago. By the twentieth, 175 organizers and 3,800 volunteers were storming fifty mills in the northeastern region. They made house-to-house canvasses, cultivated employee representatives, and held mass meetings whenever it was safe.

On July 22 S. W. O. C. decided to enroll some three hundred thousand fabricating and processing workers. Two days later U. S. Steel announced the concession of time-and-a-half pay for overtime. It sounded good but meant almost nothing, since the industry was presumably working on a forty-hour week, and "overtime" on U. S. Steel's definition did not begin till after forty-eight hours' work.

A month later twelve more U. S. Steel company union representatives, manifesting unrest, demanded a 25 per cent wage increase, and condemned the plans as "utterly futile inasmuch as they are company-dominated."

By the end of September Van A. Bittner, S. W. O. C. mid-western director, could report that forty-three out of ninety-eight employee representatives in the Carnegie-Illinois plant in South Chicago were S. W. O. C. members; thirty-seven more favored the Amalgamated, and only eighteen definitely opposed it.

The S. W. O. C. now had three regional offices: in Pittsburgh, Chicago, and Birmingham; thirty-five sub-regional branches, with one hundred and fifty-eight field directors and organizers on full-time, eighty on part-time, and five thousand volunteer organizers. The official publication—*Steel Labor*—had boosted its circulation from eighty thousand to one hundred and eighty thousand.

The S. W. O. C.'s task lay in intangibles. Director Philip Murray: "When we started the job of organizing the steel industry we found the men in the mills shot through with fear. They were afraid of the boss and of their jobs. To a large extent we have broken

C. I. O. in Steel 71

down this fear. However, the day we completely banish fear from the steel industry our job will be done."

It wasn't easy. The organizer for Beaver County, Pennsylvania, found he couldn't hold union meetings; every time he leased a hall or the upper room of a store, the steel company would buy up the land and cancel the lease. William Mitch, southeastern director, reported: "Conditions are so bad in Gadsden that when the Central Labor Union wants to hold a meeting its officers wire the Governor, who sends in state police to protect the meeting against mob outrages inspired by the employers. The last time such a meeting was arranged it was broken up when the union officers forgot to wire the Governor."

In October the steelmasters, confident as ever, dubbed the S. W. O. C. "a complete failure." But later that month Big Steel announced a wage increase "to be submitted to representatives of the employees."

Bethlehem, Jones and Laughlin, National, and Republic quickly followed suit.

The companies, not unnaturally, seized this opportunity to exhibit the genuineness of intra-company bargaining. But the employee representatives weren't at all sure they should accept the offer—since it was tied to the cost-of-living index. They had not been allowed to talk over the proposal. "They (the companies) have not discussed the proposals with us.... They say that they have 'negotiated' these pay-raises with us, but this is the first we knew of the terms they wanted us to sign." As Louis Stark, New York *Times* correspondent, reported: "Their chief objection was that the corporation's proposal would bind them indefinitely to the present standard of living, and that they would never participate in the increased fruits of productivity and of increased profits due to changes in technique and efficiency." At any rate, only three plant committees signed the clause in question.

Union leaders quickly ascribed these wage boosts to the union drive. Lewis sarcastically recalled Tom Girdler's statement of a few months back: "There is no economic justification for a wage increase," and Benjamin Fairless' dictum of September 8: "Economic conditions do not permit a wage increase."

Since economic conditions could hardly have changed so drastically in one or two months, the S. W. O. C. was left with two alternatives: either the increase had been possible all the time, or it was now justified on quite different grounds—i.e., stopping the union.

All the while revolt was rising in the company unions. Matters came to a head in December, when representatives from forty-two steel plants met in Pittsburgh and formed a C. I. O. council, proposed a national convention, and excoriated the company unions as "a Rip Van Winkle form of collective bargaining, where the company union representatives try to bargain and the management actually does the collecting."

Membership, too, was doing well. The drive which Steel executives glibly dismissed as "a complete failure" had corralled 82,315 members on November 20, 125,000 on January 9, and 150,000 members in 280 lodges by the end of February.

The time for seeking contracts had begun.

8.

For about three months, beginning in December, 1936, John L. Lewis had been negotiating in strictest secrecy with Myron Taylor, chairman of U. S. Steel. Lewis had once reminded Taylor that, after all, they would have to talk things over some time, and it might better be soon. After some thought, Taylor agreed.

C. I. O. in Steel 73

Why? For one thing, U. S. Steel hoped for contracts from English rearmament. But Walter Runciman, head of the British Board of Trade, pointed out that His Majesty must be assured of continuous delivery. Could he count on the Corporation if it resisted the C. I. O.? Thomas Lamont of the House of Morgan, which controls Big Steel, thought not. He knew quite well that the majority of S. W. O. C. members worked in the shops of the Corporation. And he could recall that General Motors recently lost vital production weeks in its unsuccessful struggle against a C. I. O. union. Lamont realized, too, that it would look a bit odd for an American firm to snap up British arms contracts while refusing to bid for United States naval jobs on grounds that it couldn't satisfy the labor provisions of the Walsh-Healey Act.

Furthermore, Lamont was not keen on Big Steel's taking the rap for the whole industry as in 1919, at the price of a drubbing in the moral conscience of the public. Half a dozen rival independent companies, where the S. W. O. C. admitted it was weak, might be in a better position to contest the issue.

Finally, Corporation stockholders, starved for sight of a dividend, were just getting a taste of prosperity; they would not lightly sacrifice it. So, Lamont concluded, Taylor must be induced to concoct the "right" policy; and it was not, apparently, too hard a job. Once the idea was suggested that he had the makings of an industrial statesman, he soon developed the "Taylor Formula" of industrial relations, which, as Mr. Benjamin Stolberg points out, "is what the average high-school boy calls union recognition."

His five or six talks with Lewis consolidated this idea in Taylor's determination, for the C. I. O. chief was glad to play along.

By February 27, Taylor was ready.

74 C. I. O. Industrial Unionism in Action

Benjamin Fairless, president of the subsidiary Carnegie-Illinois, was in the Middle West on a tour of employee representation plans, brushing up anti-union defense lines. He completed his swing at Pittsburgh, and found a telegram instructing him to come to New York.

Next day in Manhattan, Taylor told him: Here is a copy of a contract with the S. W. O. C. Tomorrow in Pittsburgh you will receive a delegation of S. W. O. C. leaders, who will ask to negotiate a contract with you. You will say "yes." You can sign it the next day.

On March 2 Carnegie-Illinois recognized the S. W. O. C. as the bargaining agency for its members, raised wages 10 per cent, established the eight-hour day, forty-hour week, with time-and-a-half pay for overtime. The C. I. O. had established collective bargaining in Big Steel.

Mr. Fairless's astonishment echoed throughout the steel kingdom and the nation at large. There had been no inkling of the negotiations. Even Mr. Lewis's organizers had been in the dark. The shock of victory was electrifying to the C. I. O. Succeeding thoughts of the immense stimulation for organization of the rest of the industry seemed even more exciting.

Steelmasters cursed Taylor as a traitor to his industry and his class. But even many who cursed were soon signing. Within three months of the Fairless contract the S. W. O. C. reached agreements with one hundred and forty steel companies, including fourteen of U. S. Steel's subsidiaries, and one of the largest independents, Jones and Laughlin, who bowed to the results of a National Labor Relations Board election. Something incredible had happened: 50 per cent of the steel industry was organized, with more to follow. By July the proportion had risen to 75 per cent.

9.

Some top-flight companies held out. Four of the largest of these formed the group known as Little Steel —Bethlehem, Republic, Youngstown Sheet and Tube, and Inland. Furious at Taylor's "treachery," they determined to fight the C. I. O. to a finish; and they built up war-chests for the struggle. Uniformly, they enjoyed a sound financial position. None of them found itself in the plight of Jones and Laughlin, which had just borrowed thirty million dollars for new mills and could not stand the drain of a strike.

Behind Little Steel stood the Guaranty Trust, which handles much of its financial affairs. Guaranty is particularly interested in financing the equipping of railroads—the coal gondolas, etc., in which Bethlehem specializes. Alloys are playing an increasingly important part in the making of such equipment—and in alloys and light steel both Republic and Youngstown shine.

Not too strangely, then, the row over Little Steel's projected union-busting broke out first within the Guaranty. The bank is under the influence of the House of Morgan. It was the Lamont followers against the Eugene Grace faction.... The issue soon shifted to a larger field, and there it found dramatic presentation.

The president of the American Iron and Steel Institute is elected each year by a majority of a board of twenty-one. Vice-presidents are customarily elected by unanimous and automatic vote to the presidency after one-year terms.

At the end of 1936, Grace, who is chairman of the Finance Committee of Guaranty, was retiring from office and Irvin, of U. S. Steel, was to come in.

Suddenly difficulties developed. The reactionaries nominated Tom Girdler of Republic Steel to oppose

Irvin. This battle over the presidency represented the struggle for control, actual or symbolic, of the industry's labor policies. Was it to go Grace's way or Lamont's?

For three days the Board balloted, and each time landed in a ten to ten deadlock—the contracted companies lining up behind Irvin, those in favor of war backing Girdler. Mr. Purnell of Youngstown Sheet and Tube was absent. On the fourth day the Board reached Purnell by phone, and he threw his vote to Girdler. It was war.

As early as March 31, the S. W. O. C. had begun sending copies of the Carnegie-Illinois agreement to the big independents, requesting negotiations to arrange signed contracts. No answers from Little Steel. In May, Clinton Golden, northeastern director, wired Republic that its men were fed up with such stalling, and that trouble could be expected if the management persisted. Girdler replied that he was willing to meet with the S. W. O. C., that he was already complying with its terms, but he would not sign an agreement. Nothing in law required it.

Golden telegraphed: did Republic expect to entrust thousands of pay-rate items and other provisions of a settlement to the memories of its foremen and the union? The S. W. O. C. saw no reason to converse with Girdler if he was determined not to enter into an agreement.

Golden got little better answers from the other members of Steel. Nobody quarreled with the wage and hour terms of the Carnegie-Illinois contract; but with one voice they cried that the Wagner Act did not require the employer to make a collective contract, that the C. I. O. was irresponsible, that its record was shot through with violated agreements.

The fact that the Auto Workers Union (jointly with

General Motors in most cases) was responsible for these abrogations, and not the S. W. O. C. which had a completely clean record with many times as many contracts, disturbed Little Steel not at all. In short, it was not a question of justice but of power. They wished not to negotiate with the union for fair or fairer terms, but to eliminate the necessity of negotiating at all. They wanted not peace but war, and a pretext for that was never hard to find.

A conversation between S. W. O. C. executives and representatives of Youngstown Sheet and Tube reveals that same ethical and intellectual bankruptcy of the steel officials. The union men, led by Philip Murray, asked Mr. Argetsinger and his confreres for one good reason why they should not sign a contract. The steelmasters requested permission to retire a moment to confer. Back they came: "We have never previously signed a union contract."

Regional Director Golden then remarked that he considered that an odd reply: hadn't they signed a contract with the United Mine Workers covering their captive mine operations? Mr. Argetsinger again went into a brief conference with his staff. The answer: "Well, that is different. One of our wholly-owned subsidiaries signed that." Mr. Golden: "All right, gentlemen, why not create another wholly-owned subsidiary to sign the contract covering your steel operations?" The conference broke up.

On May 26 the word for the strike went out to 75,500 workers in Chicago and Indiana Harbor, Youngstown, Canton, Massillon, Warren, Niles, and Cleveland. At eleven o'clock that night the second-shift workers went home as usual; but no one appeared to replace them. Next day the steel towns breathed clean air for the first time in years. The mills were as empty as a Monday-morning church.

Then, on the eleventh of June, 350 Bethlehem employees on the Conemaugh and Black Lick Railroad, which serves the Cambria plant at Johnstown, Pennsylvania, struck for a signed agreement. At once a triple alliance was formed between the trainmen, the S. W. O. C., and the miners in Bethlehem's captive coal mines. Cambria's 13,500 steel workers were called out; the mines, already shut down, were to stay down; the trainmen were to tie up shipping operations.

It is difficult to describe, to anyone who has not lived in a steel town during a strike, the atmosphere of such a community and the stark reality of its manifestations. Perhaps General Sherman's "War is hell" best sums it up.

Take it town by town.

10.

Johnstown is where the employees of the Cambria plant spend their wages; it is little else. That four hundred thousand to five hundred thousand dollars weekly payroll constitutes the life-blood of commercial Johnstown; and like most vital things it has come to be regarded as sacred by those whom it benefits.

Shortly after the strike began, vigilantes led by S. H. Heckman, head of the Penn-Traffic Store ("The largest Store Between Philadelphia and Pittsburgh"), met with the S. W. O. C. strike leaders—David Watkins and John Stevenson. According to a stenographic report of the conference, Heckman, who was one of the organizers of the Citizens' Committee, told Watkins and Stevenson that "the business men of the Greater Johnstown area will absolutely refuse to permit the employees of the Bethlehem Steel Company to organize and bargain collectively with their employer, as such procedure would be harmful to our business."

Watkins, who had been tackling Johnstown for a year, soon buckled under this and half a dozen other forms of pressure: (1) the press: the unions had nothing with which to combat the stridently anti-union blasts of the Johnstown *Democrat* and the Johnstown *Tribune*— the only papers in town and jointly owned; (2) the clergy: leading union-baiter in town was the Rev. John H. Stanton, Presbyterian, a member of the Executive Committee of the Citizens' Committee, and its spokesman over the radio; not one among Johnstown's score of ministers spoke up for the rights of the strikers; (3) the white-collar workers: these were frightened by the timely firing of clerks in the town's biggest store as soon as the strike began; by the whispering campaign that a long strike would cause Bethlehem to move its plants away from Johnstown; and by the Citizens' Committee's success at painting the S. W. O. C. as rabble-rousing Bolsheviki; (4) the small business men, who were angered at the cessation of payrolls spent in their stores, and who feared the loss of the plant altogether; (5) the upper business group who had, in addition to the fears of the lesser brethren, a close and friendly alliance with the company itself; (6) the farmers: with mortgages from the region largely held by the bank at Johnstown, it was easy for Bank President Suppes to dig up "800 farmers prepared to do for Johnstown what the farmers did for Hershey"; (7) the local government: headed by an ex-bootlegger, Mayor Daniel Shields, who was convicted two years ago on a federal charge of bribery, the city administration aided the vigilante movement and made possible the deputizing of its men.

The focal point of all these reactionary forces was, of course, the Citizens' Committee. On the Executive Board were: S. H. Heckman, president of the Penn-Traffic Store; George Fiig, manager of the Wolfe and Reynolds Store; Carl Geis, manager of Geis Store; the

80 C. I. O. Industrial Unionism in Action

Rev. John H. Stanton; Francis C. Martin, cashier of the United States Bank; and Lawrence Campbell, his secretary and head of the Chamber of Commerce, member of the Board of Merchants Board of Industry, and Citizens Council of Greater Johnstown.

Later, Martin testified that as chairman he had received $10,000 from Sidney D. Evans of the Bethlehem Company. He also revealed that Bethlehem had given $30,000 to Mayor Shields through the Committee; and Michael J. Sewak, Burgess of Franklin Borough, testified that Bethlehem's officials had offered him $7,500 to "go along with them," and when he demurred, doubled the bribe.

The Committee had about four to seven hundred of what it termed "active members" and what others called deputies or vigilantes. It set up offices in all the schoolhouses and appealed over the radio and through the press for supporters.

Picketing was rendered ineffectual by unobtrusive means. Instead of issuing a formal prohibition, Mayor Shields simply began arresting any picket who spoke the word "scab," time-honored labor epithet for a man who walks through a picket line when his mates are on strike. The police shot one crowd with tear gas, and, after putting it to flight, fired into it with side-arms, sending two men to the hospital.

When Governor Earle declared martial law, on grounds that forty thousand miners were set to march on Johnstown, the Cambria plant was closed down for a week. It opened again under control of the state troopers.

The company sent most of its men into the plant through one entrance—the lower Franklin gate. This is so situated as to make picketing almost impossible. Using the plausible argument that the road by that gate must be kept open as a highway, the head of the troopers limited the number of pickets to six. Since streetcars from town rolled right up to the gate, "scabs" had only to walk past a tiny knot of men to be inside the plant. Under those conditions the unionists couldn't declare in any effective manner their opinion of those returning to work.

By June 27, the back-to-work movement was in full swing. Workers were canvassed from house to house; one man was told that his neighbor was going back; his neighbor was told the same thing. Foremen telephoned their men to be back at work, or they would lose their identity checks. On the other hand, S. W. O. C. men were forbidden to enter any workman's house on the theory that this would constitute coercion. State troopers habitually stopped them walking on the same side of the street as a returning worker; this was called "following." The Citizens' Committee ran full-page ads, arranged by the John Price Jones advertising agency of New York, urging the strike-breaking movement along; and each day the Johnstown papers announced the demise of the walkout.

On the night of June 28 dynamite blew up two water mains leading to the Cambria plant. It was generally assumed that the C. I. O. was responsible, but conclusive evidence has yet to be revealed. There are reasons, however, for feeling that company men set off the explosions. One: they occurred shortly after the arrival at the Cambria plant of fifty Burns Detective Agency men—otherwise known as finks or strike-breakers. Two: the pipes were blown up five hours apart at points most easily guarded and most easily mended—right at their exit from the tunnels through the dams. Two weeks previously Major Adams of the state troopers had warned the Bethlehem Company to protect those pipelines; and the union claims they were normally guarded night and day all along the route. Again, hints that there might be a bombing had come from Shields on two occasions, and from company policemen.

The question—who would benefit the more by such tactics—remains somewhat murky. The company was forced to shut down for three or four days, just when it seemed to have the strikers on the run. But if the union had wanted to sabotage at all, one would expect them to do so far more effectively; and also to be aware that the reaction to such a maneuver would far outweigh any breathing-spell thus attained. One fact is clear: the bombing proved a gift to the company. Amid tremendous uproar, the C. I. O. was dramatically linked with violence, dynamite, and bloody insurrection, and its strike leaders were successfully discredited. Mayor Shields publicly told Jim Mark, white-haired miner now leading the strike, and C. R. Jones, the trainmen's chief, that he would no longer be responsible for their safety—either an abdication of civil obligation, or a plain threat. The union men accepted it as both, and chose to remain. The strike, however, was beaten.

11.

Simultaneously, the situation in Youngstown was elaborating upon the Johnstown pattern.

Control of public opinion had begun early. Three months before the strike broke the Sheet and Tube Company started "educating" the Ministerial Association, the Men Teachers Association, and the Service Clubs (the Rotary, Kiwanis, Lions), reminding them —at dinners in the plant—how much money the industry poured into their community, and appealing to them to back up the industry in case "trouble" should appear.

"Trouble" appeared in due course; and a well-fed opinion responded according to formula under the daily guidance of *The Vindicator*, Youngstown's only paper. The back-to-work movement was launched, with Ray Thomas, a district attorney once indicted for graft, returning from a sojourn in Florida to lead it. His outlook on industrial relations was simple: "Give me 200 good, tough, armed men and I'll clean up them sons of bitches on the picket line in no time."

Back of Thomas stood the Mahoning Valley Citizens' Committee, and back of the Committee stood Carl Ullman, president of Youngstown's Dollar Savings Bank. When citizens put pressure on the county commissioners against giving Sheriff Elser money to buy deputies and gunmen, the sheriff went straight to Ullman's bank. There, presumably on his personal reputation and his sheriff's salary, he was granted unlimited credit and a draft with which he purchased ten thousand dollars' worth of tear gas and other equipment.

The attack on the morale of the strikers followed customary lines at first: a newspaper campaign, house-to-house intimidation, shooting pickets, and arrests of strike leaders. Men were taken into custody without charges, and held at the police station while deputies without warrants ransacked their houses. Truck-loads of vigilantes mobilized at central points and rushed out in squads to break up meetings and picket lines.

The strikers had relied on President Roosevelt to make Little Steel come to terms. As a barely audible answer to their prayers had come the Steel Mediation Board. They felt that while it was deliberating the plants should be kept closed to maintain "the status quo." So did Governor Davey of Ohio—for a few days. When he ordered in national guardsmen to do this job, the pickets greeted them as brotherly heroes.

Then the screws were clamped down on Davey. Suddenly he discovered that the "right to work is no less sacred than the right to strike." In realistic terms that meant that the national guard would be used to get the plants going again.

A strike area was marked out, in which only six pickets were allowed at each gate. Arrests now became wholesale.

Every organizer in the region went to jail at least once, and some of them five or six times. One was arrested for being armed; he had a pair of nail-scissors in his pocket. At one time 225 men were behind bars in "technical custody," which meant that they were held without charges and consequently without bail privileges. Strikers given the third degree were booked as having fallen down the station steps, or even as having fallen off their chairs. The S. W. O. C. sound-truck was confiscated. Police raided picket headquarters on Poland Avenue, cut the telephone wires, and held the building for hours while the shifts were changing on a critical day in the back-to-work movement.

Strikers began drifting back to the mills in droves. Here, as always when mass picketing is outlawed, morale became as difficult to maintain as it was crucial. First it hung upon Roosevelt's action; he did nothing. Then it switched to the Mediation Board, which made a few well-meaning gestures and went home. It shifted to the national guard, who were to save them from the vigilantes, the police, the deputies. And their guardsmen friends turned into strike-breakers. Among the militant, experienced miners, this could not have happened. Once decided to strike, they would have pinned their faith on nobody but themselves and their own strength.

12.

In Canton the Citizens Law and Order League took the back-to-work technique firmly in hand. The League's officers: T. K. Harris, general chairman (real estate and property management); E. A. McCuskey, vice-chairman (attorney); Warren Hoffman, vice-chairman (manufacturer); R. W. Loichot, treasurer (vice-president of First National Bank).

Chief counsel for the League was Adolph Unger, convicted on a federal liquor charge, dropped from West Point, sent back from France to avoid court-martial, and eventually turned down by the Stark County Bar Association as unfit to practice.

Supporting it variously were the Chamber of Commerce, the Canton Exchange Club, Retail Merchants Board, Independent Grocers Association, the Clearing House Association, the Insurance Club, the Life Underwriters Association, and the American Legion Club. To the Rev. Oscar Mees and the Rev. P. H. Welsheimer was entrusted the job of marshaling the clergy behind the movement. The owner of the local radio station, Father Graham, was found "very co-operative" in arranging talks to the citizenry.

Middle-class opposition to the League died at birth. A Mr. Kinnison, attorney for the Pennsylvania Railroad, began urging League members to take it easy and not lose their heads. Promptly the Republic Steel Corporation heard of it, and informed the Pennsylvania. Mr. Kinnison said no more.

Then the League rounded up three hundred deputies for the mayor and the chief of police. At this juncture, however, Governor Davey's troops took over and transformed the back-to-work formula into tragi-comic reality: (1) Staged duplicate and triplicate auto caravans in and out of the plant to give the impression that the strike was broken; (2) spread the word through foremen and others that the men were to come back or lose their brass identity checks; or, if taken back, were to undergo a new physical exam—the bugbear of steel workers after a few weeks of undernourishment; (3) arrested the leaders and the picket captains and demoralized the rank-and-file.

The last operation was carried out to the full. Guardsmen mapped a strike area several miles square around the plants; no one could leave or enter without a military pass. Troops blocked off highways leading to the city, to intercept S. W. O. C. sympathizers from Akron or elsewhere. Overhead two military planes droned all day long, spotting any gathering of men on street-corners or any line of cars approaching the city. Guardsmen with new tear-gas guns and riot sticks grimly paraded the streets.

Hundreds of strikers were arrested in the Youngstown manner, and held incommunicado. Observers suggested that the strikers post a sign over the county jail—"C. I. O. Headquarters." Two small children went to the hospital with wounds in the back and stomach from bayonet jabs by young troopers who raided picket headquarters intermittently and took occupants off to jail. They beat one man to death and found two town doctors to testify later that he died of "heart-failure"—though eye-witness affidavits affirmed the clubbing.

The militia took to roaming streets outside of the strike zone and arresting people who did not "move along" fast enough to please them. Those apprehended for this were—like all the rest in the Mahoning Valley—photographed and fingerprinted. The usefulness of such procedure after the strike is obvious; no company would rehire men with those "records."

A Canton judge granted an injunction restricting the number of pickets to six at each gate. His mind seems to have been made up in advance of the hearing; for the last speaker had hardly closed his argument when the judge handed down the document fully drawn.

On July 15, Sheriff Joseph Nist forbade picketing

altogether. He had found some nails scattered on a street near the plant.

13.

Near-by Massillon proved true to type. The impetus for the back-to-work movement originated as in most cases with those not directly involved in the dispute—the leaders of the Law and Order League. They were Messrs. Whitman, merchant; Case of the Chamber of Commerce; Bordner, grocer; Arnold, undertaker; Schiadnagle, undertaker; and Roush, owner of the Rose Hill Cemetery. The last three lent a grim note not belied by subsequent events.

At the beginning of the strike men had stayed in the Republic plant, reports differing as to whether they were besieged by hostile pickets or held inside by company police. Within a few weeks, however, three hundred of them had trickled out, bored with daily rations of a can of pork and beans and a few five-cent candy bars.

Despite theatrical motorcades in and out of the plant, and the imposition of the national guard, the strike remained in good shape—from the union's point of view—up to the night of July 11. Meanwhile behind the scenes a struggle was going on that was to culminate in blood—a struggle between Police Chief Stanley Switter and the combined forces of the Republic Steel Corporation and the Massillon Law and Order League. For weeks, Switter later testified before the National Labor Relations Board, a Republic superintendent named Carl Meyers had "pounded" him to swear in more deputies and handle the S. W. O. C. pickets as Chicago police had handled their comrades in June, killing ten strikers and wounding many more. Of the Chicago force Meyers spoke admiringly: "They know how to handle the situation."

Switter persistently refused, even with Meyers' insistence that if police did not break the strike "the mills would close, the town would become a mere junction point between roads, and would not need a mayor or chief of police or any officials." Then General William Marlin, of the national guard, joined in the hunt, urging Switter to appoint deputies from the League's list which included a good many Republic employees. "This is no time to be neutral," scoffed the General, seconding Meyers' threat.

Political influence was brought to bear. On July 7 the Law and Order League threatened to impeach the Mayor, also recalcitrant at first, and to remove Switter from office. On that day the chief caved in; he had been working sixteen to twenty hours a day since the strike began on May 26, and had just spent four days and nights with almost no sleep.

"I finally told them it was up to the Mayor," he said. "They made the old boy pretty hot. Then they jumped on me. I said all right I would appoint the whole damned outfit. I would give them everything they wanted. I could see there would be a battle and bloodshed as soon as they put guns into those rookies' hands."

At the Brookside Country Club, one evening later that week, Switter accepted from Republic Steel a secret consignment of armaments which included three tear-gas guns, ninety tear-gas shells, three sawed-off shotguns and six boxes of shells.

On the night of July 11 they were used. Switter had gone out of town for dinner and "a few beers." In his absence, one Captain Harry Curley, retired contractor and ex-army officer, took command of the police and, without any authority from Switter, increased the forces watching the pickets. At about eleven in the evening the Massillon police force, plus Curley's deputies, lined up near the S. W. O. C. picket headquarters. Some two

C. I. O. in Steel

hundred men gathered there, as the picket details were changing shifts. Shortly afterwards additional police arrived from Canton.

A striker pulled up in his car, the lights trained down the street on the police. Two deputies moved toward him: "Turn those lights out or we'll shoot them out!" The driver complied, and got out of the machine. Returning a few moments later, he switched on his lights to drive off. Instantly machine-gun and tear-gas fire raked the front of his car, the street, and the ramshackle building. Fulgencio Calzada fell to the street with a bullet in his head. Nick Vadios, shot in the abdomen, died next morning. Thirteen strikers were treated in the hospitals for wounds, but there were others who took their wounds home, afraid to seek medical attention in town. The only police injured were those sickened by their own gas.

Two hours later, when the gassed C. I. O. headquarters had become safe for human lungs, troops confiscated the union's records and smashed the remaining furniture. Then started a drag hunt for C. I. O. members. All night long doors were smashed down and men routed out of bed, to be taken in truck-loads to the jail. Soon they overflowed the Massillon station, and some were carted over to Canton. Morning found more than 150 imprisoned, and many of them were detained without charges—for three or four days.

As a follow-up Massillon banned all picketing and public meetings.

The frame building in which, before that Sunday night, some fourteen hundred men had centered their struggle for a fuller and freer life; in which day after day union women served a diet of ground-hog flesh and corn that friendly farmers donated—this building now stood silent, bitter with tear gas. Next day the Massillon

Independent observed with quiet satisfaction that no pickets were to be seen there.

14.

Other points in Ohio betrayed the now-familiar pattern. At Warren, local business men and farmers formed the John Q. Public League, which undertook the same tasks as citizens' committees elsewhere. As always, the back-to-work movement formed the keystone of their efforts. Strike-breakers flooded the town in such numbers that travelers through Warren could find no accommodations for the night in its three cheaper hotels or in the Y. M. C. A.

First Republic had been forced to send supplies into the plant by airplane; later on, automobile processions moved in and out of the plants daily; but police prevented pickets and even reporters from checking the license numbers to determine how many cars were entering and re-entering in the same shift, like stage armies circling a backdrop.

Fifty men were jailed at Warren—temporarily and without charges. A court order prohibited pickets—only six allowed at any gate—to say anything to incoming workers and strike-breakers.

At Niles, too, Republic imported strike-breakers. Suddenly, during the strike, many Negroes appeared in a plant which had never hired any before. Here it was that pickets turned back mail to the postoffice if they "smelled" anything unusual. Postal authorities had adopted the policy that packages of food intended for strike-breakers were "irregular"—just as they had decreed during the General Motors strike that shipments to the Fisher Body sit-downers were "irregular." According to the Assistant Postmaster General, the government was determined to remain neutral.

C. I. O. in Steel

Early in the strike the Memorial Day massacre eloquently underlined the situation in Chicago. Subsequently police placed five hundred men around the plants to prevent further attempts at picketing, and local newspapers chanted their plaint that the murdered strikers had been attempting to "storm" the company shops. Leader of this journalistic voodoo was the Chicago *Tribune,* with Hearst's two papers and the *Daily News* close on its heels.

At Indiana Harbor, fifty miles away, occurred the C. I. O.'s nearest approach to a victory. On July 1, Inland Steel sent to Indiana's Governor Townsend a statement embodying recognition of the S. W. O. C. as representative for its own members in Inland's plants, its acceptance of the procedure of collective bargaining and seniority rights, and its willingness to arbitrate cases of alleged discrimination. Further, the company agreed to let the National Labor Relations Board decide—by election if necessary—whether a majority of its workers favored the union. The statement clearly implied Inland would sign a contract if the Board so advised.

This was no victory, though the S. W. O. C. preferred to treat it as such; but at least it held a promise of victory. And the strikers were inclined to see in it evidence of Inland's good faith, moved by a natural desire to save face by avoiding a direct contract.

Messrs. Girdler, Grace, and Purnell felt no compulsion to make a truce. Mr. Girdler, in a series of progressively maladroit press conferences, admitted that he put guns and ammunition in his plants, that he never had any intention of making even an oral agreement with the S. W. O. C.; then—in his best gutterese —he proceeded to curse the President, Governors Murphy and Earle, Myron Taylor, Secretary Perkins, and all three members of the President's Mediation Board.

By this time he had forgotten all about the Wagner Act. He would sign no agreement, he now proclaimed, because John Lewis's organization was irresponsible and broke contracts. Another reason, spoken in a rash moment: he was determined to "make wages conform to the price of steel, if it involves changing them from hour to hour." Here, at last, was a grain of truth; a statement making more sense than all his earlier sophistries and debaters' points put together.

By these words, Tom Girdler squared himself with his deeds. Both reveal a man who wants to run a gigantic business enterprise to please himself alone; a man whose outlook on modern industrial society is best summed up in the words: *Labor is a commodity*—a concept which the United States Congress expressly repudiated twenty one years ago. To preserve that outlook, Girdler and his friends waged and won the Little Steel war—for the time being.

15.

Why was the S. W. O. C. defeated?

There are some who insist that the strike was not a union defeat, but a government defeat. The argument goes that the S. W. O. C. depended on the support of those public officials whom it had helped to elect, notably Governors Davey and Earle, and President Roosevelt. If this support had been forthcoming in the measure it was due, the strikers would have won a victory.

But Governor Davey weakened quickly, it is alleged, and allowed his troops to aid the companies to staff their plants with enlarged forces. Governor Earle, after an excellent gesture of support of the union, withdrew the troops, prematurely, and because of anti-union pressure.

This made it possible for Bethlehem to reopen and wait the strikers out.

The President, the argument continues, refused to reprimand the companies before the strike, and remained aloof after it began except for a display of fine impartiality when he condemned extremists on both sides. A disastrous blow to the union.

This view has substance. Most of the allegations are true. But they are not the whole truth, nor perhaps the most important part of the explanation of the union's defeat.

The loss of the strike was based on a serious miscalculation by the leaders in charge. In the two and a half months since the signing of the Carnegie-Illinois contract, union membership in Little Steel districts had rolled up gratifyingly. The S. W. O. C. generally misinterpreted the significance of that fact. It didn't mean that even a militant membership could whip so strong a foe.

The miscalculation can be traced back to two primary factors. One was the widespread overconfidence among the steel workers, and even in the S. W. O. C. high command, because of the magnificent success already achieved and the C. I. O.'s striking triumph in the fight with General Motors.

The other sprang, as Mr. Stolberg has pertinently observed, from the background of the steel organizers themselves. Almost all of them had acquired their experience in mining regions, and the miners are a very different breed. Behind them stretches a long and continuous tradition of militant unionism. When a strike is called, they have no need for pickets: it is a 100 per cent walkout. The union by now is in their blood; they are educated. Steel workers are not—yet. Their last big strike took place years ago, and it proved a grim failure.

94 C. I. O. Industrial Unionism in Action

Racial antagonisms still divide their ranks; they have passed years of their working lives in an atmosphere of union defeatism; and unlike the miners they live in towns where the middle class remains the dominant group.

The members of the C. I. O. most keenly interested in Steel were Lewis and Brophy, ex-miners. On the S. W. O. C. staff Philip Murray, David MacDonald, and Van A. Bittner came from the U. M. W.—either loaned to the S. W. O. C. or shifted permanently. In Johnstown David Watkins, miner, preceded Jim Mark, president of U. M. W.'s District No. 2. In Youngstown John Mayo, another mine veteran, was in charge; in Cleveland were Damich and Hall; in Chicago, Bittner, Russek, and Weber.

Organizers on the spot tend to overestimate the enthusiasm of their membership, since the men they see most frequently are the energetic, aggressive front-rankers. In this case, reports streaming back to S. W. O. C. headquarters were highly misleading; they promised a solid walkout, and minimized the extent of the reactionary forces.

Even so, the S. W. O. C. command entertained a good many qualms about trying a strike. Some of the staff felt it would be a stronger move in the end to call for National Labor Relations Board elections in the plants, even if the companies refused to abide by the results; and then to press for a court ruling making it an unfair labor practice under the Wagner Act to agree on terms and yet refuse to embody them in a signed contract. But others believed they could not wait that long; the companies were forcing the issue. Republic Steel had shut down one plant in Massillon for no appreciable reason except that it was 100 per cent unionized. In other plants the C. I. O. men were being fired by the dozen.

C. I. O. in Steel

There is, in retrospect, little question now that to wait and attack in the courts would have been the wiser tactic. Given the S. W. O. C.'s fatal misjudgment of the temper and wisdom of its rank-and-file, and a consequently inadequate local preparation, the employer's violent, shrewd, and stubborn counter-attack proved unbearable.

In the name of all steel workers and the nation, but actually for the sake of economic power and industrial despotism, Little Steel carried its point against the strikers. With the assistance of the press, the clergy, the citizens' committees and their vigilantes, city, county, and state authorities and the national guard, Little Steel broke the strike—"in the worker's own best interest." As Governor Davey expressed it to a strikers' delegation protesting the violence of deputies: "After it's all over, I hope you'll love me as I love you, because I love you all!"

IV. C. I. O. IN AUTOMOBILES

1.

IN the fall of 1926 the American Federation of Labor held its annual Convention in Detroit. In seven years, Mr. Green's "Family of Labor" had dwindled to a modest two-thirds of its post-war figure of four millions. The Convention assembled in the capital of the automobile industry of the United States; but it was not the capital of unionism. Auto workers claiming membership in the A. F. of L. numbered but a few hundred. Detroit and the automobile industry were not only non-union; they were militantly anti-union.

The time had come, the Convention decided, to plan for the belated organization of auto workers. So they put through a resolution defying the open-shop employers, and called for a meeting of all interested craft unions.

Reaction rolled like a fog from the columns of the Michigan press. Editors wrote vigorously of the coming "Struggle of the Titans." The Automobile Chamber of Commerce issued pronouncements warning against this "un-American undertaking." The Employers' Association of Detroit beat out the slogan "Detroit is Detroit because of the Open Shop," while the more inclusive Citizens' Committee, backed by the local Chamber of Commerce, proclaimed the formation of a union of fifty local business men's associations to oppose the A. F. of L. Committee leaders accused Mr. Green and his associates of being "against the government." They warned, they indicted, they attempted to prevent Mr.

C. I. O. in Automobiles 97

Green from speaking in local churches. To "maintain the American Plan of employment in Detroit" they solicited a large fund, pleading that "if the A. F. of L. is successful, it will mean untold hardship for our workmen and the expenditure of millions of dollars by our employees."

Their worries and their solicitude were needless. The Federation talked big. Later, however, the crafts' meeting found the difficulties so great that, in the words of one delegate, "the question of attempting to organize the auto workers was temporarily laid aside." The program "should be undertaken from a different angle and direction." This "different angle" was a curious one, betraying the Federation leaders as either touchingly innocent or paralyzed by a sense of the hopelessness of their task. The plan amounted to this: that Mr. Green should write letters to the militantly anti-union auto magnates "with a view to inducing them to enter into conference for the purpose of trying to negotiate an understanding that might result in lessening the opposition of the officials of these companies to their employees being organized." Of course employers either did not reply at all, or wrote that they were satisfied with things as they were. The industry remained non-union.

Ten years passed. The same anti-union city of Detroit with its neighboring automobile principalities was besieged by a very different foe—the C. I. O.—acting through the United Automobile Workers of America. In a few short months the U. A. W. forced two of the nation's three giant motor concerns to reverse their labor policies, and put the third squarely on the defensive. Union membership mounted in a year from thirty-five thousand to almost four hundred thousand. Employing new techniques and manifesting an impres-

98   C. I. O. Industrial Unionism in Action

sive solidarity, the United Auto Workers fought and won a series of prolonged and bitter strikes.

2.

The auto penetrates every fiber of American civilization. It has altered the tempo of an era, the cohesion of a continent, the morality of a generation. With puckish impartiality it has profoundly affected a thousand facets of our culture—attendance at movies, the technique of war, the sale of clothes, the tax policies of the government, suburbanization, the growth of the insurance business, the winning of elections at home, the extension of imperialism abroad, the size of the farm unit, the solvency of trolley lines, profits in cement, rubber, and glass, the standards of rural education.

One certainty emerges: the auto is the golden calf of the machine age, the pet of millions and the god of many. Who touches the idol, touches a nation to the quick. And the auto workers undertook their spectacular campaigns of organization and the pyrotechnical strikes which followed with the uncomfortable realization that they were operating on a stage, closely watched by a tremendous and potentially inimical public.

The United States makes eight of every ten automobiles in the world, and of these 75 per cent are built in Michigan. At the hub of this universe, Detroit thrives on an international traffic: its population has grown 500 per cent since 1900 while its satellites—Flint, Highland Park, Pontiac, Hamtramck—have become major cities of one hundred thousand or more.

The industry itself belongs to a race of giants. In 1935 General Motors, Chrysler, and Ford together showed assets of two and a quarter billions, as compared with a total for all public utilities of five billions, for the

C. I. O. in Automobiles

large chemical companies of less than two billions, and for the coal companies of three-quarters of a billion. If all the minor auto companies were added to the Big Three, their combined assets would closely match steel's proud boast of four billions. Revolutionizing our industrial past, Motordom now sharply contests Steel's traditional domination. Car and truck output mounts by hundreds of thousands of units annually: two and a quarter millions in 1920, five and three-quarters millions in 1929; after the Great Depression, four and a half millions in 1936. Dollar value of the product reached three and a half billions in 1929. This year it will amount to two and one half billions at the least.

3.

Three names control the auto industry. Between them General Motors, Chrysler, and Ford produce 90 per cent of the cars sold in the United States. Their share of the total has grown steadily for many years, the last depression serving to accentuate the trend. By 1935 the smaller companies were reduced to a diet of crumbs from the tables of the Big Three.

The world's largest auto firm is General Motors—in capital, number of stockholders, employees, plants, and market extension. An operating enterprise, its affiliates fall into several classes: "Eight passenger and commercial car companies with eighteen plants; twenty body and parts companies with thirty-seven plants; a national service company; Delco Appliance and Frigidaire; two airplane plants; eastern, western and transcontinental air lines; Ethyl gasoline; four members of its own financial group; four real estate companies"; and a network of sales and assembly companies around the world. In 1934, 20 per cent of the world market outside the United States and Canada went to General Motors.

It owns Vauxhall Motors of England and Adam Opel, A. G. of Germany. Through the former it does nearly 10 per cent of the British business, and through the latter a good 40 per cent of the German—where its plants occupy a strategic position in the military plans of the Hitler government. G. M. is an international enterprise.

From 1909 to 1937, G. M.'s net sales have exceeded sixteen billion dollars, two billion of which have been available for dividends among its three hundred and forty thousand stockholders. Preferred dividends in that period have amounted to one hundred and seventy-five millions, while common stock has received over a billion and a half. In addition, stock dividends have frequently been distributed as a device to make cash dividends seem smaller than they really were. About six hundred millions of profits have been plowed back into the business.

The largest single stockholders are the Du Pont family. With eighty million dollars, much of it borrowed from J. P. Morgan and Co., they acquired a quarter interest in the corporation in 1921. These eighty millions have yielded them over two hundred and fifty millions in dividends up to date—a generous 300 per cent in fifteen years. Du Ponts have dominated the company since its birth. Eight of the family or near-family sit on the board of thirty-five. The president, chairman of the board, and chairman of the important Finance Committee are known as Du Pont men. Seven Du Ponts and four Morgans control the fourteen-man Finance Committee. The full directorate, if its connections were traced in all directions, would reveal intermarriage with most of the elements of industrial and financial power in the United States.

Ownership is widely scattered, but control highly concentrated. Management rests with G. M.'s officers,

C. I. O. in Automobiles

the most highly paid in the world. In 1935, while the hourly rate of employees rose 5 per cent (or about three cents), the eleven top officers were granted increases ranging from 50 to 100 per cent. Twenty-seven executives got salaries in excess of fifty thousand dollars in that year, fifteen in excess of one hundred thousand dollars, ten above two hundred thousand dollars and two—President Sloan and Executive Vice-President Knudsen—were paid about three hundred and fifty thousand dollars apiece. Each reached a half million in 1936.

For its owners and officers, General Motors has been an Aladdin's lamp. We shall see later that the story runs somewhat differently for its two hundred and eleven thousand workers.

FORD: The Ford Motor Company is a family domain, with chief estate at Dearborn, Michigan. The biggest manufacturing plant, the River Rouge factory, employs ninety thousand men, and houses a power, light and heat plant, fire department, telephone and telegraph exchange, glass factory, freight and express offices, laboratories, machine shops, a boys' trade school, hospital, safety and hygiene departments, and a motion-picture studio. Here are blast furnaces, foundry, body plant, motor assembly plant, coke ovens, steel plant, cement factory, and repair shops for locomotives. Ford is now erecting a rubber plant for the manufacture of tires.

Ford assembles his cars at seventeen plants located at strategic points from coast to coast. Within sixty-five miles of Dearborn twenty villages live by producing small parts for Ford. Factory, sales, and service branches are located in eighteen countries; manufacturing plants in Canada, England, and Germany. The company owns iron ore and lumber resources, coal mines in Kentucky and West Virginia, and lake- and ocean-going steamers.

102 C. I. O. Industrial Unionism in Action

Supplementing its own supplies, Ford buys from seven thousand firms throughout the United States, and pays them a billion dollars a year. Many a distant merchant marches to the music of Ford's money.

In 1914 Ford made over a quarter of a million cars and trucks. For five years, starting in 1923, he turned out an annual stint of two million units. In 1937, the number will probably reach a million and a half, produced by a working force of one hundred and twenty-two thousand men and women.

The Ford family's profits have been colossal. In the thirty-three years of the company's existence, thirteen billion dollars of sales have left a profit for the owners of seven hundred and eighty-two million. As the four millionth V8 came off the assembly line in 1936, the United States could acclaim a citizen who had amassed a private fortune of a billion dollars, with all the breath-taking powers and prerogatives such wealth confers.

CHRYSLER: A new-comer. His success has titillated even the jaded interest of the automobile industry. His company has become the outstanding competitor of General Motors and Ford. In 1922, Chrysler sold only fifty thousand cars. In 1929 he sold four hundred and fifty thousand and netted an income of over twenty millions. In 1936 that high was bettered with 1,066,229 cars produced, sixty thousand workers employed, and a profit of sixty-two millions or $1,425 per share.

4.

The lesson of these figures is multiple, but it can be summarized in one word: power. Power over materials, money, and men. It is worth asking how that power over men has been exercised.

The workers engaged in actual production of cars number about four hundred and fifty thousand men and women. Most of these—young, strong, adaptable—have come into the Detroit area from the farms of the Mid-West and the back-country of the South, many at the direct solicitation of the auto companies. In 1934, forty-seven out of every hundred workers in the Detroit plants were found to have migrated there between 1922 and 1929. Less than one per cent were native.

The entire country has invested this vital resource in the auto industry, that everyone may ride. These thousands of workers have pitched their lives in tune with the hum of the belt-line.

Let it be emphasized that the enterprise in which these lives have been invested is at once a marvel of mechanical efficiency and an arrogant despotism. The hundreds of items that make up the daily life of the worker in the factory—wage rates, hours, speed of machinery, routing of materials, hiring, promotion, firing—have been determined solely by the managements of the companies without consultation of those affected. Strictly speaking, this has been government without the consent of the governed. And judging by the long and varied record of complaints, this industrial plutocracy has been anything but beneficent.

In 1935 a government report by Leon Henderson on the automobile industry reviewed the status of the workers: "Labor unrest exists to a degree higher than warranted by the depression. The unrest flows from insecurity, low annual wages, inequitable hiring and rehiring methods, espionage, speed-up, and displacement of the workers at an early age." And this antedated the appearance of the C. I. O. Let us investigate these charges briefly.

As to wages, the industry seems to have enjoyed a somewhat undeserved fame. Since 1914 when Mr. Ford announced a five-dollar minimum day for his employees, writers and speakers everywhere have popularized the high-wage story as though it were unalloyed truth. No one would deny that hour, piece, and day rates have been relatively high. In 1934 the average hourly rate stood at seventy cents; and it has since been raised from 10 to 20 per cent. Thus in 1934 a worker might make twenty-eight dollars in a forty-hour week; perhaps thirty-five dollars today.

But these are average figures, from which there are departures downward and upward. The former far outnumber the latter because the workers in the industry are chiefly unskilled. Years ago Ford figured that 43 per cent of all the jobs in his plant could be learned in a day, 36 per cent required from a day to a week, 6 per cent from one to two weeks, and 14 per cent from two weeks to a year. Recently a Chrysler official claimed 75 per cent of his employees had been trained in a day or two. And the less skilled the job, the less it pays.

Average rates are high, relative to those in other industries. But it is the annual wage that is important to a family's life, and automobile annual earnings are subject to a grievous instability. Cars are made in abundance in some months, and little or not at all in others. Keeping pace with this monthly fluctuation of production, employment oscillates violently. Regularly each year, thousands of auto workers are turned off for periods of a few weeks to two or three months. Most of them fail to get other work during this time.

Here we find the explanation for the low actual earnings, and they are not quite what the public supposes. Reliable estimates placed them at thirteen hundred dollars in 1926, nine hundred dollars in 1933. The government report referred to above estimated that 45 per cent of all auto workers were making less than one thousand dollars a year in 1935.

Not surprising, therefore, that the motor men clamor

for greater stability of employment and income. They ask, so to speak, for the "right to work," annually denied them by the prevailing characteristics of the industry. Inevitably, too, with seasonal unemployment an omnipresent threat to income, workers have urged their protection by a seniority system, giving the greatest stability of income to those longest in the industry. The instrument they have been forced to use to secure these measures is—the union.

A second target for workers' complaints has been the speed-up. This practice wears a varied guise. The simplest kind is the foreman's threat that if a man does not step lively, another will take his place. Unless checked by union restraints, foremen utilize such threats universally. Another brand is the slack-season custom of laying off the slowest men first and the fastest last, regardless of seniority—a terrific inducement to speed. Again ambitious department supervisors or plant superintendents push the men by increasing the revolutions of the machines.

Most important of all, however, has been the speed of the assembly lines. Production work in automobiles is largely carried on by means of conveyor belts. There the workers stand, each prepared to do his trick as the frame passes down the line. The car begins, scarcely more than a skeleton held together by a few bolts. Moving along, it reaches someone who places a wheel on the nearest axle. His neighbor tightens the bolts that hold the wheel in place. Another puts in a steering wheel, a fourth sets a fender—each man doing the same thing over and over with grim regularity.

Mr. Ford has observed that "no work is so rude that the worker may not exalt it." A trade journal editor compares the assembly line to a modern dance. But workers, possibly unaesthetic, object that the speed of their dance leaves little breath for exaltation, and life is a torment and a misery. One worker writes from a General Motors plant that "the men work like fiends, the sweat running down their cheeks, their jaws set and eyes on fire. Nothing in the world exists for them except the line of chassis bearing down on them relentlessly ... The men move like lightning; some are underneath on their backs on little carts propelling themselves by their heels all day long, fixing something underneath the chassis as they move along." There seems to be no set speed for these assembly lines. If for some reason the line is shut down for a short while the foremen may increase the speed of the belt—and the men—to make up for the lost time.

The system puts a premium on youth. Life in the industry ends before fifty. The companies deny having such a policy of discharge, but the fact is clear to anyone who stands at a factory gate when shifts are changing. Small loan companies in Detroit refuse loans to auto workers unemployed and over forty years of age: they are not a good risk. Having done their ten-, fifteen- or twenty-year stint for the industry they are pushed out, industrially aged, while still in middle life. The individual worker has no means of combating this scrapping.

Related to the pressure upon workers for speed in production are "incentive" systems of payment based on the familiar piece-work plan. Under the group system, participants in a multiple process share a lump sum for the job. The more produced, the more each gets. The fastest man urges on the others. The bonus system works to the same end, but rates of pay lag farther and farther behind output. The Henderson report charged that both systems have been administered so as to drive men at top speed in a relentless competition, the company profiting at their expense.

Both systems of payment, and particularly the bonus

C. I. O. in Automobiles 107

plan, are further objected to because they make calculation of earnings difficult. Complaint is frequent that men do not know how much they will receive on payday.

The workers have not kept these grievances to themselves. They have made a noise. But to their protests the companies have turned a remarkably deaf ear, refusing effective consultation with the men, and reserving sole decision to management.

The viciousness of this one-sided government manifests itself in petty tyrannies of foremen, unchecked by any authority on the part of those whom they direct. A foreman can make a worker's life on the job unpleasant in innumerable ways: assigning him the less congenial tasks, or failing to deliver materials promptly. He can exercise favoritism in layoffs and in rehiring. He can capriciously victimize workers by outright discharge. Such powers are critical, and need constant check. All employers are familiar with this kind of corruption of authority and can prevent it. Judging from the frequency of complaints against foremen, the auto industry has nurtured the vice in its most exaggerated form.

On top of all these sources of discontent—unstable employment, insecurity of income, the speed-up, complicated systems of payment, and irresponsible tyrannies on the part of foremen—the industry has imposed an extensive espionage system. Confirming bitter observations already current among students of industrial relations, the Henderson report charged that it was an endemic practice in the big companies.

The Senate's La Follette Committee (investigating civil liberties during the last year) corroborated this charge in specific detail.

The experience of auto-worker Richard Frankensteen may be taken as typical. An employee for years in the

Chrysler Dodge plant of Detroit, he had a good record, was a popular man among his fellows, and three years ago they elected him as one of the representatives in the Chrysler company union. Later he became chairman of the group of over a hundred delegates.

Under Frankensteen's leadership, these men quickly learned the shortcomings of this form of employee organization. They found that it secured many small concessions from the company: clean windows, ventilated lavatories, and sanitary milk caps. But when it came to the basic questions of wages, hours, speed-up, and seniority the organization simply did not function. These questions were taboo; they were management problems solely. Frankensteen and his fellow representatives finally formed an independent union, the Automotive Industrial Workers' Association.

All during 1934, Frankensteen worked hard as union president, speaking continuously at meetings of the locals and inspiring in the men a determination for a strong organization. In the course of such after-hours work he met John Andrews. They became close friends. Andrews seemed a militant, fearless union man with ideas congenial to Frankensteen. Day after day, week after week they talked the union problems; and this interest stimulated a friendship between their families. Picnics, dinners at each other's houses, movies, and in 1935 a two weeks' vacation, were shared together. To Andrews Frankensteen gave his unreserved confidence.

But each day Andrews was delivering a complete report of his friend's union activities to his real boss, the Corporations Auxiliary Company, an industrial spy agency in the employ of Chrysler. Andrews' job was to seduce Frankensteen and systematically sell his confidence, in return for ten dollars a week and a padded expense account from Corporations Auxiliary. That concern in turn charged Chrysler nine dollars a day.

It is almost bromidic to remark that Chrysler was interested in Frankensteen because it wished to destroy the union of which he was a leader.

Chrysler was Corporations Auxiliary's best customer, in 1935 alone buying $72,611 worth of its service. General Motors, although employing this concern among others, favored the Pinkerton Detective Agency. With it, they spent $839,764 for spies from January 1, 1934, to July 31, 1936. Half of this went to Pinkerton —and the figures are known to be incomplete. General Motors had bills submitted to it in such form as to make them appear to be charges for quite different services. The spy agencies themselves made their records as difficult to obtain and understand as possible.

In 1933 Corporations Auxiliary had 38 operatives in Chrysler plants; by 1936 there were 430. The expenses of these spies increased as union activities quickened. Chrysler went so far as to spy on the engineers in its Detroit plant, with the result that the Society of Designing Engineers was soon reduced to a fraction of its earlier membership.

With many more spies in its shops than Chrysler, General Motors found matters complicated in the extreme. It even employed G. M. Pinkertons to trail G. M. Corporations Auxiliary men, fearing that the latter might be selling its trade secrets to competitors.

All this elaborate espionage, designed to keep unionism out of the industry, only capped the arch of the employees' accumulated grievances. It was inevitable that they should band together for action. Under the New Deal's encouragement, auto workers formed scores of protective organizations under many different auspices.

Led by General Motors, the companies promptly countered with company-dominated unions. These attracted workers for a while, but their bogus character

110 C. I. O. Industrial Unionism in Action

provoked an inevitable disgust. Outstanding strikes in Toledo Auto-Lite and Toledo Chevrolet in 1934 and 1935 forecast shadows of coming events. In August of the latter year the A. F. of L. chartered the United Automobile Workers of America. In the following spring the U. A. W. elected its own leadership and achieved its first exclusive bargaining agreement—with the Packard Company. In July, 1936, to escape the craft threats that were implicit in continued A. F. of L. connection, it affiliated itself with the C. I. O. Six months later the accumulated discontents of decades burst into the open.

5.

Mr. William S. Knudsen, then executive vice-president of the largest motor company in the world, spoke to the Indianapolis Chamber of Commerce a few days before Christmas, 1936. He asked his audience to "understand that there is no attempt on my part to discourage organization of any sort as long as it is done on legal and constructive lines. I think collective bargaining is here to stay, but I do think collective bargaining ought to take place before a shut-down rather than after."

These remarks are interesting in the light of the following facts, subsequently revealed to the La Follette Committee:

(1) At that moment all five officers of the Lansing local of the United Automobile Workers were Pinkerton undercover agents in the employ of Mr. Knudsen's company. At least one organizer for the union, Arthur Greer, was on the Pinkerton payroll. (2) Under the irritations of the spy system, membership in the Lansing Fisher Plant local had fallen from almost 100 per cent of the workers until only the five officers were left.

The Flint local went from 26,000 members to 122 in the course of a few months for the same reason. (3) Lawrence Barker, a Pinkertonian, had been employed by G. M. during 1936, not only to demoralize unions but also to work among the men for the defeat of Mr. Roosevelt. (4) Mr. Knudsen's personnel director in Chevrolet believed that the use of stool pigeons was a "company habit," and already G. M. was projecting a private detective service of its own. Men were being instructed to use any means "short of bribery" to obtain information on company employees. (5) Chevrolet at Flint had recently bought large quantities of tear gas and tear-gas guns for the local police department, through a complicated billing intended to conceal the identity of the purchaser. (6) Flint workers were required to furnish information concerning union affiliation when soliciting relief from Genesee County authorities. This information was turned over to the General Motors Corporation. (7) After the Toledo Chevrolet strike in 1935, the company settled with a promise to respect the union and bargain collectively in good faith. Six months later, the company moved its machinery to Saginaw, leaving nine hundred Toledo employees without jobs. (8) At the moment Mr. Knudsen was speaking, G. M. strikes were in progress in Kansas City and Atlanta, provoked by alleged discrimination against union workers on the part of local officials of the company.

The day after Mr. Knudsen's reassuring speech, Homer Martin announced for the U. A. W. that Knudsen would soon have the opportunity to make good his words. The union by letter asked for a general conference with the company for collective bargaining. The letter recited the failure of local efforts to negotiate important questions of speed-up, job insecurity, seniority, and piece-work abuses.

112 C. I. O. Industrial Unionism in Action

G. M.'s reply was a refusal to meet in a general conference, and a recommendation that the union take up the grievances with the local authorities of the various plants. It was an evasion of the issue, because everyone knew that the matters listed by the union were beyond the competence of local officials.

Through sheer disgust union workers in the Cleveland Fisher Body Plant sat down spontaneously on December 28. On the twenty-ninth, the manager of the two Fisher plants in Flint was presented with a union contract, with the request that he sign it or at least discuss it within a week. Next morning, workers in Plant Number 2 saw inspectors transferred to other jobs because, it was believed, they would not quit the union. A sit-down began in protest. That afternoon the men in Plant Number 1 took alarm as they saw what appeared to be tools and dies essential to production loaded on box cars for shipment to Pontiac and Grand Rapids—weaker union towns than Flint. They, too, sat down. Plant by plant the G. M. tie-up spread to Norwood and Cleveland, Ohio; to Anderson, Indiana; to Kansas City and Atlanta.

Thus began the first great auto strike, one of the most dramatic labor conflicts in our history. The C. I. O. high command, preoccupied with the drive in steel, tried in vain to prevent the strike; it was fed by deep springs of resentment among thousands of men against a corporation grossly derelict in its obligations. Whether the sit-downs caught G. M. officials by surprise is difficult to say. Certainly their strategy remained confused during much of the conflict.

Following its usual ritual, G. M.'s first act was to apply for an injunction. A Judge Black ordered the sit-downers to leave the plants, and enjoined all picketing of company property. In sum, he told the workers that they should not conduct a strike within, nor defend a strike without the plants. The sheriff, attempting to serve the court order, was "laughed out of the plant" as a band of pickets marched defiantly in the streets below. Nothing more was heard of this injunction, although the judge later suffered severe criticism for sitting in a dispute in which he was actually a participant. Challenged by union lawyers, he admitted ownership of nearly a quarter of a million dollars of G. M. stock. Although he did not seem to think such a status disqualified him to act as judge, sentiment generally sustained a contrary conviction.

The company had declined a general conference before the strike began. On January 3, 1937, it changed its mind. But still it offered only to *discuss* general matters, not to bargain about them. It was still its position that actual negotiation of agreements must be carried on with each plant separately. The union was not interested. Two days later came the first gunning for public favor. With the sit-downs spreading in Ohio and Indiana, President Sloan wrote a letter "To all employees of General Motors Corporation." Posted on plant bulletins and published in several newspapers, it suggests G. M.'s tone at this point in the strike. The company policy, he said, was to allow full freedom of organization to employees. He charged that workers were being forced out of their jobs by the "ruthless" sit-down strikes, union intimidation, and shortage of materials caused by the strike. "The real issue is perfectly clear and here it is: Will a labor organization run the plants of G. M. Corporation or will the management continue to do so?"

On this issue, Mr. Sloan's mind was made up. He had determined that the management should run things, that work was to continue to be given to men according to their abilities; never would the company recognize any union as sole bargaining agency, and so far as G. M. was concerned, "no man will have to pay tribute to any one for the right to work."

His statement was a model of autocratic paternalism, overlaid with shrewd obfuscation. It consistently pretended that the union was demanding a closed shop, and would require men to "pay tribute for the right to work." The union at no time during the strike asked for a closed shop. And it doesn't help much to call voluntary dues to a union "tribute."

Sloan's letter produced little effect. The strike spread to Janesville, Wisconsin, and Cadillac in Detroit, which with closures forced by lack of supplies brought the number of idle employees to ninety thousand by the company's own figures. Any favorable public reaction to Mr. Sloan's appeal was vitiated when the disclosures concerning Judge Black were made public at the end of the week.

The union meanwhile had formed a board of strategy, comprising the general officers of the U. A. W., national representatives of the C. I. O., and the president of the Flat Glass Workers' Union—a C. I. O. affiliate then on strike against the two great glass companies, Pittsburgh Plate Glass Co. and Libbey-Owens-Ford. (These two companies practically own the industry, so that the supply of auto glass was for the time almost completely stopped.) The board quickly set up strike machinery: a national relief committee, speakers' bureau, national citizens' committee, publicity bureaus for Flint and for the whole country. To systematize the feeding of the sit-downers, the U. A. W. hired a chef. Digging in for a long siege, the union tightened its grip on strategic bottleneck plants and effected general paralysis of the whole company.

6.

The strike's second week opened with a company overture. Leading officials offered a conference for *general* negotiations, with the proviso that the company would not recognize the union as sole bargaining agency, and on condition that the sit-downers first evacuate occupied factories. This latter condition, to be repeated many times in ensuing days, undoubtedly appealed to a public disconcerted by this strange new strike tactic which seemed replete with vaguely dangerous possibilities.

But the union declined to take the company proposal in complete good faith, fearing that once the sit-downers had left the plants the company would undertake to start production again. The strategy board replied with a counter-proposal to the governor: they agreed to evacuate, provided the company promised not to remove dies or equipment outside the strike zone, and not to resume production. They offered also to drop temporarily their demand for sole recognition, reserving the right to bring the matter up in conference. Knudsen refused to promise anything and the overtures collapsed. G. M. paused once more, evidently relying on winning wider public support as business groups in the strike communities began to grow restive under loss of trade.

This policy proved fruitful. On the eighth of January there came into existence an organization destined to play a critical role—the Flint Alliance. Flint is a city of one hundred and sixty thousand population, of whom forty-six thousand are on General Motors' payroll. Eighty per cent of the families of the town depend directly upon their jobs at the motor factories. By the

116 C. I. O. Industrial Unionism in Action

second week in January, thirty thousand of them were idle.

Ostensibly the Flint Alliance was born as a "voluntary movement of employees who wish to return to their work, and are against the strike." There is no way of telling how many of the twenty thousand members claimed next day actually worked for General Motors. Certain it is that *membership in the organization was open to all citizens in the town.* Headed by a one-time mayor and former Buick (G. M.) paymaster, it was at once proudly endorsed by a group of two hundred business men, many of whom joined. Housed in an imposing suite of offices in a prominent business building with additional rooms in an expensive hotel, the Alliance was represented by men who had been or still were affiliated with the company, and was assisted by a high-powered publicity agent from New York. As an organization of workers, free of company influences, it was suspect from the start.

But with its aid the Works Council of the Flint Chevrolet Company secured several thousand signatures to a petition condemning the strike. Certainly the Alliance scored in its persistent efforts to label the strike a minority undertaking. Russell B. Porter, antiunion reporter for the New York *Times,* was persuaded, after attending meetings sponsored by the Alliance, that the strike could not claim a majority of the workers. Indeed he doubted that it was backed by even a substantial minority.

The company discovered many odd friends; and the drollest now appeared. Four A. F. of L. craft unions, claiming a jurisdiction (previously unexercised) over certain skilled workers in the industry, denounced the United Automobile Workers as an outlaw union. They charged—adducing no evidence—that a majority of the employees in certain plants disapproved the strike.

Next day eight Federation internationals, among them the Machinists and the Brotherhood of Electrical Workers, wired G. M. officials protesting any agreement which would permit the U. A. W. to bargain on behalf of craft-union members. This too was a claim concerning a paper right. John Frey, for the A. F. of L. Metal Trades, said that "we don't intend to allow the Auto Workers to run away with our union." Martin of the U. A. W. replied that Mr. Frey had no union in the industry with which they could run away. No craft union held an agreement with G. M., or possessed more than a handful of members in the industry. But the company gained from the interchange, for it could answer the U. A. W. demand for exclusive bargaining rights with the Federation's telegrams.

The first violence occurred on January 12—"The Battle of Bulls Run." Changing its tactics about the sit-downers, the company ordered the heat turned off in a Flint Fisher Body plant. City police moved out to the factory while a company force undertook to starve out sit-downers on the second floor, removing ladders by which food was passed to them from the street.

Rallying a storming-party the sit-downers captured the plant gates from the company police, precipitating an attack by the city gendarmes outside. In the mêlée tear-gas bombs hurtled against the strikers inside and outside the plant, the besieged replying with streams of water forced through company firehose. These had the double effect of bowling over the cops and diluting the tear gas.

For hours the battle swirled with clubs, riot guns, tear gas, hinges, and pieces of pavement warming the air. Every window in the plant was broken. The end of the fight found the sit-downers completely victorious, in possession not only of the second floor of the plant but of the first as well.

118 C. I. O. Industrial Unionism in Action

Both parties now turned from brickbats to propaganda. Mr. Lewis launched a bid for overt support of the U. A. W. by Washington. He called for a congressional investigation of General Motors—its finances, watered stock, salaries and espionage. G. M., he charged, was in violation of the National Labor Relations Act.

Meanwhile mass meetings of "loyal" employees in Saginaw, Detroit, Flint and elsewhere gave G. M. a talking-point. These bodies passed resolutions, signed petitions, and solicited government officials. Some light may be thrown on these affairs by a similar demonstration in a St. Louis Chevrolet plant. There forty-five hundred of the five thousand workers signed a petition to the management, protesting their satisfaction with conditions and their intention not to strike. A week later three thousand of them walked out. Union officials maintained that foremen and company officials forced workers to endorse the petition.

7.

The strike's third week brought a curious chain of events in which the Flint Alliance played an unenviable part, while Mr. Lewis shocked a nation by open solicitation of the President.

All along Governor Frank Murphy had been in constant attendance on both union and company officials. His efforts at mediation were tireless. He had been subjected to great pressure to "take a firm stand," to send in troops, to declare martial law, to "crack down on the strikers." But he held fast for patience and a peaceful solution. And on the fourteenth of the month, G. M.'s Mr. Knudsen knuckled under. He told the governor that he would meet with the union officials, even though their men still occupied the plants. This, he emphasized, was to explore possible exits from the situation, not for collective bargaining.

The announcement was widely hailed as the first step toward settlement. A conference held next day produced a tentative fifteen-day truce: the union to evacuate the plants by the eighteenth, the company not to remove equipment or resume production as long as both parties were participating in negotiations "looking toward an agreement on all other matters in dispute." Ostensibly the management had come round to the union proposal of a week earlier.

Sit-downers trooped out of the Detroit and Anderson plants to the tune of band music, singing, and cheering. The general jubilation that followed was marred by only one sour note—the truce collapsed. The Flint Alliance had asked for a conference for collective bargaining and Knudsen had granted the request. Stunned, the union at once called off the evacuation in Flint.

Considering the U. A. W.'s profound suspicion of the semi-vigilante, semi-company union character of the Alliance, Knudsen's action was either a blunder of the first magnitude or evidence that G. M. was not to be trusted. Governor Murphy gave the company a "strong hint" that it had acted stupidly, and that scheduled bargaining with the Alliance should be canceled forthwith. Mr. Lewis summed up the irritation of union leaders: "No half-baked compromise is going to allow G. M. to double-cross us again. We are willing to confer, each side holding its arms." Blandly the company announced that the conference had broken down because the union failed to carry out its agreement.

The Flint Alliance offered to withdraw from the bargaining picture for the time being—a tardy performance. The C. I. O., "holding its arms," began to consolidate its forces. (1) Quickly it arranged a settlement of the Flat Glass Union strike, surrendering a demand for sole bargaining rights and the check-off in return for recognition of its right to bargain for members, and promises from the two companies that they would not bargain with any other organization for the duration of the agreement. Clearly the C. I. O. hoped by ending this strike to relieve G. M.'s competitors of any production difficulty caused by shortage of glass. Free of this restriction, Ford and Chrysler would be able to slash into G. M. sales and contracts. (2) The C. I. O. made a major bid for Washington assistance, as Lewis released what was dubbed an "ultimatum" to Roosevelt: "We have advised the administration through the Secretary of Labor and the Governor of Michigan that for six months the economic royalists represented by General Motors, the Du Ponts, Sloan and others contributed their money and used their energy to drive the President of the United States out of Washington and this Administration out of power.

"The Administration asked Labor to help it repel this attack, and Labor helped the President to repel the economic royalists. The same economic royalists now have their fangs in Labor and Labor expects the Administration to support the auto workers in every legal way in their fight."

Instantly the press concluded that this open call to the President to pay an alleged political debt was a first-class tactical blunder. The New York *Times* noted abruptly that "Mr. Lewis had a full supply of impudence with him." Messrs. Sloan and Knudsen broke off their conferences with the Governor and Miss Perkins, declaring that Mr. Lewis had made it "futile" to continue. Ears turned toward Mr. Roosevelt, who obliged at his next press conference with the vague comment that "there come moments when statements, conversations, and headlines are not in order." Which was interpreted as a well-deserved rebuke to Lewis.

C. I. O. in Automobiles

But Lewis was cannier than his critics. He knew the President, and he had spoken with care. For some time Mr. Roosevelt had avoided him. It was rumored that he was not going to intervene in the dispute in any way, that he wanted—understandably—to avoid making any C. I. O. commitment which would anger A. F. of L. officials and alienate the public. So Mr. Lewis decided to bolster Mr. Roosevelt's morale by reminding him of the truth: that he had been opposed viciously by the very men now fighting the union, and that it was for support in just such circumstances that the C. I. O. had thrown its money and votes to his assistance the preceding November. Yes, the President owed a debt.

Further, Lewis wished to have the administration maneuver the company into an open show of bad faith.

A few days later the President sharply rebuked Mr. Sloan for refusing to return to Washington for conferences under the auspices of Miss Perkins. He said that he "regarded it as a very unfortunate decision on his (Sloan's) part." Encouraged, Miss Perkins observed: "An episode like this must make it clear to the American people why the workers have lost confidence in General Motors."

Events hurried to a crisis. On January 21, G. M. estimated the strike idle at one hundred and thirty-five thousand. The company took to the radio to popularize a theme heard frequently in subsequent months: the "right to work," an "age-old, universal, and eternal principle." The Flint Alliance took up the refrain. Mass meetings in all the struck towns, and tireless petitioners claiming 123,724 signatures, shouted that the workers wanted to return to work.

The Flint Alliance made a formal call on the Governor. To their new-found slogan, "we want to work," he replied that the strikers wanted to work too, and

122 C. I. O. Industrial Unionism in Action

the company was preventing it. Had the Alliance not broken the truce, Murphy reminded them, "it is likely that all of you would have been at work today." Neatly and with justice he tossed the responsibility back to the Alliance.

But it didn't stick. A public impatient of issues and rights knew only that the strike was irritatingly long-drawn-out: people inclined to pin responsibility on the most exposed scapegoat—and that was the union. Anderson and Saginaw registered unmistakable defeats against the union. Moreover, the company seemed to be discriminating against union members in the Flint Chevrolet plants, which had never been struck. The union strategy committee saw that something was needed to buck up strike morale and turn the tide against the company.

The committee drew up an exceedingly shrewd plan. The union leaders knew that if they could capture Chevrolet Plant No. 4, where all Chevrolet motors are made, they could paralyze that whole G. M. division. But the company knew it, too, and stationed a heavy detachment of guards there.

The union held one trump—its familiarity with company stool-pigeons. The leaders arranged to have them present at critical meetings which decided to storm Plant No. 9. This seemed likely enough to the "stools," since the U. A. W. claimed a majority of members there: they duly reported the plan of attack to G. M., which shifted its forces from No. 4 to No. 9. At the last moment, of course, the U. A. W. strategists sent a crowd to No. 4, and quietly took possession of the motor plant.

This proved the pivotal point of the strike. The union had taken the offensive again; its success electrified the rank-and-file, and correspondingly dismayed the company.

C. I. O. in Automobiles

Next day Judge Paul V. Gadola issued a severe injunction against the sit-downers in the two Fisher Body plants (Chevrolet No. 4 was occupied too late to be included in the court order). Under threat of a fifteen-million-dollar fine, he forbade picketing or any interference with G. M. plants, and gave the sit-downers twenty-four hours to get out.

"Shock troops" from Detroit, from Ohio rubber factories, and Pennsylvania steel and coal companies arrived to prevent the enforcement of the injunction. The sit-downers themselves wired the governor: "We have decided to stay in the plant. We have no delusions about the sacrifices which this decision will entail. We fully expect that if a violent effort is made to oust us many of us will be killed. Unarmed as we are, the introduction of the militia, sheriffs, or police with murderous weapons will mean a blood bath of unarmed workers."

A tensely dramatic moment. But the sheriff wisely declined to enforce the injunction without state assistance; and the governor, concentrating on a peaceful settlement, ignored the formal requests of the sheriff's office. The company's legal efforts to break the strike remained abortive.

As a result, and following the remarkably peaceful demonstration of thousands of visiting unionists, sentiment for direct action speedily crystallized among Flint business men. Word went round the town that "the union has taken over the city with its out-of-town men, and we had better think about getting it back." Plans for a citizens' army one thousand strong were never carried through to completion: the conclusion of the strike cut them short.

Mr. Lewis came to Detroit bringing the full weight of his C. I. O. prestige to bear. At the urgent request of the governor and President Roosevelt, Mr. Knudsen conferred with him early in February. Once more the issues were defined. Lewis renewed the demand for recognition of the union as sole bargaining agent, a demand that had not been made for some time. He took the position that the union had enrolled a majority of the workers (denied by the company), that in fact the union was the only bona fide agency ready to take the responsibilities for collective bargaining, and that contracts with more than one workers' organization would be impracticable anyway. He emphasized that sole bargaining status would not mean the closed shop, that men might join the union or not as they pleased; it meant only that a contract signed with the union would cover all workers alike.

The company's contribution to compromise was a refusal of sole bargaining status, and an insistence that the men must first evacuate the plants. Deadlock.

The governor, however, meant in grim earnest to achieve a settlement. Roosevelt wired, urging that the dispute be resolved in the interest of the public. All attention concentrated on the conversations in Detroit, as though a collective will could resolve the conflict. Union shock troops withdrew from the streets. The special city police were sent to their homes. Simultaneously the company deferred its request for a court writ to oust the strikers.

The deadlock held for long and weary days. News trickled out that the governor was hopeful. Mr. Lewis contracted a severe cold. Men left the conference room with tense, drawn faces. Finally the company abandoned its evacuation stand; the union whittled down its demand for sole bargaining rights to the twenty plants actually struck.

Still seeking an exit, the company on February 9 urged a ballot of the workers, to find out how many wanted the union to represent them. Lewis refused on grounds that the heavily-charged atmosphere made a fair vote impossible; the U. A. W., he said, was the only agency qualified to bargain; also, "if we are the bargaining agency to start these plants in operation, we must be the bargaining agency after an agreement is reached." Two days later, after long and perplexed prodding, Governor Murphy finally pushed the right key into the lock—the formula of the Flat Glass Workers settlement. General Motors recognized the U. A. W. as bargaining representative for its members only, and promised the governor in writing not to deal with any other group before consulting him.

It was over—the strike which for forty-four days had gripped the attention of the nation and gradually paralyzed the greatest motor enterprise in the world. No one doubted that its terms gave the union a substantial victory—no one except Mr. Green. With a fine inappropriateness he told the nation's newspapers that the settlement signified a surrender by the union, because no direct agreement was signed, no closed shop granted, and the sole bargaining idea "completely abandoned."

He was not well informed. Lewis, Knudsen and others signed an agreement before a roomful of reporters and cameramen, who flashed the scene to all the world. The closed shop had never been demanded. And the company's letter to the governor established what was understood to be sole bargaining status for a probationary period.

The contract carried the following provisions: (a) recognition of the U. A. W. for its members only; (b) straight seniority for every worker in his department after six months' service with the company; (c) grievance machinery in the form of shop committees; (d) the speed-up to be studied with the object of eliminating injustice; (e) the forty-hour week to be retained, thus denying a union demand for the thirty-hour week; (f) continuance of time-and-a-half for overtime; (b) uniform minimum wage scale denied, due to the variety of businesses and conditions under which G. M. operates.

Operation of the plants was to resume at once, with no discrimination against the strikers. Both sides promised not to coerce men into or out of the union, and the company dropped its court action. The agreement was set to run "in full force and effect until terminated by either party or changed by consent of both parties," and to hold in any case until August 11, 1937.

The result of more than fifty hours of exhausting conference, the settlement constitutes a personal tribute to the pertinacity and courage of the governor. Haggard from the strain of keeping tempers in check and preventing raw feelings throughout the state from exploding into violence, he was asked his impressions of the negotiations. He replied that all he could remember of the nightmare was men reaching for their coats to leave the room, with threats that they would never return.

8.

Walter Chrysler came next, and from him the U. A. W. expected little trouble. A good majority of his seventy thousand workers belonged to the union and Chrysler, they felt, had recognized this by jumping wages 10 per cent just a few days before the G. M. settlement. Generally it was assumed that Chrysler had sufficient acumen to capitalize upon the mistakes of his competitors and assure himself of peaceful and continuous production.

These expectations proved too sanguine. When the union asked for negotiations and a sole bargaining status, Mr. Chrysler answered yes to the first and no

C. I. O. in Automobiles

to the second. Promptly Mr. Frankensteen, U. A. W. organizational director, tendered to the Chrysler management the resignation of 102 of the 120 Works Council representatives, each of them stating that the overwhelming majority of his constituents favored the union as their bargaining agency.

Since 80 per cent of these employees had voted for the employee representation plan only two years before, Mr. Chrysler was a trifle taken aback. But discussions respecting seniority, minimum wages and hours got nowhere. On March 8, the company standing pat on its refusal to give the union sole bargaining rights, some sixty thousand workers suddenly struck. Two-thirds of them chose to occupy almost all of the Chrysler factories—far and away the largest sit-down in labor history.

Though all but seventy-five hundred of the sit-downers were sent home after the first few days, the union held the plants tight for thirty days. Massed pickets surrounded the buildings. When the sheriff attempted to enforce a court order for evacuation, the union either ordered or permitted thirty to fifty thousand cheering, singing strikers to encircle the plants. When a Judge Campbell ordered the arrest of several thousand sit-downers—plus John L. Lewis and seventy union officials—the sheriff scratched his head and put his feet on the desk. There was nothing else he could do.

Alarmed at this "anarchy," citizens appealed to the governor to send in troops. He refused to do so without a formal plea from the sheriff and only after the latter had exhausted his deputization powers. Mr. Murphy had no intention of appearing in the role of strikebreaker.

But Murphy's difficulties were greater here than in the case of General Motors. The country had become perturbed over a second great strike with its accom-

128 C. I. O. Industrial Unionism in Action

panying evidences of mass strength, and had launched upon an emotional discussion of the sit-down. Governors of Texas, Mississippi, New Jersey and Connecticut spoke against it. The Senate rocked to the denunciations of Mr. Vandenberg and others. A proposal to issue a senatorial ukase against the sit-down failed by a narrow margin, while the House finally quashed a proposed inquiry into this new type of strike. It was a month of intense feelings, openly-spoken fears for the safety of the Republic, and spectacular oratorical achievements.

Emotions were inflamed, but thought was rather superficial. As Senator Wagner remonstrated in a sturdy speech: "The sit-down has been used in protest against repeated violations of industrial liberties which Congress had recognized." In other words, strikers were using the sit-down to enforce laws which corporations had broken and which the state power had failed to enforce. The workers were sitting down on their own property, their jobs; the possession of company plants was incidental to that act of self-protection.

Mr. Murphy resumed his role of arbiter. By March 24 he had brought Chrysler and Lewis into the same room, and for nine hours he held them together until an agreement was reached. Lewis, probably moved by public clamor against the sit-down, agreed to ask the strikers to evacuate; in return Chrysler promised not to remove machinery or undertake operations during the ensuing negotiations. Next day, after President Martin and other leaders had pleaded with them in the various plants through a long night, the workers marched out jubilant behind their bands and banners.

From Lewis came an earnest reminder that the conference had better settle the strike soon, or the workers might again take matters into their own hands. Reluctantly leaving the plants, they might less reluctantly return. Chrysler replied that the central demand of exclusive bargaining status would not be granted. And here matters stood for several days while Lewis and Chrysler, the two chief protagonists in the drama, attended to duties elsewhere.

The change apparently did them good. Returning on April 3, they settled the strike in three days with a signed contract designed to run for a year. Sole bargaining rights, strictly defined, were denied the union. But the contract contained a promise that the company would abstain from all support of or agreement with any other organization which purposed to undermine the U. A. W. In effect, if the U. A. W. was sufficiently popular to prevent the appearance of another bona fide union it would remain sole bargainer for all employees. Reflecting the unauthorized stoppages that had sporadically interrupted production at General Motors in preceding weeks, the agreement pledged the union to prevent such strikes. A supplementary contract provided a system of seniority and adjustment of grievances.

Thus ended the second great auto strike. It was costly in wages lost by workers and temporarily in profits foregone by the company. It failed to gain the union's central demand. But its demonstration of mass strength invigorated the entire C. I. O. movement, and the auto workers themselves trooped back to their machines self-confident in solidarity and their manifested unity.

9.

"A man loses his independence when he joins a labor union, and he suffers as a result." This sentiment, expressed by Mr. Ford as his family corporation closed its thirty-fourth year of profitable existence, provides the basis of one of the most relentless anti-union programs to be found anywhere in industrial America. The U. A.

W. respects Mr. Ford's power, but has carried its drive for members to the Ford empire, nonetheless—with some success on the periphery and violence at the center. The union has obtained agreements in several assembly plants, notably in Richmond, California; St. Louis; Kansas City; and to some extent in Chicago. Meanwhile, in Dearborn, at "the world's largest industrial unit" employing nearly ninety thousand men, the union's first public gesture met with almost incredible viciousness from the delegated agents of Ford.

The U. A. W. has long cried out against his labor policies; but it remained for a government agency to reveal their brutal outlines to a skeptical public.

On June 26, 1937, the National Labor Relations Board cited the Ford Motor Company for interference with independent unionization, domination of a workers' organization (the Ford Brotherhood), and discrimination against members of the U. A. W. More than a hundred witnesses testified in hearings which followed the citation. Ford's counsel, denying the constitutionality of the National Labor Relations Act, announced that the company would resist the application of the law to its employee relations up to a judgment by the Supreme Court—a sit-down strike in advance.

The decision of the Board has not yet been published, but the hearings overwhelmingly uphold the accuracy of most of the charges. Former Ford employees reported the River Rouge plant overrun with service men, or spies, and that their number had been augmented during the General Motors and Chrysler strikes. Many stated that they had been warned by foremen against unions. Others alleged that their discharges were due to their union membership and activity.

But the outstanding measure of the militancy of this concern was the violence used by Ford agents against union men and their wives at River Rouge.

The U. A. W. planned a distribution of circulars to Ford workers at shift time, and obtained a city permit. On the afternoon of May 26, Frankensteen and Reuther, U. A. W. officials, mounted a street overpass leading to one of the plant gates. (The company claims this overpass is private property; the union contends it was leased to the Dearborn Street Railway.) The two men paused for a moment to allow newspapermen to photograph them, and noted some hundred and fifty men loitering on the platform.

"They did not look as though they were entering or leaving," testified Reuther, "as they had no lunch baskets and wore no badges... After the pictures were taken we were approached by some of these men from all sides... One called out that we were on private property and to get to hell off of there. Frankensteen and I turned to get off the bridge in obedience to the command. I had hardly taken three steps when I was slugged on the back of the head. I tried to shield my face by crossing my arms. They pounded me all over the head and body... I was knocked to the ground and beaten...

"They picked me up and threw me down bodily on the concrete floor of the platform. Then they kicked me again and again. They tried to tear my legs apart. Seven times they raised me off the concrete and threw me down on it. They pinned my arms and shot short jabs to my face. I was dragged to the stairway. I grabbed the railing, and they wrenched me loose. I was thrown down the first flight of iron steps. Then they kicked me down the other two flights until I found myself on the ground where I was beaten and kicked."

Frankensteen got similar treatment. Responsible persons—among them Dr. Sanford representing the Chicago Federation of Churches—corroborated both incidents. "Two individuals grabbed Frankensteen," Dr. Sanford said, "one by each foot, twisted his body, threw him down, one stepped on him, and one ground his heel in his abdomen."

The testimony wound on through all its hideous details. One man had his "innards smashed," and suffered hemorrhages for twelve days. Another had two vertebrae broken. Women were pushed and knocked down; at least one was kicked while on the ground. Newspaper reporters and photographers from such papers as the New York *Times* gave general or specific corroboration.

Through its attorney the company insisted that loyal employees led the attacks, enraged at being called scabs. There is no record of this provocative epithet. Furthermore, many of the attackers were recognized as professional thugs, "typical of the hoodlums I have known while covering the police courts," according to an Acme News Service photographer. Back of these thugs almost certainly stands the Ford Service organization and Harry Bennett, ex-pugilist personnel director. To him is attributed the formation of the "they shall not pass" brigade to beat back inroads of the union. A Grand Jury has indicted some of his staff and the company itself for assault with intent to do great bodily harm.

Indubitably, Mr. Ford has carried out in practice his convictions on the menace of unionism. Elaborate espionage covers his plant within and follows his employees without the plant. Harry Bennett boasts that he knows every time a Ford member pays his U. A. W. dues. Men detected in union activity lose their jobs.

Faced with a drive by a strong and determined union, Mr. Ford has met its first overture with a resistance amazingly aggressive, vicious, and cynical. Ford is accustomed to victories. He has won his important patent cases in the courts. He has defeated Wall Street and the bankers. He successfully defied the government in its efforts under the National Recovery Administration. He now stands defiant before the union of workers in his own industry. He may force a momentous struggle, as he has already begun a brutal one.

10.

The United Automobile Workers of America is one of the newest unions in the labor movement. In the course of a single year it has grown from thirty-five thousand to over three hundred and fifty thousand members; has won written contracts with two of the three largest auto companies, a few agreements from the third, and scores of contracts with companies serving the industry. The U. A. W. stands now as the third largest international in the C. I. O., only the Mine Workers and the Steel Workers surpassing it.

Its growth has enormously heartened workers in the Mid-West. During the winter and spring of 1937, applications from workers in cigar, furniture, fountain-pen factories; in power houses, garages, and dairies—all wanting to flock under the generous spread of the Auto Workers' tent—swamped the youthful leadership of the union. The C. I. O. has since put all these groups under separate regional offices in Detroit, Chicago, and elsewhere.

The U. A. W. has had troubles of its own—the growing pains of a new organization heady with victory. Time is necessary to mold the mores that hold any organization together for the long pull, that keep it from dissipating its energies, or breaking away from the advice of leaders pledged to contracts. Time is what the auto workers' union needs.

The unauthorized strikes of the power-house employees, which cut off electricity from a population of five hundred thousand in thirteen counties of Michigan and drew condemnation from Governor Murphy as well as a rebuke from the union president, stems from this lack of self-discipline. In part the Lansing labor holiday—the U. A. W. local called out all workers in plants, offices, and stores for a day—is attributable to a sort of adolescent ebullience. But it was caused, too, by a union membership outraged because the sheriff dragged eight of its people out of their beds after midnight on warrants accusing them of the crime of picketing.

The General Motors stoppages in violation of the agreement of February further demonstrate the youth of the union, and the unionists' youth—both of which are traceable to G. M.'s own policies of union-busting and of employment age limits. But there are other important factors. It is true that the number of these stoppages ran over two hundred by the end of June. It is true that the company protested more than once. It is true that Mr. Martin for the union promised punishment of union men who were responsible, and probably did impose some measure of discipline.

But it is also true that these stoppages were inevitable in the circumstances, for the grievance machinery was new and inadequate. Long years of pent-up irritations and anger—consistently ignored by the company—gushed out with little regard for formal devices. The failure of foremen and department heads to change their ways overnight enhanced difficulties. Some of these company officials were embittered by union recognition and set out on their own to discredit the union. At least one superintendent instigated a sit-down of the workers with just such a purpose; it was so bald a case that the company felt obliged to dismiss him.

Assuming that the G. M. high command has sincerely tried to build up a collective bargaining institution, it still will take patience on their part and long training of their subordinates in the plants before harmony can be sustained. If the higher officials themselves are not sincere (as some of Mr. Sloan's utterances would indicate) then trouble is bound to come, for they, too, will have to be educated.

11.

The U. A. W. is not only young but exuberant. Much of its surplus energy has been canalized recently in various social activities. Five cents out of each worker's dollar-a-month dues are set aside in national and local treasuries for an educational program. An educational director has designed an elaborate program of classes in the various auto towns on history, economics, trade unionism, and parliamentary procedure. A summer school in 1937 provided the services of five teachers to forty prospective union leaders. Six union members will go to Brookwood College in the fall for a year. There are bands, a union paper, dramatic groups, women's auxiliaries, boy brigades, and a score of other quasi-social undertakings. And there is local political action.

The Lansing local has a "Flying Squadron" of five hundred of its most active members, with insignia, rules of personal conduct, and considerable emphasis on discipline. These men stand ready for any special work that the union requires. In particular, being organized by city wards they constitute an inherently potent machine for corralling voters of the community. The union now claims a membership equal to one-fifth of the town's population—which means a voting strength of about two-thirds.

In Flint, the union stewards, whose job is the handling of grievances in the shops, are organized on city-wide lines. Every ward can thus be covered. The Saginaw local has a similar system, and in Jackson both the shop-steward and the flying squadron systems will be used.

These intimations of labor parties with their base in the local unions, and with loose ties between the cities, are insufficiently developed to be evaluated. But potentially they are all-important. The importance to the union of favorably-disposed state and city officials was unforgettably borne home to them during the auto strikes.

Anti-union sentiment will play a decisive part in the future of these political organizations. During the strikes, all the auto towns witnessed the formation of groups ostensibly designed to preserve "law and order," which in effect meant to break the strikes. These groups ranged from the curious American Labor League to the crop of Law and Order Leagues which sprouted everywhere.

The latter, perhaps the most likely of all to persist, are invariably sponsored by men prominent in business life. The League in Flint has as its officers a successful attorney and a former commander of the American Legion Post, the owner of a dairy, a hardware merchant, an officer of a commercial bank, a doctor, a manufacturer of china closets, a jeweler, a restaurateur (this ardent patriot is quoted to the effect that "I could clean up this country by getting my rifle and killing Roosevelt, Murphy, and John L. Lewis"), an owner of a transportation company, the president of an insurance company, and a bank director. Its executive committee is composed of two bankers, five merchants, two real-estate proprietors, two manufacturers, and one clothing merchant.

The aim of this League, as well as its counterparts in other towns, is "to advocate and secure strict enforcement of existing laws, . . . to uphold the courts and public authorities in a just administration of such laws . . . to supply law enforcement agencies, at their request, with sufficient personnel volunteers, who shall be deputized

C. I. O. in Automobiles 137

to help carry out their duties under any and all circumstances." The last item is the fundamental one. It means simply that the League will furnish volunteers to the sheriff and police chief for strike-breaking, and will encourage large deputy forces in times of labor disturbances.

As yet these Michigan leagues have shown little interest in inter-city or national organization. Under stress such a development would almost certainly occur. Nor have they proved as effective in influencing city and state officials as have similar organizations in Ohio and Pennsylvania. But the union locals are watching them closely, and their own political evolution will in some measure reflect the actions of the leagues.

12.

The U. A. W. has been fortunate in its high command; perhaps less so in its subalterns. Its president, re-elected in August, 1937, for his second term, is Homer Martin. In his middle thirties, idealistic, humanitarian, he left a Baptist pulpit when his congregation balked at his social preaching. Becoming a production worker in a Kansas City General Motors plant, he quickly assumed leadership of the workers and suffered the usual punishment of discharge. Events quickly lifted him to prominence in union circles, and the newly-formed U. A. W. elected him as president in 1936. His services to the union have been those of the spellbinder, the exhorter, the public relations officer. His forte is evangelism in the union cause. His shortcomings appear in the conference room, where he seems insufficiently skeptical of a bluff and not hard-headed enough to wait it out.

Wyndham Mortimer, his first vice-president, is a man in many ways his complement—older, with a full life of the worker behind him, and longer union experience than has his chief. He is a shrewd bargainer, a man whose talent in negotiation proved crucial during the auto strikes. After a few trials Martin transferred this activity to Mortimer.

Most of the other leaders are still in their period of probation. Some, like Frankensteen, hold considerable promise. One of the auto manufacturers remarked last winter: "I would gladly enter into an agreement with you if you were headed by a Philip Murray." The answer must be apparent even to enemies of unionism; it takes a long term of union experience for Philip Murrays to develop, and so far the auto industry has done its best to prevent such schooling.

V. OTHER FIELDS TO CONQUER

BY July 4, 1937, everyone knew that Little Steel had defeated the S. W. O. C. Editors across the country asked if Mr. Lewis had reached the apex of his power, and was now headed downward. Many with satisfaction answered their question in the affirmative.

Their hopes marred their judgment. They failed to note that while the steel strikes were C. I. O., the C. I. O. was not simply the steel strikes. It is thirty-two organizations, and not the least important are those least heard about. Among them lie the C. I. O.'s major possibilities, major implications, and major problems.

1.

Rubber is one of those unions. Organization began under the A. F. of L. Up to September 1935, the Federation had enrolled about four thousand of the one hundred and twenty thousand workers in rubber, and divided them among thirty-nine loosely-federated locals. Then the rank-and-file reared up, overrode Green's remonstrances, and won an international charter.

They now had an organization, but few men in it. Workers were waiting to see if this new union had any offensive power and stamina. In January 1936 the United Rubber Workers pulled a strike. With eight hundred members among the fourteen thousand employees of Goodyear's Akron plants, it staged a successful sit-down after the management had refused to meet its representatives, laid off its men, and threatened to reduce wages.

The stratagem won. Workers flocked into the union; and it removed the sit-downers to the picket line. After five bitter weeks Goodyear gave in, agreeing to reinstate every striker, recognize the union, correct its lay-off policies, inaugurate a thirty-six-hour week in the tire-and-tube divisions, and set up shop committees in the various plants.

The bitterness did not disappear immediately. Raw union recruits preferred striking to negotiating; the company continued to rely on spies, its Law and Order League, and its company union. Sit-downs broke out recurrently. Now, however, stability is appearing. The union's increasing discipline, coincidental with its own great growth in the industry, has reduced strike interruptions to negligible proportions; and Goodyear is learning to use the grievance machinery with some equity and smoothness.

The militant rubber workers' natural inclination turned them toward the C. I. O.; and their union formally affiliated in July 1936. What is the prospect for the U. R. W.? Already it has enrolled seventy-five thousand of the industry's one hundred and twenty thousand, won its first signed agreement (with Firestone), overwhelmed its opponents in a Goodyear Labor Board election, and has sewed up Akron, capital of the rubber kingdom. Two lines of development open up before it: the extension of organization into the resistant South, and the tightening of its control of the North so that it may begin to repay to the C. I. O. some of the strength it has borrowed.

2.

The C. I. O. risks a great many battles to gain a great deal of territory. Nowhere is that more apparent than in shipping. The prize is big: three hundred thousand seamen and longshoremen, and the organization of a sector peculiarly vital in our national economy. The obstacles are equally impressive: Joe Ryan and his A. F. of L. longshoremen in the East and South; a rankling rivalry between two industrial union leaders on the Pacific; and their common foes, the Industrial Associations, and the ship-owners.

Agents for the C. I. O. are Harry Bridges on the Pacific, and Joe Curran on the Gulf and Atlantic. Bridges—a tireless young Australian, seventeen years in this country, spellbinder, shrewd bargainer, leader of the 1934 maritime strike and a determined progressive—has won the loyalty of the Pacific longshoremen and other sea-going groups as well as the confidence of John Lewis, who made him coast director. All of this, however, has made him hateful in the eyes of Harry Lundberg, secretary of the Sailors Union of the Pacific. At the last convention Lundberg let his rancor persuade him to table a motion to join with the C. I. O.—even though he himself is an industrial unionist and his six thousand seamen had just voted for affiliation.

Joe Curran faces an even tougher situation. Up from the ranks in the 1936 revolt against "old-line" A. F. of L. collaboration with the ship-owners, Curran formed an independent National Maritime Union for unlicensed seamen, deck hands, engine-room men, cooks and stewards on the Lakes, Gulf, and Atlantic. Behind him now stands the C. I. O.; but squarely ahead looms Boss Ryan, who has turned his International Longshoremen's Association into a hybrid industrial union in order to recruit marine workers of every description. Ryan's sea-change would be irrelevant if he didn't control some twenty-five thousand to forty thousand eastern and southern dock-workers; if he weren't a close ally of Daniel Tobin, czar of all the teamsters; and if he hadn't developed a sinister system of collusion with the ship-owners, operating his own strike-breaking agency for them.

However, the C. I. O. is relying on the National Labor Relations Board.

The National Maritime Union and Bridges' Federation—which are soon to form a national maritime federation—can consolidate their forces through secret Board elections to determine sole bargaining rights disputed by Ryan or the A. F. of L. Sailors Union. This means a probable end both of the costly "quickie" strikes that the rival factions have called against each other, and of Ryan's own power. Dictatorial control over unwilling men will be more difficult when they have an alternative union and a protected means of choosing it, as Mr. Ryan will doubtless discover when the returns come in from the gigantic poll the N. L. R. B. is now conducting among seventy-five thousand seamen in the East and South. Early results show an overwhelming sentiment for Curran's union.

3.

The C. I. O. has also taken to wheels, guided by a New York subway worker named Michael Quill. Another of that large group of union leaders who have been restive under craft restraints, Quill brought his N. R. A.-born Transport Workers Union over to Lewis when the A. F. of L. tried to split it between the Machinists and the Street and Electric Railway and Motor Coach Employees. His sixteen thousand followers formed a nucleus of a new international union for all land transportation workers except those on railroads.

Ninety days after joining the C. I. O., Quill had shot his membership to ninety thousand and had forced closed-shop agreements covering almost every one of

Other Fields to Conquer 143

New York's seventy-five thousand transport employees. All this Quill achieved through elections, without a single strike of any magnitude. For the first time in their meager lives, the taxi drivers (with the exception of those in the Parmelee Company, whose case remains unsettled) have an organization, a guaranteed weekly wage of fifteen dollars plus commissions, regular hours, and vacations with pay.

Using New York as his base, and drawing upon it for funds and experienced leadership, Quill has now set out to organize the rest of the country's one million five hundred thousand transport workers. Already the T. W. U. boasts regional offices and a staff of organizers in Pittsburgh, Cleveland, Detroit, Los Angeles, and other major cities.

In states which have their own Labor Relations Boards governing intra-state commerce, Quill expects to use elections to win the right to bargain for employees. In less advanced areas he will undoubtedly have to resort to the strike, because opposition will be unrelenting. Company unions constitute one stumbling block; recently in Philadelphia the Rapid Transit Employees Association roundly trounced several craft unions and the T. W. U. The A. F. of L. itself, unless labor's breach is soon healed, will train a battery of heavy guns on Quill's men: its various railroad craft unions—the Street and Electric Railway and Motor Coach Employees, the Teamsters, and especially the Machinists—who now enroll every worker who will sign a card, no matter what his job.

The factor most likely to inhibit Quill's use of the strike, and possibly jeopardize the success of his whole drive, is the quasi-public nature of the industry. That amorphous but omnipotent group—the public—will not long tolerate interruption of service, especially if caused by inter-union skirmishing.

4.

These far-flung drives mark out for the C. I. O. much rich and virgin territory, but also some nasty problems. The rubber workers and transport men had their difficulties throwing off craft unionism and penetrating wholly new fields. The seamen and longshoremen struggle against internal wrangling and political machines.

But when the C. I. O. set out to organize textiles, it tackled a quite different proposition. Textiles is a sick trade; and it displays the hostile irritability of invalids. Between 1926 and 1933 cotton textiles alone showed an aggregate deficit of one hundred million dollars. The whole industry has been in the doldrums for years.

Two factors are responsible: migration of firms from North to South, and persistent overexpansion. One condition, cheap southern labor, links the two.

At the turn of the century New England operated 67 per cent of the nation's cotton spindles, the South a mere 24 per cent. Thirty years later the ratios were almost exactly reversed. Why? Southern operators cut their cost by continuing the night ("graveyard") shift which the War had introduced. Southern legislatures wrote no labor laws at all, or only lax ones, while the North put sharp restrictions on hours and night work. Finally, the South could in 1928 pay workers $6.71 a week less than the North and get away with it. Southern mills can turn out a standard print cloth at 19.9¢ a pound, which would cost 28¢ in Massachusetts.

As migration to warmer climes proceeded year after year, northern owners blundered through bankruptcies, recapitalizations, second starts, and partial closures—to the inevitable abandonments which have left New England towns, without an economic base, breeding-places of misery for entire populations.

Other Fields to Conquer   145

On a national scale, however, textiles have plunged deep into the morass of overproduction. Since the industry is highly competitive, low prices follow naturally. This tendency has been furthered by a clumsy marketing machinery, large ("on the safe side") inventories, misjudgments of demand, and consequent stock losses. But the real devil in the textile drama has been drastic reduction of costs accomplished by the most suicidal tactic the industry could have devised: competitive wage-slashing.

No firm, however competitive, could long stand out against it. Repeatedly the industry fell into a vicious spiral with employers cutting wages and prices, causing other employers to meet these prices by cutting wages, thus forcing other employers—etc., etc. "Overproduction," in the sense that the price of the product kept shooting below its cost, was the only possible outcome.

The Cotton Textile Institute tried recurrently to break into this spiral by attempting to impose production control and price maintenance. But by 1933 the industry was still hopelessly demoralized, and hastened to embrace an N. R. A. Code which placed a floor under wage rates, a ceiling on hours. Average rates rose from twenty-three to thirty-nine cents within the half year; hours dropped from forty-six to thirty-three. Weekly earnings rose from $10.90 to $13.03.

Unprecedented though they were, these requirements "are not believed to have imposed excessive burdens on the industry," reported the Code Authorities. Textiles revived. For the first time in years the industry seemed on the road to stabilization—until Mr. Schecter's chickens downed the Blue Eagle.

The problem which the Textile Code faced remains to be solved. A bottom must be put under prices, and as in the bituminous coal industry, only one practi-

146 C. I. O. Industrial Unionism in Action

cable means lies at hand: production control and maintenance for all firms. Only one practicable agency —government excepted—exists to enforce that means: unionism.

"Hard-headed" employers, of course, are not likely to agree, since they tend to think by concerns and not in terms of the collective industry. They see only that for their plants a wage rise necessitates a boost in prices, putting them at a competitive disadvantage. With this complaint the union sympathizes, and suggests a national scale. But here the employer hastens to point out that higher prices will discourage the national demand for textiles. This statement is ill informed: the combined personal and industrial demand for textiles is relatively insensitive to price—an "inelastic" demand. For a given increase in price the amount of textiles purchased will not fall proportionately, and the total income of the industry will be increased rather than diminished. Low wages can be raised—and at once— without a depressing effect on the industry.

National wage-scales negotiated by union and management would put a nether limit to national costs, stabilize prices, prevent unscrupulous employers from undermining established firms by setting up new plants in low-wage areas, slow down the disastrous rate of increase of firms and spindles, reduce cut-throat competition, and as an end-product restore profits to owners.

What chance has a union to bring about this stabilization of the industry, since the initiative must certainly come from it and not from the very practical business men? So far, there has been none. The A. F. of L.'s United Textile Workers never made a perceptible dent on the crucial southern sector, despite heart-rending efforts and some bloody strikes. The complexity of the industry, the docility of southern workers,

Other Fields to Conquer 147

inter-union conflicts, the innocuousness of the A. F. of L. command, the crushing of civil liberties through the unqualified resistance of the mill-owners, all combined to dictate defeat.

Now comes the C. I. O., through its Textile Workers Organizing Committee. The T. W. O. C.'s assets: (1) adroit leadership, captained by Sidney Hillman of the Amalgamated Clothing Workers; (2) extensive financial backing from the garment unions; (3) an elaborate organization—regional offices in Chicago, Minneapolis, Allentown, Philadelphia, Rochester, Passaic, Roanoke, and Boston; eighty-seven sub-regional offices; five hundred organizers with hundreds of additional volunteers; (4) and its bold belief that the entire industry can be organized.

Inaugurated in March 1937, the T. W. O. C.'s campaign had netted four hundred thousand members by September. Charters had been issued to one hundred and seventy-five local unions. Over four hundred firms had signed agreements covering one hundred and fifty thousand workers. Hillman found only one large strike necessary—that of fifty thousand silk workers, most of whom won recognition from their employers by September.

The T. W. O. C.'s proving-ground, however, is the South with its suspicion of northerners, its old prejudice against unionism, and its tendency to view all change as inherently radical and disruptive. The committee claims that workers there were joining in August at the rate of one thousand a day. But only fifteen southern plants and ten thousand workers operated under contract—a small fraction of the region's five thousand mills and four hundred and fifty thousand textile hands.

5.

The kind of industrial statesmanship the C. I. O. exhibits in a chaotic industry like textiles indicates its maturity. Even more significant eventually will be its campaign in the newest and most crucial sectors of the economy: the white-collar group.

In 1880 there were only six hundred and fifty thousand "clerks." Today nearly eight million persons take dictation, type letters, keep records and accounts, answer telephones, tend shops and stores, transmit telephone and telegraph messages—and in innumerable ways perform the immense amount of administrative labor by which modern business functions, and on which it depends increasingly as the productive and distributive processes become more complex, more technical.

This white-collar class, making up one-sixth of the working population, may be as well labeled the silk-stocking group: nearly 40 per cent of them are women; and in certain fields such as stenography, typing, and bookkeeping, men stand very much in the minority.

More striking than the emergence of this stratum has been the rise of the "productive professions"—highly trained technicians, engineers, chemists, cost accountants, specialists in management, industrial psychologists and business economists. Closely related to these "brains of industry" are those workers outside of commerce proper who perform much the same function for society as a whole—teachers, nurses, librarians, writers, editors, artists, lower governmental officials, and experts in social, economic, and political problems.

Together these two groups compose what might be termed the nervous system of the economic organism. Professional employees now fulfill the traditional functions of ownership—the development of new products and processes, the combination and supervision of the various factors of production—while the clerical group administers the details.

This situation carries revolutionary as well as evolutionary significance. It means that the section of our economy which keeps the wheels turning from day to day has become an employed instrument. Ownership has hired out its former duties (and its justification) to people who live by the sale of their brains and skill, as manual laborers live by the sale of their bodily energy. Classified by the basic socio-economic test—the relation of production to ownership—this "new middle class" is not *middle* class at all but essentially a wage-earning, propertyless group. That its members receive weekly or monthly salaries rather than daily wages in no way alters the fact.

The import of this condition lies rather with the future than the present. White-collar employees have always up to now thought of themselves and been thought of as kinsmen to ownership, indifferent or hostile to labor. Their interests—social, cultural, and economic—lay above them rather than below. But the Great Depression proved educative. An increasing fraction of this semi-bourgeoisie came to feel an even more binding relation with the wage-earning class, because the two groups shared a common experience of pay cuts, insecurity in their jobs, unemployment with consequent loss of skill, and an insistent doubt of the ability and economic usefulness of private ownership in the modern world.

Since 1933 journalists, teachers, government employees, screen actors, and writers, retail clerks, office workers, and technicians of all kinds have sought protection and advancement in unionism. Three organizations illustrate the progress as well as the peculiar

150 C. I. O. Industrial Unionism in Action

stumbling blocks of this whole class: office workers, newspapermen, and government employees.

Office Workers. America has four million of them. Only recently have some of them begun to look through the outward evidences of their well-being (their clothes, their education, their tastes) to the realities beneath.

(1) *Salaries.* In 1926, during the bloom of Mr. Hoover's New Era, the National Industrial Conference Board reported the median salary for chief clerks as twenty-six hundred dollars a year, for mail clerks eight hundred dollars. The remainder lay between those two. In all the office occupations studied, "the approximate average salary (was) close to $25 a week or $1260 a year. *This is slightly less than the average weekly earnings of manual workers in 25 industries,* which in the first quarter of 1926 was ... $27.27."

(2) *Tenure of jobs.* During the years following 1929, employers vigorously reduced what they called "mass production's pain in the neck"—the overhead of clerical and executive staffs. The result, in 1933: 35 per cent of the country's salaried employees had no jobs. In New York City in 1934, 40 per cent of all relief applicants were white-collar workers. In mid-1935, the Federal Emergency Relief Administration reported that 12 per cent of the workers on full relief had been office workers, and by 1936 10 per cent claimed clerical training and another 10 per cent classified as professional and proprietary. Because of the reluctance of the average white-collar man to apply for relief, it is safe to assume that the unemployed of this class exceeded the number reported.

(3) *Technology.* The machine is bidding against the office worker. Of all clerical jobs about 80 per cent can now be mechanized, and in large offices much of this robotization has already taken place. The tabulator, billing machine, calculator, mimeograph, multigraph,

photostat, and comptometer have divided work, specialized jobs, leveled salaries by reducing the higher and raising the lower. The job itself has become less interesting, more routine, more subject to speed-up. At the same time that college graduates have flocked into offices for "any kind of a job," the need for that education has decreased.

(4) *Personal status.* The great distinction of the office worker in the past was her relationship to her employer, a kind of recognition of individuality. Now only the private secretary still enjoys the daily conference of management, knows the inner machinations of the business, and is permitted to identify herself with the firm. Like the factory hand the "girl in the office" is a cog, as unimportant individually as the desk at which she works.

Facts penetrate in time. Prejudices, like debts, are liquidated. Awakening to the meagerness of their salaries, the menace of unemployment, the march of the machine, the increase of routine, the depersonalization of status, office workers are beginning to turn toward the labor movement for help. From 1934 to 1937 local A. F. of L. unions of office workers increased only from thirty-three to forty. The New York City unit of Bookkeepers, Stenographers, and Accountants tripled their membership—to twenty-five hundred. Numbers, however, were less significant than drift.

In the spring of 1937 the C. I. O. gave ten thousand rebels from A. F. of L. locals an international charter as the United Office and Professional Workers of America. Their field is immense; likewise their expectations. Two current tendencies will aid their drive: the breakdown of the office workers' middle-class ideology under the pressure of economic realities; and the increasing tendency of women to regard their jobs as

152   C. I. O. Industrial Unionism in Action

positions permanently worth protecting, not merely preludes to marriage.

Journalists. Formed in 1933 under the genial guidance of Heywood Broun, the American Newspaper Guild has always inclined toward the left wing of the labor movement. Although the Guild accepted a charter from the A. F. of L. in 1936, its Convention a year later voted overwhelmingly to affiliate with the C. I. O. on an industrial basis. A subsequent referendum sustained the Convention's decision by 2-1.

From its first timid tactic of holding parties for publishers, the A. N. G. has grown into a full-fledged business union. During the past year it has tripled its membership to fourteen thousand of the country's sixty thousand editorial workers and two hundred thousand eligibles. The Guild reports forty-seven signed contracts, among them sixteen Scripps-Howard papers; it has agreements or "statements" from most of the Hearst press. Within the last year it has gained substantial pay-increases on eighty papers.

Newsmen are hard to organize, not because they are cynical as the movies would indicate, but because of their curious and traditional romanticism. Publishers have found it feasible to pay them in excitement rather than currency, and to exploit the mingled glamor and megalomania that surrounds the writer's trade.

Journalists are becoming less gullible by reason of certain obtrusive and unromantic facts. In 1934, 27 per cent of the editorial employees of the country made less than twenty dollars a week; almost half were under thirty-two dollars a week; only 10 per cent enjoyed fifty dollars or more—these being mostly executives and key deskmen.

In 1930 a large majority of newspapermen worked a forty-five- to fifty-hour week. Only 14 per cent put in less than forty hours. Today the Guild lists an almost universal five-day, forty-hour week on metropolitan dailies as its "Number 1 achievement." Other gains include seniority ratings, standards of severance pay, and increased protection from editors who used to "sack" at the drop of a hat.

Sensitive to these facts, American publishers have banded together to obscure the Guild's drive for better economic conditions with an oratorical mist about the freedom of the press. Focal point of their plaints is the A. N. G.'s demand for a "Guild Shop." As a convention of eleven large newspaper associations resolved recently: "A closed shop means a closed editorial mind."

To this red herring, the Guild has a threefold reply: (1) As a labor union, the Guild's business does not deal with editorial policy, but in the improvement of wages and conditions of work for its members; (2) the Guild shop does not impair the employer's right to hire whomever he fancies, but merely obliges anyone who *is* hired to join the Guild after thirty days on the job; (3) the Guild in no way prescribes or interferes with the opinion of its members on any subject; specifically, its Constitution forbids any discrimination against a writer because of "sex, race, or religious or political convictions, *or because of anything he writes for publication.*"

As Mr. Howard Brubaker snorted in *The New Yorker:* "The newspaper publishers oppose the Guild Shop, fearing that the reporters and editors might color the news. Under our constitutional right to a free press, nobody can do that but the owner of the paper." Consider the difference in editorial "slant" between the New York *Times,* the *Herald Tribune,* the *Post,* and the Hearst *Journal.* Does this represent any bias but those of the particular owners? There are big Guild units on all of these papers. Can it be their members who color the news?

Possibly Guild units on particularly rabid papers may

154 C. I. O. Industrial Unionism in Action

in the future refuse to handle copy which they believe libelously anti-union. Is the owner's right to misrepresent worthy of preservation regardless of the effect of those lies upon the public and upon the employees who must concoct them? A good journalist has an intense interest in the ethics of his profession. Are such principles less safe in his hands than in those of men to whom journalism is not a profession but a business, men whose interests are closely allied with one group—the wealthy?

Government Workers. The administration of the government in the United States employs some three million persons, most of them dependent upon their salaries. Entertaining the familiar phantasies of white-collar workers, and with somewhat higher wages, better tenure, and longer vacations, they have not proved an easily organizable group. Their wage is modest—on the average less than fifteen hundred dollars a year. It changes slowly, netting a pleasing gain in times of falling prices and a painful loss when prices rise. Security of tenure as a principle lacks adequate machinery for protection against unfair dismissal.

There now exist three unions of federal workers. The largest, the National Federation of Federal Employees, is independent of any labor affiliation. With fifty thousand members it has for twenty-one years devoted itself to the enforcement of civil-service regulations, welfare problems, old-age pensions, and similar activities. It is frequently referred to as the government's company union.

The second organization is the four-year-old American Federation of Government Employees, affiliated with the A. F. of L. From the first its leadership, composed mostly of high-ranking administrative and personnel officers, has met opposition from a progressive wing interested in more active support of union de-

Other Fields to Conquer   155

mands. The quarrel, after several skirmishes, ended with the suspension of seven rebellious lodges and their affiliation with the C. I. O. This formed a nucleus for the country's third union—the United Federal Workers of America, numbering three thousand members out of a potential four hundred thousand. (Army, Navy, and Postal employees are ineligible.)

In addition the C. I. O. has chartered another group to compete with the A. F. of L., the State, County and Municipal Workers. So far it has enrolled forty thousand out of two million eligibles.

In these fields the C. I. O. will have to adapt its tactics to peculiar conditions. Contrary to President Roosevelt's recent statement, federal law does not deny the right to strike to unions of government employees. But strategy demands self-imposed restraints such as the constitutional limitation of the A. F. of L. union, and John Lewis's statement of policy that strikes and picketing in this area are "inappropriate." The employer is the government; it sets the terms of employment legislatively. Therefore the union's pressure must be exerted upon the legislators, by demonstrations, publicity and a lobby.

August 1937 marked one year since the Executive Council of the American Federation of Labor voted the suspension of the C. I. O. In that brief time American unionism has pushed through the most extensive organization campaign in its history. To describe that effort in greater detail is impossible within the limits of this book. The table on page 156 presents a rough statistical and chronological picture—as good a snap as can be shot of a rapidly changing scene. The breakdown of membership by unions is not official, as some figures are contested and others are highly unstable.

With the exception of the Typographers and the Cap and Millinery Workers, the first twelve C. I. O. unions

156 C. I. O. Industrial Unionism in Action

CHART OF MEMBERSHIP IN THE C. I. O.

Original 8 Unions	Date of Affiliation	Approx. Membership Before Affiliation(1)	Approx. Membership Sept. 1937(2)	Maximum Potential Membership(3)
1. United Mine Workers	Nov. 1935	400,000	600,000	620,000
2. Int'l. Typographical Union	"	73,400	80,000	82,000
3. Amal. Clothing Workers	"	100,000	200,000	200,000
4. Int'l. Ladies Garment Workers	"	160,000	250,000	300,000
5. United Textile Workers (T. W. O. C.)	"	100,000	400,000	1,250,000
6. Oil Field, Gas Well and Refinery Workers	"	42,800	100,000	1,000,000
7. Cap and Millinery Workers	"	21,400	35,000	60,000
8. Mine, Mill, and Smelter Workers	"	14,600	50,000	150,000

Nationals and Internationals Added Since Formation of the C. I. O.

9. Federation of Flat Glass Workers	April 1936	14,000	18,000	18,000
10. United Automobile Workers	July 1936	19,000	375,000	500,000
11. United Rubber Workers	"	3,500	75,000	120,000
12. Amal. Association Iron, Steel, and Tin Workers (S. W. O. C.)	June 1936	9,200	500,000	800,000
13. United Electrical and Radio Workers	Nov. 1936	30,000	130,000	347,000
14. Marine and Ship Building Workers	"	10,000	25,000	75,000
15. United Shoe Workers	April 1937	20,000	51,000	300,000
16. American Communications Assoc.	"	......	10,000	350,000
17. Aluminum Workers of America	"	12,000	15,000	40,000
18. Transport Workers	May 1937	16,000	90,000	1,500,000
19. Architects, Engineers, Chemists, Technicians	"	6,000	7,000	250,000
20. National Leather Workers	"	15,000	15,000	80,000
21. United Retail Employees	"	15,000	40,000	3,000,000
22. Int'l. Fur Workers Union	"	30,000	35,000	......
23. Office and Professional Workers	"	10,000	25,000	3,800,000
24. American Newspaper Guild	June 1937	5,000	14,000	200,000
25. United Federal Workers	"	25,000	5,000	485,000
26. Nat'l. Die Casting League	"	......	5,000	......
27. State County and Municipal Workers	July 1937	......	40,000	2,000,000
28. Agricultural, Canning, and Packing Workers	"	......	100,000	4,400,000
29. National Maritime Union	"	38,000	38,000	300,000
30. Woodworkers Federation	"	100,000	100,000	1,000,000
31. Marine Engineers Beneficial Association	Aug. 1937	......	7,000	......
32. Int'l. Longshoremen and Warehousemen's Union	"	......	25,000	75,000

525 industrial local unions in Bakery, Food, Meat Packing, Tobacco, Lumber, Furniture, etc., with about 200,000 members. Total members for the C. I. O.: 3,718,000. There are over 50 Industrial Union Councils and at least 4 State Industrial Union Councils on the verge of receiving charters. West Virginia has already received a charter. These Councils bring together the C. I. O. unions in the cities and in the states.

1 Figures taken from the report on membership of the American Federation of Labor Convention, 1936.
2 Figures from the offices of the Committee for Industrial Organization and the individual unions.
3 Figures drawn from the Statistical Abstracts of the United States.

Other Fields to Conquer 157

were suspended from the Federation at its 1936 Convention. Their membership totaled slightly more than one million. Subsequently the C. I. O. gained international, national and local unions with a November 1936 membership of 250,000. By September 1937 this 1,250,000 had grown to 3,718,000, almost three times the figure of a year before.

The suspension order left the A. F. of L. with about 2,500,000 members. Withdrawals have since reduced this by another 250,000. According to Secretary Morrison 666,360 new members joined before the end of July 1937. This would make the Federation total for that date 2,900,000—less by 200,000 than Morrison claimed. In September, the Executive Council announced that its new members totaled a million, and the total 3,600,000. There are discrepancies here, which may be accounted for in part by the fact that the Federation still lists certain unions as affiliates, although they have gone over to the C. I. O.

In addition their figures include several unions whose fidelity wavers. The Brewery Workers' 42,000 members are militantly industrialist. Their official news-organ constantly advocates the C. I. O. program. The Fur Workers Union has already voted its 30,000 into the C. I. O. The Boot and Shoe Workers Union has recently lost at least 15,000 to the C. I. O. Morrison counts the International Typographical Union. Its 80,000 members may vote soon on C. I. O. affiliation. President Howard, secretary of the C. I. O. from the beginning, has urged his union to follow him.

Included also in A. F. of L. figures are the Newspaper Guild, now C. I. O.; the Hatters, whose president is a member of the C. I. O.; the International Longshoremen, 20,000 of whom have already gone C. I. O. with their leader, Harry Bridges. Several thousand machinists have joined the New York section of the Trans-

158 C. I. O. Industrial Unionism in Action

port Workers; another 15,000 have joined eastern lodges of the United Electrical and Radio Workers. From 75,000 to 100,000 woodworkers have left the Carpenters and joined up with Lewis; while the International Seamen's Union has lost virtually its entire membership to Joe Curran's N. M. U. Retail clerks have departed from the A. F. of L. in large numbers, to form a C. I. O. international; the Hotel and Restaurant Employees International Alliance in New York and several large cities are strongly C. I. O.; and several hundred local unions among aluminum, distillery, office and optical employees have formed C. I. O. locals.

There may be other defections from the A. F. of L. membership. The total of withdrawals not already included in the sum given above reduces the Federation figure by another 50,000. Further secessions may approach 200,000—an outside guess on future A. F. of L. losses. It is very unlikely that they will be that high.

In both the C. I. O. and the A. F. of L. (particularly the latter) there exist large marginal blocs whose allegiance will depend upon the events of the next few months.

6.

The C. I. O.'s set-up is provisional: no convention has met; no constitution prescribes officers, powers, structure, or function. This will probably be done before the close of 1937.

The C. I. O. is designed for rapid, effective action in winning members to two kinds of unions: nationals or internationals, and local industrial units not yet provided with a national charter.

The functional relationship between the C. I. O. and its local industrial charges resembles that between the A. F. of L. and its federal units. These industrials draw

Other Fields to Conquer

on the National Committee for supervision, advice, and assistance in negotiating contracts and defense in strikes. If they survive, they will become units in national unions.

National and international unions are autonomous in all internal affairs—dues, standards of collective bargaining, powers of officers, and strike calls.

The C. I. O. acts as liaison officer between the unions, pooling ideas and resources. In addition, the Committee uses its prestige to settle internal controversies in and between the unions. It adjudicated a dispute between garment unions over jurisdiction in knit goods. At least temporarily it ironed out difficulties between automobile leaders, and after considerable storm and stress effected an amicable shift in officers of the Flat Glass Workers.

With all forty-eight states covered by fifty regional and sub-regional offices, the C. I. O. is prepared to send men quickly into new territory. On the C. I. O. payroll, as distinguished from those of affiliated unions, are 458 organizers, 241 of whom have been assigned to the several unions and organizing committees. At their own expense, the unions which originally set the C. I. O. in motion have provided hundreds of organizers for particular campaigns. The Mine Workers supplied most of the paid organizers in steel; the Garment unions those in textiles, where 500 are said to draw full-time pay.

A few unions, brawling with new strength—the Auto Workers, for example—have their own paid organizers.

Doubtless the C. I. O.'s permanent structure will take the form of a federation of essentially autonomous unions, the parent Committee exercising unrestricted authority only in new fields. At present this Committee consists of the presidents of the affiliated organizations listed on page 37: Messrs. Lewis (chairman), Howard (secretary), and Brophy (director). On the basis of the reports from organizers, regional directors, and the Steel and Textile Workers Organizing Committees, they make the plans, chart the course, delegate tasks, and co-ordinate the whole enterprise.

C. I. O. funds come from two sources: (1) gifts from affiliated unions, particularly to initiate the major drives. The S. W. O. C. started with five hundred thousand dollars from the Miners alone; the T. W. O. C. received an appropriation from the Amalgamated Clothing Workers and the International Garment Workers of at least as much; (2) charter, initiation, and monthly dues from affiliated unions and their members. Regular dues are five cents monthly per member from the treasuries of nationals and internationals, and fifty cents from industrial locals. The latter charge their members one dollar dues; while the autonomous unions set their own figures.

Although the dues of most C. I. O. affiliates are markedly lower than those in the A. F. of L., the per capita tax of the C. I. O. itself is considerably higher than that paid to the Federation. Mr. Green's organization receives but one cent a month (in May a special conference of A. F. of L. representatives recommended that the per capita be stepped up to two cents): Mr. Lewis's C. I. O. gets a nickel. *If dues are paid by all members,* perhaps one hundred and sixty thousand dollars flows monthly to the C. I. O.; to the A. F. of L. from thirty thousand dollars to fifty thousand dollars. (Official figures are unobtainable.)

Despite the size of its income, the C. I. O. has been forced for lack of funds to forego some departments necessary to a thoroughgoing labor movement: a full-fledged research bureau, adequate publicity, a national newspaper for general distribution. More will be said of these in our last chapter.

7.

A review of the C. I. O.'s leadership yields one outstanding conclusion: the organization is a group of workaday unions, not a labor movement built on theory. The leaders are workers up from the ranks, not "intellectuals." The C. I. O.'s general staff, then, can be expected to map its course more by yesterday's experience than by tomorrow's vision.

Above all of them towers John Llewellyn Lewis. Admire him or hate him—Lewis is probably America's public figure Number One. Like an iceberg, he looms large but the biggest part of him is submerged and unrevealed. Nobody knows him fully, probably not even John Lewis.

His background is easier to spot. Born in 1879 in an Iowa mining town, he entered the pits at twelve; later he roamed around the United States digging coal, silver, gold. He saw strikes, took part in them, and came to be a young hopeful in union politics. Samuel Gompers made him a field and legislative representative of the A. F. of L. at thirty-one; from this new angle Lewis saw a great deal more of America, learned lobbying, and investigated a dozen industries. By 1917 he was vice-president of the United Mine Workers; by 1918 its acting head; in 1919 he became president.

Lewis got little formal education; during the years he has acquired a great deal of book knowledge. His speeches swell with phrases from Homer, Shakespeare, and the King James Version—inserted perhaps because Lewis likes the language, and because it appeals to that dramatic sense which makes him a magnificent orator.

Lewis's past is innocent of corruption but full of rumpuses and not a little violence. Ruthless with those who opposed his policies and regardless of personal con-

162 C. I. O. Industrial Unionism in Action

siderations, he kicked Brophy, Hapgood, Germer, and other progressives out of the U. M. W. in the twenties. Now he has drawn many of them into the C. I. O. Insincerity or conversion? Or is it simply that Lewis knew when to be progressive and when to sit tight? He was branded a reactionary in the twenties for not unionizing the bloody West Virginia area; when the N. R. A. gave him his chance he organized it 100 per cent.

Lewis has a Napoleonism within him; but as yet there exists no indication that he runs or intends to run the C. I. O. as he does the U. M. W. He is far too valuable to be discarded for his excesses; the C. I. O. needs his gifts of oratory, strategy, bargaining, and bludgeoning. It needs his tentative, untheoretical intelligence, his conviction that history is a complicated process that will bear watching; and it needs his bold gambler's determination, once he sees the alternatives, to push his program through hell and high water.

Second only to Lewis in executive stature comes Sidney Hillman, president of the Amalgamated Clothing Workers—immigrant, Jew, brilliant leader. He combines an old interest in social philosophy with a practical military and organizational ability. His intellectual background was radical, but his day-to-day record shows a close co-operation with capitalism. He has supplied industrialists with a valuable and free efficiency service, put credit at their disposal, and taken over shops to put them into the black again. His union has built apartments, run a bank, and provided unemployment insurance for its members.

Hillman doesn't orate; he speaks. His flair for bargaining is strong, and his administrative work of the very first class. He supplements Lewis in many ways. At present he is giving his energy to the textile drive.

Hillman's associate in the garment trades is David

Dubinsky. Because his personal feelings dictate unity in the labor movement, and because his used to be the only clothing union in the A. F. of L., Dubinsky has served as chief liaison man between the hostile camps. Such he is likely to remain, despite rumors that he would like to return to the A. F. of L.

Charles P. Howard heads the most literate, articulate, and argumentative union in the movement: the Typographers. With an intelligence sharpened by the active democracy of his followers, he enjoys an acute perception of issues and a special capacity for their logical presentation. A craft union leader, he sees beyond craft barricades.

Homer Martin, once national hop, skip, and jump champion, once a Baptist minister, once a worker in a Chevrolet plant, now heads three hundred and fifty thousand auto-unionists. Largely through the impress of his driving, plain-spoken but idealistic eloquence upon unorganized workers craving expression, he shot out of the ranks quickly. Three years after leaving the pulpit, Martin won the presidency of the U. A. W. His ideas are hazy but humanistic; in private, at press conferences, before public meetings he talks about "life" and the realization of human values. His aim is a democratized, controlled capitalism. If anything about Homer Martin does more for the U. A. W. than his oratory, it is his being an ex-minister of the Gospel. That makes an appeal in the Middle West.

The roster of leaders reads too long for a full roll-call. Of Philip Murray, director of the S. W. O. C., little need be said; already his reputation for probity, sound judgment, and an unselfish capacity for command has made itself known. Under him, such men as Clinton Golden, Van A. Bittner, and Jack Lever couple resolute understanding with tactical flexibility.

Then there is the baby of the C. I. O.—James Carey,

able president of the electrical workers at twenty-six. Powers Hapgood, Harvard graduate, Socialist, idealist, hardened in many a contest within and without his Mine Workers Union, administers the New England area. West Coast Director Harry Bridges has come triumphantly through the flames of as severe contests as any C. I. O. leader. Joe Curran, his maritime colleague on the Atlantic, is a rough-hewn captain thrown up by an emergency and likely to stick there on his own abilities.

That the C. I. O.'s leadership proves effective in a fight, its own history records. Will it tend, in times of peace, to an official bureaucracy or to rank-and-file democracy?

The delicate problem of democratic government is the attainment of efficiency, notably in crises, without losing touch with the governed. "Pure" democracy does not exist in the labor movement—or on any other political stages. Probably the Typographers come closest to it with frequent conventions and elections, rank-and-file newspapers, and the use of the referendum.

There is no easy formula. Born of mass pressure the C. I. O. unions are demonstrably, vociferously democratic now. But as the shouting gives way to dull familiarity, when compromises must be swallowed willy-nilly, the test will come. Understandably leaders will grow impatient at the chore of persuading the lowest common denominator in the union, and will long to centralize decisions in their own hands. Moreover, the simple matter of administrative efficiency will press centralization. These new unions are big. Can a local of twenty-five thousand conduct its business like a New England town meeting, without surrendering control to demagogues and manipulators, or else blundering ahead in mass confusion? Big business breeds authority for the sake of accomplishment. So too will big unions. The need for

Other Fields to Conquer

efficiency will swing the pendulum over to oligarchy until the rank-and-file pulls it back in the name of democracy. Political history is oscillation.

First and last the C. I. O. is an American phenomenon and will have American virtues and vices. It will preach democracy, and will practice it within its unions as much or as little as suits its needs.

In the long, secular run of things, however, its weight in society will be thrown inescapably upon the side of democracy: it is a mass movement; it deals with problems collectively; its very life depends upon its success in serving the many, not the few.

VI. C. I. O. TACTICS

1.

THE thirty-fifth floor of the Grant Building, in Pittsburgh, city of the Golden Triangle, is the headquarters of the new Steel Workers Union.

Equipped with its two-toned rugs, a battery of telephones, steel-tube furniture, silent typewriters, filing cabinets and directors' tables, it is a model modern office. Presiding over it are two men, quiet, devoted, self-assured. They are Philip Murray and Clinton Golden, of the Steel Workers Organizing Committee.

As a business office it is simply efficient. As a union office it is an innovation—a sharp contrast to the small, dingy, out-of-the-way quarters of its predecessor. The change underscores the first and basic quality of the C. I. O. in its young adventure. It says at once that the C. I. O. is an important institution, that the government is behind it, and that the workers need have no fear. Labor unions have usually worn the air of unwanted stepchildren, existing as they have in communities which held them suspect, where employers were hostile and workers browbeaten. In those wide stretches of industry to which the C. I. O. has turned its organization efforts, fear has deep roots. That fear has had to be understood and conquered.

Fine offices and all the tangible and intangible evidences of a brisk efficiency have helped. Confidence in support from the state and national capitals has reassured. The worker from the feudal steel towns of

C. I. O. Tactics

Ohio or Pennsylvania could not fail to sense that this union, no matter what the boss said, had strength, sufficient, perhaps, to make a man of him and to protect him on his job.

But the attack upon fear has had to be carried right into the steel towns themselves. Peripheral assurance was not enough.

2.

Fear was endemic in Aliquippa, steel town of thirty thousand people. Along the left bank of the Allegheny stretches the mill of Jones and Laughlin, fourth largest of the "Independents." Source of income directly or indirectly for all the inhabitants of the town, J. & L. represents economic, social, political power. Its community injunctions: labor unions must not be tolerated, union members must not be hired, and union meetings must not be held. For many years these rules were observed to the letter. Tom Girdler, once the dominant official of the plant, saw to that. Civil liberties, so far as they related to workers and unions, did not exist in Aliquippa.

After an abortive attempt at reform in the days of the N. R. A., Aliquippa relapsed into its feudal ways. Then in 1936 the S. W. O. C. sent in one of its hardiest organizers, Joe Timko.

Timko adapted his tactics nicely to the timidity of the workers, the fear psychosis of the town. He rented a vacant store in a workers' section as a union meeting place. There on a hot summer night he held a public meeting. The seventy-five persons who came to hear the talks of Timko and his friends were unhappy specimens of the free American. Worn, tired, with shoulders bent, the men seemed drained of hope. Their listless eyes momentarily brightened under Timko's sardonic comments about their bosses. Then the light would fade. Their wives seemed more eager, more easily touched, more ready to respond. One wondered at the sanguine daring of the organizer, that he should come to such uncompromising country as this.

Loudspeakers poked their gaping mouths out through the open windows. Timko's greatest audience was not in sight at all. Hundreds had gathered—unseen by company eyes—in the houses that cluttered the neighborhood. In these retreats they were free to listen to the leaders analyzing their jobs, denouncing the company. The promises of the union poured into the night.

Later in the same town, as elsewhere across the steel wastes, the organizers again reached those timid workers without subjecting them to the bosses' reprisals. Before the plant gates a sound-truck drew up at shift time. As hundreds of workers filed in and out, the air vibrated with the gospel: The union can help you! They were told that it was no longer a risk to join: the law and the union would protect them from the anti-union employer. If a man were fired as punishment, he need not worry. The union would care for him, get or give him another job. And in Harrisburg, the State Relief would see to it that he did not starve. For, the loudspeaker would boom out, "the Lieutenant-Governor of the State is a vice-president of the United Mine Workers, and he won't let you starve."

The men could not help hearing; and they could scarcely be accused of responsibility. They were simply coming to and from their work.

It might still have been disastrous to have joined the union unless a man were protected by numbers. How to get a substantial membership while protecting individuals from stool-pigeons and spies was a problem that had to be solved at once. And solved it was. No local record must exist in Aliquippa (or any other locality) of the names of workers who joined the union. Application blanks were therefore published in the steel workers' paper. All the worker had to do was to cut the blank from the paper, fill it out and mail it to headquarters in Pittsburgh. For months a vault safe in the Grant Building was the only repository of these names. Not even the local organizer knew when a man became a member. No means were left by which the boss could get the news. An effective technique, which did much to counter fear.

The great day came in Aliquippa when membership was large enough to set up a lodge of the union; officers were elected, and under the banner of numbers men no longer hid their union buttons but wore them openly, albeit nervously. The time had come to visit the employer as an operating business organization. And thus Timko did his job in "Little Siberia." Fear allayed, numbers grew; and courage took fear's place. On May 23, 1937, the workers of Jones and Laughlin won exclusive bargaining rights for the S. W. O. C.

This pattern was duplicated a hundred times. The methods varied, but everywhere it has been much the same story of overcoming timidity and suspicion. The union must get workers to listen; so sound-trucks and loudspeakers have proved enormously effective. But in some industries, notably southern textiles, it has been necessary to go beyond the factory gates; systematically the organizers have canvassed the homes of the workers. Chosen with an eye on prejudice against the Yankee, the organizers have been men who have lived in the South, speak the language, understand and are considerate of southern attitudes.

Sometimes, however, it is impossible to talk with the workers at all. Henry Ford's are not the only employees afraid to attend meetings, stop in the street, or receive strange callers at home. For such as these the circular, the pamphlet, the paper are the only means of

170 C. I. O. Industrial Unionism in Action

communication. Pamphlets carrying union appeals have been printed by the million: a description of industrial unionism, an analysis of the major industries, information of workers' rights under federal law, and what the union is doing for men in particular industries.

Newspapers are more ambitious. Steel, auto, rubber, textile, and other unions publish their own. The C. I. O. puts out an excellent Union News Service. Volunteers hand these out to men at plant gates. Ford employees hesitate to take issues as they are going in, so the union concentrates on them as they leave. Sometimes workers have been afraid to take them at all; so bundles have been dropped at street corners, to be scattered, picked up, and passed from hand to hand.

On one or two occasions airplanes have broadcast the literature. Mr. Lewis and other officials have used the radio. And finally great mass meetings have been called, in which the individual was swallowed up in the crowd and his identity safely obscured.

Such was the meeting in South Park near Pittsburgh on the first Labor Day of the C. I. O. Two hundred thousand workers, their wives and children, came, a jostling, dusty crowd. This was a holiday, but a holiday with a difference. A U. S. senator, a governor, and Director Murray of the S. W. O. C. were to talk about the steel drive, about unions, about workers' rights. From early morning the men and women wondered what was to come.

The crowd filled the great amphitheater and spilled over to the hills beyond. Each of the speakers spoke challengingly. Each extolled the union as the worker's best friend. Each shouted assurance that workers' rights would be protected until the organized would march in a great army of free men across the land. Pretentious oratory, rich with drama and designed for effect. Oratory received with a roar of approval from thousands of bursting throats.

The climax came when Governor Earle, intense, choosing his words with care, told them that never during his administration would the state troops be used to break a strike. The skies returned the crowd's response. In Pennsylvania, where unionism had been fought for years with the assistance of the armed forces of the law, this promise had revolutionary significance, and these people knew it. They knew that few strikes are won after troops appear on the scene. They knew that the Governor's words held enormous import for them all.

Again a technique to dissolve fear, extend assurance, fortify the individual by identifying him with the group to which he belongs.

3.

After unions in steel, autos, and rubber were organized, they asked employers for recognition and collective bargaining negotiations. This characterizes nonradical unionism everywhere. To secure bargaining status in industry is its ràison d'être.

The C. I. O. unions have frequently accompanied this request with a demand for what is called "sole bargaining rights." As we have seen, Mr. Sloan and Mr. Girdler twisted this into the bogey of the closed shop, and denounced the unions because they "levy tribute on the workers for the right to work." This accusation has served to popularize a misconception. What do these demands mean? Why are they made? The closed shop requires that no one may work in the plant unless he joins the union with which the employer deals. But this is not the case with a sole bargaining agreement. The latter requires the employer to make an agreement with one organization and no other. But it does not require any employee to join the union if he does not wish to. A closed shop hires none but union workers; the "sole bargaining" shop might, conceivably, have no union workers at all.

The rationale behind both of these institutions, however, is the same. It is desirable to understand it. Each is designed to protect the union from competition with other employee organizations, inspired by the employer to weaken and destroy unionism. The history of General Motors, for example, made the workers suspect that, given an opportunity, the company would break their union and abrogate its contract. For years the corporation had been militantly anti-union. As late as 1936, it had used company unions to break up any possible cohesion among employees. The U. A. W., with reason, did not believe that the corporation had changed its mind overnight. Therefore they demanded protection in the form of a sole bargaining contract. Only with this guarantee of stability, the C. I. O. believes, will unions grow strong and develop that responsibility and discipline about which employers talk so much.

As to the closed shop, not yet requested generally by the C. I. O. unions, the reasoning runs much the same. A closed shop shuts out all possible company stooge-unions. The idea is this: as long as a union shop employs some non-union men, the employer has an opportunity to build up a skeleton force of non-unionists. In depression he can lay off the union men first, and by the time recovery arrives give the decimated union a knockout punch.

Whenever a union believes the employer will break the union if he can, it will demand the closed shop. Strong unions like the Railroad Brotherhoods do not ordinarily make the demand. Deeply entrenched in the industry, they entertain no fears for their existence.

C. I. O. Tactics 173

The closed shop rests on another impulse: union men, like most Americans, do not like dues dodgers. When unions spend money and strength to improve working conditions for an entire shop, they quite naturally want all workers to share in the expense as well as in the fruits thereof. They do not care for perpetual hitch-hikers.

4.

Many people believe that unions are functioning only when they are striking, that union officials must keep trouble brewing between workers and employers if they are to last long. In short, that strikes *are* the labor movement.

Although their members comprise but a small proportion of the workers in the country, it is true that unions carry on three-fourths of all strikes. The strike is the most important weapon labor has. If it wishes to drive good bargains with employers, it must keep the weapon polished and ready for use.

But it is by no means true that unions want strikes. John Lewis, strike provoker No. 1 in the opinion of many Americans, is pretty emphatic about it: "I never wanted any strike if I could avoid it. I would much prefer to avoid a strike—I abhor strikes." At best, strikes are expensive. Wages are lost. Strikers must be fed. The longer a strike lasts, the more the needs of the strikers must be met from funds supplied by the union. In some of the strikes this year, C. I. O. unions have spent hundreds of thousands of dollars on benefits to workers.

But another factor is even more deterrent. A strike is a slippery weapon. Defeated union members are open to discharge and the blacklist, and the union itself is likely to be blotted out. Not unnaturally, then, the records demonstrate that most unions make every effort to settle disputes without recourse to the strike. Many unions guard against hasty strike judgments by taking from their locals all authority in such matters, and concentrating it in the hands of national officers. Frequently the national office controls finances for the same reason. High officials, removed from the heat of a dispute, are much more likely to be reasonable and willing to mediate than are local officials, or an irritated rank-and-file.

Oddly enough, employers are usually not aware that national officers—whom they call "outsiders"—are much easier to deal with than union committees from the shop. Far from fomenting trouble, they spend most of their time settling disputes before the strike stage is reached.

Unlike most English strikes whose purpose is preponderantly to improve wages, hours, and working conditions, American strikes are now mainly for union recognition. Of the 2,156 strikes settled during 1936, 50.2 per cent arose over recognition—that is, the right to exist. Of the 709,748 workers affected, 51.4 per cent were fighting towards this objective.

In the first five months of this year over 1,900 strikes were declared, affecting nearly one million workers. More than half of them, comprising over two-thirds of the workers, sought recognition. The two great auto conflicts and the strike against the steel companies were all fought for effective recognition, in one way or another denied the union.

The greater portion of all these strikers were affiliated with the C. I. O., but before the conclusion is drawn that the C. I. O. is more inclined to strike than the A. F. of L. unions, one should remember that the C. I. O. has been organizing industries where the right to build unions has rarely if ever been permitted. That right had first to be established, by strikes if necessary.

C. I. O. Tactics

5.

On a Sunday afternoon two years ago a baseball game was called between two factory teams of Akron rubber workers. Just as they were taking the field, someone remembered that the umpire was not a union man. All members of the Rubber Workers' union, the players refused to continue until the umpire was replaced. They *sat down*. The crowd sat down, everyone sat down, until presently the umpire was changed and the game began under union auspices.

The sit-down had come to Akron.* On their return to the shops the workers, it appears, recognized that the same stunt could be pulled on recalcitrant foremen. Why not sit down when things went wrong? And next day they did. Spontaneously, without orders, workers suddenly dropped their work and relaxed beside their benches, cauldrons, or machines. The foremen, the department heads, the superintendent—all the people who had looked so important before—were on the spot.

As one worker laughed, "Those birds looked awful silly running around trying to fix things up. And we knew they couldn't until they came across with the goods." "The goods" in this case consisted in the reprimand of a foreman who had been too colorful in his abuse of a worker. The men thought the evidence was with the man. Before they set the machinery in motion again they saw that the foreman was rebuked and temporarily laid off.

---

* The sit-down of course is old. Only its extended use is new. Historians have found sit-downs of cobblers, printers and textile workers in the sixteenth, seventeenth and eighteenth centuries. The workers at Rouen engaged in a sit-down at the cathedral in 1485. In the United States what were called stoppages, but might have been called sit-downs, occurred in the garment shops. They were not, however, stay-ins, for the workers went home at night where the stoppage was longer than one day.

176   C. I. O. Industrial Unionism in Action

Since that day in Akron, the rubber companies have suffered an epidemic of sit-downs, most of them lasting but an hour or two. More recently sit-downs have been staged by seamen on harbor-bound vessels, clerks in the five and tens, busboys and waitresses in metropolitan hotels, berry pickers in Wisconsin. The institution has gone round the world to be embraced by Coptic monks in Egypt and Geisha girls in Japan.

Harder hit than rubber, the automobile industry has endured upwards of four hundred sit-downs. Many lasted only a few hours, while workers at the White Motor Company sat for fifty-seven days and nights before they won a signed agreement.

A modification of the sit-down is the slow-down. Louis Adamic relates an amusing instance in an automobile factory. The assembly-line was geared to 140 hoods an hour. The superintendent stepped up the speed of the conveyor to 160. Figuring this as an increase of 20 an hour, or one-seventh, the men systematically jumped one hood in seven. The result at the end of the line was appalling. Swallowing his irritation, the superintendent reverted to the original speed.

The sit-down strike imposes problems upon the union, too. Food, sleeping quarters, sanitation, and recreation must be carefully provided to maintain the morale of the strikers. In large strikes the food has been supplied by strikers' wives, union funds, gifts from sympathetic organizations, and by the "chiseling committee." The chiselers, an important part of the strike machinery, solicit donations from friendly merchants. In the rubber strikes, near-by farmers gave generous quantities of food.

If a sit-down lasts only a short time, meals may be provided by wives who do the cooking at their homes. In more prolonged strikes the union sets up a strike kitchen, hires a cook, and puts the enterprise on a pro-

C. I. O. Tactics 177

fessional basis. At Flint the U. A. W. spent one thousand dollars on kitchen equipment. The chef, loaned by the Cooks' Union of Detroit, reported that "the amount of food the strikers use each day is immense: five hundred pounds of meat, one thousand pounds of potatoes, three hundred loaves of bread, one hundred pounds of coffee, two hundred pounds of sugar, thirty gallons of fresh milk, four cases of evaporated milk."

Comfortable sleeping accommodations are all-important. The auto factories were ideal. With cushions and cotton padding the floors of the cars were easily adapted to strikers' needs. In some plants burlap became hammocks; in others, benches and tables were made to serve.

Usually a barber can be found to renew his trade. Where the strikers are women, a beauty parlor may make its appearance. Orchestras, dancing, basketball, boxing, wrestling, and card playing grow out of needs and ingenuities. Workers have amused themselves by composing ballads telling the strike's history, immortalizing outstanding aspects of the dispute like "The Battle of Hellhole," more generally known as Fisher Plant No. 2:

> "In the office they got snooty,
> So we started picket duty,
> Now the Fisher Body Shop is on a strike..."

And so on through the history of the strike.

A rough discipline is maintained: hours allotted to various tasks, and set at regular times. The plant must be cleared, the gates policed, the strike committee must meet, the strikers gather to review the essentials of the conflict, buck up morale, and solve new problems. Drinking is ordinarily prohibited, and violators of the rule punished. Women are not permitted where men are striking. A sit-downer's absence from the plant may be permitted for a short time, but only for important reasons. A dodger is dropped from the ranks. Day and night a strikers' police force must watch for dissension within and danger without. When outsiders threaten to attack, special precautions are taken: alarm systems are set, and entrances barricaded.

6.

As a strike technique, the sit-down disconcerts many union leaders. Mr. Green disowned it from the first, and ordered a Federation inquiry into its use. In his effort to cast discredit upon the C. I. O., he claimed that A. F. of L. unions had not used the device. At least twenty sit-downs by his own men have been reported in the New York press.

But undoubtedly Mr. Green voiced a sincere conviction shared by many of his associates in the labor movement. Some C. I. O. leaders confess to a private anxiety, and hope that the sit-down will give way to more familiar tactics.

Whatever its ultimate legal status, the sit-down deserves better treatment from the chiefs of the labor movement. As a union weapon, it possesses great advantages over the usual type of strike, advantages which explain its recent popularity. A strike is useless to a union unless it succeeds in at least crippling the production of the plant. It is desirable that production stop altogether, not only that the utmost economic pressure may burden the company, but also to keep morale at high pitch. Nothing pleases a striker like the sight of smokeless chimneys. The sit-down does the job most easily and surely.

Suppose that the workers of General Motors had struck by walking off their jobs. They would have established a picket line at the gates, to persuade men from going back to work. The company in turn would have tried to run the plant with non-striking employees and imported strike-breakers. Success would spell an open declaration of union defeat, and possible loss of the strikers' jobs. Such a situation sets men on fire, most of all when legitimate grievances have provoked the strike in the first place. Violence follows.

Let the picketing be peaceful, say the courts. But, reply the unions (privately), if picketing is peaceful under such circumstances, pickets must be kept so limited in number and restrained in conduct as to surrender all advantages in the dispute. However, if pickets are massed sufficiently to be effective, violence is likely to occur. In the charged atmosphere of a picket line it is difficult to keep tempers checked, tongues from insult, and stones from flying. But violence is an open invitation to the courts and the police to scatter the pickets in the name of order—which means the breaking of the strike.

The sit-down is much more efficient. The occupation of the plant prevents strike-breaking; and the men can also repel police attacks. Even tear gas may be useless. When police used tear-gas bombs against strikers in the Fansteel Metallurgical plant of Chicago, the strikers used the ventilating system to turn the gas back upon the police. Only with the power turned off was a second police attack successful.

Of the thousand-odd sit-downs reported in the press since 1935, only twenty-five were broken by police intervention. In most of these strikes the workers won part or all of their demands.

Not only is the sit-down highly effective; in itself it is non-violent. If violence occurs it can be precipitated only by the employer and the police. An employer, however, will hesitate to start a battle if

180 C. I. O. Industrial Unionism in Action

machinery may be damaged, and he may alienate the public support to boot.

Superficial in its judgment of the issues in industrial conflicts, the public is quickly aroused by overt violence, its antipathies readily mustered against those seemingly responsible. On a picket line adept strike-breakers can easily make violence appear the fault of the pickets themselves, thus turning the public's curse upon them and their cause.

Such a consideration may prove of the utmost importance. In the big General Motors strike the sit-down tied up the plants as a walk-out could never have done. The company found the risk of losing public sympathy too grave to undertake eviction by force. Experience in the later steel strikes turned out precisely the reverse, thus pointing the identical lesson.

A healthy spirit among strikers is a critical necessity. Maintaining morale becomes a difficult matter after the ardor of the first few days has cooled and last week's pay has run out. Outside picketing in dirty weather, the sight of other workers or strike-breakers taking jobs, and the very real risk of injury combine to lower enthusiasm rapidly. The sit-down offers immense advantages in this respect. Strikers are protected from wind and weather. They are insulated from demoralizing influences outside the plant. They have little to fear from attack—so little, in fact, that the slight possibility lends a thrill to the affair. Days are filled with both union work and recreation. Wives are relieved of the worry about violence that acts as a drag upon a walk-out strike.

The sit-down, of course, has its limitations. It is much better adapted to a plant opening directly on the street, with windows accessible to strikers' friends on the outside, than to the remote and separated units of a steel mill, entrance to which may be a half-mile from the gate. Contact with the outside *must* be maintained; food *must* be delivered. At the plants of the rubber or automobile companies this was a simple process. Conceivably the police might have prevented it, but the public would not long have tolerated a campaign of starving out strikers.

In the steel strikes sit-downs would have been difficult, possibly out of the question. But as yet it seems that no one—even among the C. I. O. officials—has given adequate thought to more general adaptation of this strike device.

That this instrument is susceptible of abuse by a minority no one would deny. A handful of workers may shut down an entire plant over a small complaint. As observed in the General Motors experience, the better the machinery for the adjustment of grievances, the less likely it is that such interruptions will occur. The very threat of "wildcat" stoppages will stimulate the creation of machinery which will render them unnecessary. Secondly, a few workers will be able to interrupt production only when they have considerable support. Otherwise their fellow-workers won't let them get away with it. Unionization itself already shows signs of developing a discipline which in time will make this kind of problem a minor one.

7.

Inevitably the novelty and effectiveness of the sit-down exposed it to wide criticism, directed as well toward all its "friends." Among these were Miss Perkins, who observed that during the General Motors strike the legality of the sit-down strike had not yet been determined (she was being strictly accurate), and Mr. Landis, chairman of the Securities Exchange Commission and newly appointed Dean of the Harvard Law

School, who said that the sit-down might come to be held quite as legal as other kinds of strikes.

Neither Miss Perkins nor Mr. Landis gave outright approval to the sit-down. But a storm of abuse and denunciation greeted their remarks. Both houses of Congress throbbed for days to shocked speeches. Newspapers bulged with editorial and reader comment about public officials who gave encouragement to an outlaw movement. A typhoon broke over the head of the President of Harvard, who had but recently appointed Mr. Landis to his deanship.

Interpreting the opinion of many, Mr. A. Lawrence Lowell, President-Emeritus of Harvard University, wrote that the sit-down strikes constituted "an armed insurrection... defiance of law, order, and duly elected authorities... spreading like wild-fire." Professor Magruder of the Harvard Law School entered a calm reminder: "One who exhausts his emotional reservoir at the 'wild disorder' has no capacity for indignation at the social conditions, the misuse of the forms of law, often the downright illegality and over all the stupidity that provoked the disorder almost inevitably." It might also be recalled that in all the "armed insurrection" of the sit-downs, no deaths and only negligible violence were reported.

Is the sit-down illegal?

There is no federal law which explicitly outlaws the sit-down. The State of Vermont in April 1937 made persons engaged in such an "occupation" of property liable to heavy imprisonment and fine. Similar bills have been introduced into the legislatures of Florida, Massachusetts, Michigan, Minnesota, New Hampshire, Texas, and Ohio. In the last named, the statute took the form of an amendment to the State Labor Relations Act, which was lost at the end of the session.

Without specific authority, however, many courts

have found against the sit-down and issued injunctions against the strikers. Ohio, California, New York, and Michigan state courts have so held. The Court of Appeals for the Third Circuit is as yet the only federal court to act on the question. It, too, asserted the sit-down's illegality.

The grounds of all these judgments were similar. Judge Wilson of Los Angeles, allowing an injunction against an A. F. of L. union engaged in a sit-down, declared: "The right of an employee to be upon his employer's premises is by reason of his employment therein. When the employment ceases, his right to remain upon the premises is no longer that of an employee and his privileges are no greater than those of the members of the general public...." Sit-down strikers, he continued, "not being on the premises as owners, employees, or customers, but occupying the same against the owner's will and for the purpose of enforcing demands upon him, are trespassers."

The issue is a simple one: do employees, when they strike, lose their employee status? The courts say yes, and almost certainly will continue to do so for some time. Labor says no.

The unions maintain first that employers whose plants are struck do not enter the court with "clean hands." Since it is the business of an equity court to issue decrees only when justice can be done both sides, the union maintains that the court may not act unless it bring justice to the strikers as well. Secondly they point out that the National Labor Relations Act affirmed it public policy to encourage the organization of workers into independent unions; that the major sit-down strikes have been called against employers who refused to abide by that law; and that the strikes have had as their sole intent the peaceful enforcement of the law. They argue that the purpose is identical with that of a walk-out strike, which is legal in most jurisdictions.

Unionists maintain finally and basically that trespass upon the employers' property is only incidental to the protection of the strikers' jobs, and that jobs are a prior kind of property, fundamentally important to workers only a few days removed from starvation. As Chief Justice Hughes decreed: "The legality of collective action on the part of employees in order to safeguard their property interests is not to be disputed." If the job *is* property, and if a strike is legal to protect it, the unions argue that the sit-down strike can but incidentally be viewed as a trespass on the property of the employer. Competent lawyers including Leon Green, Dean of the Northwestern University Law School, have given their support to this position.

The sit-down is logically related to the facts of modern industry. Backed by substantial economic and legislative force, it will probably be found legal eventually. And if the old parties prove wary of pressing the fight, labor may well turn to independent political action. Which recalls again that the C. I. O. is a mass movement, that its appeals are addressed to great numbers of workers, and that in countless ways mass strength will tend to develop and apply its own mass tactics to economic and political problems. Mass picketing as at Chrysler, mass visits to a hostile court as at Toledo, mass street demonstrations as at Lansing, mass boycott of anti-union papers as at Milwaukee, mass boycott of an entire state as in Maine—all are expressions of a movement whose power will spring from numbers, its philosophy from democracy, and its strategy from solidarity.

8.

To its battery of techniques, the C. I. O. has added an appeal to law and an appeal to public authority to a degree unprecedented in the American labor movement.

Long ago unions in the United States developed a habit of reliance upon their own economic strength and a suspicion of the courts. Their experience with laws ostensibly passed in their interest has not been reassuring. On the receiving end of the hated labor injunction, their acquaintance with police, sheriffs, and militia has too frequently been achieved through the medium of the nightstick and the riot gun. So the rule has grown: "Take care of yourself; fight the employer with union weapons; leave the law to others; and give the courts a wide berth!"

The last four years have witnessed a profound change. The National Recovery Act and its Labor Boards were solicited and used by the A. F. of L. Federation unions supported the Social Security Act (many of whose provisions it had scorned not many months before), the Walsh-Healey Act, and the Guffey Coal Bill. During the last session of Congress both the A. F. of L. and the C. I. O. gave support (mild in some instances) to the Wages and Hours bill—later lost in the quarrels of the Democratic party.

The principle, however, has been established beyond retreat that in the future the labor movement will rely more upon government. Deliberately and officially the C. I. O. has approved such action. Its constituent unions have worked vigorously to elect New Deal candidates to public office. In return they have expected concrete assistance. Murphy in Michigan and Earle in Pennsylvania have contributed greatly to the movement in those two states. If Roosevelt's failure to admonish the independent steel companies was a blow for which the S. W. O. C. was unprepared, his public comments during the General Motors strikes proved a direct contribution to the union cause. His knuckle-rapping of

186 C. I. O. Industrial Unionism in Action

"economic royalists" and the general tone of his administration won him the C. I. O.'s outright support in the last campaign.

These unions have used the courts. They have applied for injunctions to restrain employers from violating the National Labor Relations Act, and the police from evicting sit-downers. They have petitioned governors to declare martial law in strike areas, as in Pennsylvania, in the hope that it would serve the strikers' cause. All these appeals and petitions indicate what may prove for labor a dangerous departure. Unionists have always contended that injunctions are not appropriate in labor disputes, and that martial law and troops aid their enemies. To invoke these instruments will lend them an approval which may subsequently be used against the unions. The troops in the steel areas were in the end bitterly regretted.

One other instrument the C. I. O. has gratefully utilized—the Senate Committee which has been investigating civil liberties under the chairmanship of Mr. La Follette. This has been of priceless assistance, not only to the C. I. O. but to the entire labor movement, in flashing an impartial light into the darker places of industrial America where organization is only now penetrating.

Finally the C. I. O.—and the A. F. of L. as well—has employed the services of the National Labor Relations Board. Set up by an Act of July, 1935, the Board has been particularly active during the present year. It has contributed enormously to clearing away obstacles to organization and union recognition. Inevitably this assistance has gone chiefly to the more active unions, leading a good many politicians to criticize the N. L. R. B. as "partisan," and an "adjunct to the C. I. O." Accordingly we shall need to examine the Board's work in some detail.

9.

The National Labor Relations Act represents no innovation. The United States has a long history of government intervention in the field of industrial relations. Largely confined to the railroads, this policy reached a culmination in the Railway Act of 1926, amended in 1934. This Act holds explicitly that amicable relations between roads and employees depend upon the establishment of strong labor unions, capable of entering upon collective contracts with the management. Accordingly the Act outlaws employer interference with employee organizations. Employers are forbidden to promote company unions or to give financial aid to any labor associations.

A National Mediation Board is set up to conduct elections among workers to determine whom they wish to represent them, and to provide voluntary mediation and arbitration facilities. An Adjustment Board, if asked, rules on grievance cases—notably those concerning interpretation of agreements between the two parties. Nothing limits the right to strike, except that under certain conditions both sides must maintain the status quo for a limited period while efforts at mediation are being made.

The Act has been a success. The Board's report for 1936 states that in the two preceding years no strikes or interruptions of service occurred, with the exception of a "wild-cat" stoppage of forty men on a small industrial railroad. "Serious differences" had arisen constantly, for "railroads are not different from other industries in the number and character of disputes.... Over two hundred disputes were serious enough to require the intervention of the Board and over fifteen hundred were referred to the four divisions of the

Adjustment Board. For every dispute submitted... there were many others considered and settled in conferences between representatives of carriers and the employees. Eleven railroads took strike votes after the first attempts at mediation had failed and voted to withdraw their services." But in every case the issues were resolved by the efforts of the Board without resort to the last drastic gesture.

Since this Board's inception others have cropped up. By virtue of N. R. A.'s Section 7A, guaranteeing self-organization rights to workers, the President set up a Labor Relations Board. It had a rocky time. The law was ambiguous, the Board had no enforcement powers and no effective administration support. With the Supreme Court decision against the N. R. A., this Board died. Then in July 1935 the present National Labor Relations Board took its place.

Considering recent agitation for its amendment, let it be noted that the Wagner Act received as thoroughgoing an examination as any legislation in recent years. Public hearings covered 2,285 pages of printed testimony. Over two hundred witnesses testified, representing almost every major organization and enterprise directly connected with industrial relations. Committee members studied the statute line by line. Sixteen months, covering two sessions of Congress, elapsed between the introduction of the bill and its approval by the President.

Like the Railway Act which it follows closely, the National Labor Relations Act states that when employers deny workers their right to organize and bargain collectively, strikes result which obstruct interstate commerce. Experience shows that protection of these rights encourages industrial peace. Therefore, it concludes, the policy of the United States must be the

C. I. O. Tactics

mitigation and elimination of these obstructions by protection of the rights in question.

To accomplish this end, Section 8 enumerates certain unfair practices in which the employer may not engage: any interference with workers' rights; domination or support of labor organizations; encouragement or discouragement of unions by discrimination in regard to employment or terms of employment; discharge of employees who file charges under the Act; and the refusal to bargain collectively with the employees' representatives.

The Board may receive complaints from workers, in accord with these violations of law. It may conduct hearings, make findings of fact, and issue "cease and desist" orders against employers found in violation of the Act. No penalty is attached. Should an employer fail to obey the order, the Board may petition a federal court for a decree enforcing the order. Further refusal to obey becomes contempt of court. The Board further may conduct elections among employees, to discover the representatives in any unit considered appropriate for collective bargaining: craft department, shop, or company. Those elected by a majority become the representatives of all.

The Act applies only to industries affecting interstate commerce. The expectation of its sponsors that it would apply to manufacturing was fulfilled in the Supreme Court decisions last spring. The Act was declared applicable to the enormous manufacturing enterprise of Jones and Laughlin Steel Company. It was held also to apply to a small clothing company, the Friedman-Harry Marks concern in Virginia, whose business runs to about two million dollars a year. The court justified this decision on the ground that the company belonged to a large and important industry. If the company denied workers their union rights, it might disrupt the industry and do severe damage to the interstate commerce of the nation.

The court has not been called upon to review the Act's provision which gives exclusive bargaining rights to the representative of a majority of workers—a provision that has received much criticism. But in an earlier case involving the Railway Act, the court observed that such a procedure was not only sensible but necessary. According to this decision, only one contract with one scale of wages, hours, and conditions of work was practicable for a railroad. Inferentially this would apply as well to a factory. Employers who oppose this principle in industrial relations, in the name of the minority of workers, are really fighting unionism under a fine-sounding slogan.

The fifth unfair practice under the Act is a refusal to bargain collectively. The question has become acute: Do employers violate the Act by refusing to *sign* an agreement? Officials of Little Steel took the position that they do not. The court has not reviewed the question, but will probably be obliged to do so. Already it has twice ruled that employers must make every reasonable effort to reach an agreement. The word "reasonable" is clearly a word difficult to apply to a specific situation. But it seems likely that Girdler's blunt refusal to sign the company's name to an agreement whose terms he accepted will be interpreted as a sign of "bad faith" and a violation of the Act.

No sooner was the National Labor Relations Act passed than critics began to clamor for its amendment— without waiting to try it out. They have leaped into renewed activity since the Supreme Court freed the Board from the restraint imposed by doubt as to the Act's constitutionality.

The most frequent charge made against the Act is that it places burdens upon employers without imposing

C. I. O. Tactics 191

corresponding responsibilities on the unions. This is an empty rebuke. The law is no more one-sided than laws requiring that employers pay wages in U. S. money and not in company scrip, or requiring them to install safety guards around machinery to protect operators. The Labor Relations Act is intended to be "one-sided"—in order to redress a pre-existing imbalance. It was passed deliberately to strengthen workers that they might approximate the strength of the companies with which they bargained. That a serious inequality existed—and still exists—in favor of employers is a commonplace among students of industrial relations.

There are many proposals for additional legislation: unions should be required to incorporate; they should be made subject to damages for illegal acts of officers; the Act should state unfair practices of unions as well as of employers; unions should be required to publish financial statements; strikes should be outlawed.

The demand for incorporation of unions is an odd one. It comes from people who want to make unions "responsible." Yet unions are already responsible before the law, and incorporation would, if anything, reduce their liability. Members of a corporation stand liable for claims against the corporation only to the extent of their investment in it (except for occasional double liability as in banks). Members of unincorporated organizations are subject to unlimited liability. Since 1908, when the first decision of the Supreme Court on the Danbury hatters' case was made, unions have been subject to damage suits under the Sherman Act. Since 1914, according to one authority, "there have occurred at least 23 criminal prosecutions, 6 damage suits, and about 40 suits for injunctions." In two of the cases "there have been settlements for large damages."

So far as state courts are concerned, unions may be

sued in many jurisdictions as unincorporated associations. Finally, the Labor Relations Act cannot be said to be one-sided in this matter: it does not require employers to incorporate.

As to the suggestion that unions be required to publish their finances, it should be emphasized first of all that most unions do publish to their members audited reports of receipts and expenditures. Union leaders oppose such a federal requirement, not on the ground that it would embarrass them to be honest, but that publication of information on union resources would enable employers to single out the richest, bring suit for one cause or another and tie up their funds at critical periods. As long as unions feel that employers are hostile to their very existence they will resist pressure to give their enemies any facts which could be used against them. The Labor Relations Act is not one-sided on this matter either. It does not require employers to publish accounts. It does not lay such an obligation even upon those associations of employers who make it their chief business to harass and destroy the union movement.

The proposal that the Act list unfair labor practices of the unions is especially beside the point. Common law amply covers coercion and intimidation of employees by unions, but takes no notice of the less tangible coercion by employers in their control of jobs. It was to bring such practices under the law that the Act was passed.

The suggestion that strikes be outlawed may have the virtue of simplicity but it would not "balance" the Labor Relations Act. If strikes were outlawed, the lockout would have to go too. That would mean subjecting both sides to compulsory arbitration. The United States has had experience with arbitration. The record is clear: employers do not want it and unions do not either. With both parties opposed to such machinery, it seems obvious that the consequences would be worse than the trouble it was intended to cure. Further, such a federal requirement without an enabling amendment would be flatly unconstitutional as a violation of due process. The court so ruled in the Wolff Packing Company cases.

The United States has embarked on a policy of encouragement of collective bargaining through the development of strong unions. To rob these unions at the outset of the most effective weapon in their arsenal —the strike—would reduce the entire program to an absurdity.

When pushed from one proposal to another, the critic of the current governmental policy on labor relations will invoke the lesson of England. Well, what about England? First, English unions may incorporate, but are not required to. They may register and gain certain privileges in return for certain responsibilities. This again is voluntary.

After two decades of complete statutory immunity (which did not bring the empire to ruin) Parliament in 1927 subjected unions to certain limited restraints. The Act made two kinds of strikes unlawful: that which "has any object other than or in addition to the furtherance of a trade dispute within the trade or industry"—i.e., the sympathetic strike; and that which is "designed or calculated to coerce the government." The second of these is certainly unlawful in this country, and the first, through court precedent, almost as clearly so.

Thus strikes that are illegal in England are already illegal here. And, in addition, a good many others which *are* legal in England are not lawful in America. For example, many states do not permit a strike for a closed shop. Most states hold a strike unlawful that violates a collective agreement. Everywhere strikes that are held conspiracies in restraint of interstate commerce violate the law.

In the United States, it is illegal for a union to persuade or attempt to persuade customers from patronizing a firm against which the union is striking. The union may not even tell its friends about the strike, orally or by published statement, with the intent of reducing the employer's business. England knows no such restraint.

As to damages, English practice is simple. Except in the case of the two strikes which are illegal, funds of English unions may not be attached, no matter what the means employed to carry on a strike or how illegal they may be.

American unions are subjected to innumerable other restraints of which English unions are free. A maze of city and state laws restrains picketing in the United States. The labor injunction is a unique tool by which American courts, at the request of employers, prevent unions from carrying on activities essential to their program. The familiar contract requiring workers NOT to join a union has been a favorite among employers. By means of these "yellow-dog" contracts coal operators in West Virginia for years strangled all union "agitation." Organizers were prevented from talking unionism on the grounds that it would induce breach of contract. Only recently has the government taken steps to wipe out the practice by denying the contract enforcement in federal courts; and some of the states have followed suit. Of all these union shackles the English know little or nothing.

The appeal to English practice is based at best on ignorance. Anglophiles among labor critics would find themselves disappointed and aggrieved if they followed their noses to Merrie England.

C. I. O. Tactics

When discussion on these matters gets well bogged down, and England seems a delusion after all, the critic is apt to inveigh against the racketeering in the labor movement. There are racketeers in unions. And the labor movement has not acted as strenuously in their eradication as it might have done.

But three comments are necessary. First, trade unions are American institutions, with American vices as well as virtues. Anyone who can recall the last six years will remember a little racketeering among eminent bankers and utility executives. Secondly, there are far fewer racketeers in unions than some newspapers would lead us to believe. News is built upon the spectacular; city editors do not find honesty spectacular. Finally we do not need more laws to deal with whatever extortion exists in unions. As New York's experience under Prosecutor Dewey attests, whenever a community determines to drive out such illegal practices, existing federal and state statutes prove more than sufficient.

Our discussion of law has gone far afield. But so too has the C. I. O. The importance of the C. I. O.'s resort to law extends beyond any immediate gains it may have achieved thereby. Its significance lies in the reorientation of the labor movement from its traditional suspicion of courts and legislatures to an open-eyed desire to exploit both of them to the limit of their usefulness.

VII. THE EMPLOYER FIGHTS BACK

1.

THE United States is a non-union country. In almost any year of the last half-century one could have selected a hundred workers at random and found ninety or more without any union affiliation whatever.

The explanation of this state of affairs, odd in a rich and vigorously industrial nation, is multiple. Fundamentally it is the country itself. Fecund in opportunity, the wide-stretching continent invited a man to swing up the ladder of success by his own unaided efforts. The philosophy of "once a worker always a worker" has been abjured. American mores have been emphatically individualistic. So too have those of American workers.

Again our industrial technology has been a rapidly changing one. The development of the machine has repeatedly emasculated craft abilities. The center of industry has moved away from the skilled trades where unionism has had its strongest hold to the amorphous mass-production plants. The craft structure of the A. F. of L. has grown steadily less adapted to the country's industrial make-up. Meanwhile, the secular rise of real wages has made men believe that capitalism was already serving them well enough without the prodding of unions.

To all these considerations must be added one crucial factor: the opposition of the employer to unionism—

The Employer Fights Back 197

itself the product of his individualism, his unwillingness to surrender any portion of his power, his wish to believe that the interests of himself and his worker are not antagonistic but mutual. Some of this opposition has been well-disposed and sincere. It has been expressed in a benevolent paternalism, by which workers have benefited.

Much of it, however, has been militant, disingenuous, brutal and cynical. If in what follows the militant opposition is dwelt upon, it is not to suggest that this is a complete picture of employers' attitude toward workers. It is only that this opposition is the more overt, the more sinister, and possibly the more likely response to the C. I. O.'s militancy itself.

In 1919 the United States Steel Corporation, as we have seen, faced a national strike. For years it had blithely indulged in a tyranny unparalleled in the annals of large industrial enterprise. But now the back bills of three decades' grievances were about to be presented. Yet the company took no steps to consult its employees, discuss complaints, consider their demands. There was literally no system by which the company and its thousands of workers could communicate effectively with each other.

Mr. John D. Rockefeller, Jr., an ardent sponsor of the employee representation plan—or company union—was worried. He was an old friend of Mr. Frick of the Corporation. One morning, the newspapers occupied with the coming struggle, Rockefeller called on Frick, whom he caught at the breakfast table. He urged that the strike threat was evidence of something wrong, that the company should realize the need of consulting its workers, and that the employee representation plan could meet this need. He did not propose independent unionism, note. He advised a company union. But it was too strong for Mr. Frick. He pounded out: "This is my business. I will run it as I please."

One might have supposed he was talking of a peanut stand, not an enterprise employing two hundred thousand people and very largely dictating their lives. His was a flawless enunciation of the despotic conception of industrial government—still embraced by a majority of American employers.

Consistently, employers have forged a number of weapons to defend their conviction. Notably in the past they have used industrial espionage and company unions. The advent of the C. I. O., the Senate investigation of espionage and the federal government's opposition to company unions have forced a change of tactic. For the time being industrial spies are under a cloud, and company unions are on the run. In their place industry aims two other guns squarely at the Lewis men: "A. F. of L. company union," and the Citizens' Committee. But first of all, and most of the time, *American employers have unionized themselves* to defeat the workers.

2.

Of these employer groups partially or exclusively devoted to anti-union activity, some are confined to single industries: the National Erectors' Association for the manufacturers and erectors of structural steel, the National Founders' Association among the makers of cast-iron products other than stoves, the Metal Trades Association for the fabricators of metal products. Some cut across industrial lines: the National Industrial Council, the League for Industrial Rights, and the National Association of Manufacturers.

The N. A. M., for example, has some four thousand members. Through individual contact or affiliation

The Employer Fights Back

with state organizations, its influence spreads nationally, and is devoted to an intractable opposition to unions. Within its own industry the American Iron and Steel Institute has performed this same function.

But the brashest of the employers' anti-unions are in coal and the metal trades. The Harlan County Coal Operators' Association of Harlan County, Kentucky, is a regional industrial enterprise. The County lives on coal. The Association sees to it that the miners live none too well. Every coal operator belongs to the Association and pays dues based on his monthly tonnage —which means an annual income to the Association of sixty to seventy thousand dollars.

With news of the C. I. O. campaign of 1936, dues were doubled "to fight unionization of the miners" according to the testimony of the secretary, Mr. George Ward, before the La Follette Committee last spring. Ward confessed he had kept no records of receipts and expenditures, because "to be frank, I have been anticipating an investigation for the past three or four years."

The Association had reason to avoid the light as the Committee hearings disclosed. The Association had been employing regularly at one hundred and fifty dollars a month one Ben Unthank, known throughout the county as the "road killer" of the organization. Poverty-stricken, bewildered miners, brought to Washington to tell of anti-union activities of the operators, pinned a succession of brutal attacks and several murders on Unthank and his associates.

Legal cover for this terrorism was easily arranged. The Association simply bought out the law. The Sheriff boasted that his force consisted of 379 deputies, 37 of them ex-convicts, 64 indicted at various times for serious crimes. He said he had "sold out" to the mine owners, in exchange for numerous perquisites amounting to over one hundred thousand dollars in the three

200   C. I. O. Industrial Unionism in Action

years 1934-37. The local judge was an operator himself. The prosecuting attorney for the region was on the payroll of the largest coal company.

A peer among the lawless coal barons of Harlan was Pearl Bassham, owner of the Harlan-Wallins Coal Company, and chief contributor to the Association. Asked if he had ever given murder instructions to the thugs employed by the Association, the best reply he could muster was that he could not remember! In common with other operators he made it clear that he was against workers' unions. He inveighed against the closed shop and the check-off. Yet, somewhat humorously, it was brought out that his company regularly employs the check-off for the support of the company's medical service. A monthly $1,800 to $2,400 is deducted from the workers' pay. The three physicians carrying on the service are paid a total of $1,250.

Mr. Bassham evidently favors the check-off when it pays him. He even obliges his workers to buy lottery tickets on second-hand automobiles discarded by himself and his friends. It's the most profitable way they have of getting rid of their old machines. Needless to say, the Association has kept Harlan County pretty free of the taint of unionism.

A more respectable organization is the Metal Trades Association. Organized forty years ago it was not originally intended as a union-busting agency. Its first important action was to sign a national agreement with the machinists in 1899-1900. But after a short honeymoon the agreement broke down, and an anti-union program was projected, to continue unremittingly to the present day.

About one thousand members constitute the Association roster, many of them units in larger companies; hence, the channel of influence for a much wider constituency. Membership is granted only on the under-

The Employer Fights Back

standing that the employer will not deal with unions, will co-operate in the program of sabotage to which the Association is dedicated, and in crises will turn over its labor troubles to the Association. Dues are collected at the rate of twenty cents a month per employee. A large Defense Fund is maintained, amounting currently to over two hundred and fifty thousand dollars.

Mr. Sayre, a valued executive officer of the Association for thirty years, claimed that "our primary interest in all things is to try and get the employer and employee to believe that their interests are mutual." To encourage this mutuality, the Association furnishes spies to its members to ferret out union activities, report on union men, secure their discharge, and blacklist them throughout the industry. The Association spends, on this industrial espionage, from fifty thousand dollars to sixty thousand dollars a year. That they have had success is seen in the low estate of the Machinists Union in the metal shops of the country.

But the Association's big guns are reserved for those occasions when unions appear and strike to gain recognition. The M. T. A. is the strike insurance agency of its members.

First of all it stands ready to supply strike-breakers up to 70 per cent of the total staff of the company. It arranges bank and commercial credit for the struck concern. It enlists other members of the Association to fill the orders of the company, that valuable customers may not be lost. And if the strike-breaking provokes resistance, the Association at its own expense provides special "guards," ostensibly for the protection of employers' property.

Judging from the recent instances of M. T. A. strike-breaking at the Black Decker Plant of Ohio and the Columbian Enameling and Stamping Company, of Indiana, a further function of these guards is to provoke violence, a call for the national guard, and the suppression of civil rights of the strikers. This insures the defeat of the union.

The Association further promotes the mutual interests of employers and workers by "combatting adverse class legislation." It notifies members promptly when such legislation is threatened, and proposes appropriate action. The record charmingly tells what is and what is not "adverse class legislation." The National Labor Relations Act is, but anti-picketing ordinances (as in Terre Haute) are not. The Walsh-Healey Act enforcing minimum hour and wage requirements on government contracts is, while laws to compel unions to incorporate and publish their finances are not.

Some notion of which class the Association considers "adverse" is revealed in its opposition to the Social Security Act. After that Act was passed, a bulletin was sent to Association members, to be posted where employees could read the bitter truth. The Act's taxes on wages, it stated, were to be used for the *general* purposes of the government. This was a simple untruth. It omitted altogether to mention that employers too were required to contribute to the fund. Throughout, the bulletin was a tissue of confusion. As Mr. La Follette remarked to the Association's officer, "If wage earners were as unfamiliar with the Social Security Act as you seemed to be at the time you prepared this bulletin, they would be completely mixed...." Mr. Sayre was embarrassed.

The "mutuality" of the M. T. A. is of the "heads-I-win, tails-you-lose" variety.

In its anti-unionism the Association does not confine itself to its members. One or two years ago an Association member, S. L. Allen of Philadelphia, suffered a walkout of his employees. The M. T. A. stepped into the breach. It put in sufficient "finks" to break the strike. At this point Mr. George Deming, vice-president of the Philadelphia Storage Battery Company, owners of the Philco Radio and Television Co., severely criticized the Allen concern for not settling with the union. Deming, it seems, has considerable sympathy with unionism, and considers it the business of the workers and not of the employers whether they form a labor union or not.

Deming's remarks drew a letter from Mr. Stringham, eastern representative of the M. T. A., to his chief, Mr. Sayre, of the Chicago office. Deming was "the yes man for the labor racketeers" on the Mayor's Labor Board. Deming was the "best thing the A. F. of L. has in Philadelphia, and his constant agitation for the A. F. of L. is adding strength to the organized labor movement. This man should be *broken down*. Can you suggest anything...?"

The kindly Mr. Sayre replied to his staff member that "the next time you see Mr. Keller, give him the benefit of your opinion regarding Mr. Deming's attitude toward labor problems."

Who is Mr. Keller? He turns out to be a member of the Executive Board of the Metal Trades Association and an officer of the Chrysler Motor Company, owner of Philco stock, and one of Philco's best customers. The suggestion is all too clear. The M. T. A. carries its organization gospel even to the heathen outside its fold.

3.

Industrial espionage is the business of at least two hundred and thirty agencies in the United States employing thousands of operatives. Estimates of the number of spies vary from a minimum of forty thousand for all the agencies to one hundred and thirty-five thousand for the Burns, Pinkerton, and Thiel agencies alone. An old student of the business believes that the mininum cost of this service to American employers is over eighty million dollars a year.

Take Corporations Auxiliary, referred to in Chapter IV. Here is a profit-making concern, interested in extending its business whenever and wherever it can. When the N. R. A. proffered some mild aid to labor organization, the agency succeeded in running its list of clients up to two hundred.

The trick of getting business from employers is crude but effective—get them worried about possible labor troubles. In a nice way, of course—as in the following form letter: "... organized labor misleaders have found a rare opportunity in the C. I. O. Misrepresentation, stretching of the truth, and general chicanery of labor organizers ... all this is very confusing to the workmen, who need leadership to tell them what their rights are with respect to being forced into organizations." Always the worker's friend, Corporations Auxiliary stands ready to furnish that "leadership," that the employees may be taught their rights.

In some instances an employer, slow in taking the agency's tip, was encouraged to make up his mind by insinuating spies into the plant, through the regular employment office, and without his knowledge. These spies (the Auxiliary officials prefer that their operatives be called "Industrial Psychologists") then persuaded the workers to start a union. This done, the Auxiliary Company opportunely arrived to offer its advice and sell its services to the company.

It might be thought that a spy company, with a staff of "Industrial Psychologists," would be acquainted with labor problems and the students in that field of economics. Unfortunately, however, Mr. Ross, the general manager of the Auxiliary agency, had his say before the La Follette Committee as an expert on labor. At one point in his testimony he remarked that "every authority is agreed that to avoid serious labor disturbances it is up to the employer to keep himself fully informed on the sentiment among his employees."

Senator Thomas was interested, and asked who Mr. Ross meant by "authorities." Ross referred vaguely to "articles by newspaper columnists and economists, in fact Roosevelt."

"Do you think President Roosevelt a good authority on labor relations?"

Mr. Ross on second thought was not sure. Mr. Thomas then inquired if Ross read books on such matters, and received the quick reply that he not only read them, he "studied them," that he made it his business to keep up with "scientific studies" in order to train his operatives. The Senator quite naturally asked Mr. Ross to name an outstanding authority in America on labor relations.

"An outstanding authority?" hesitated Mr. Ross. "I am poor in recollecting names or the volumes either." Then, puzzled, he suggested tentatively the name of "Bassett." The Senator encouraged him to name some "particular book." A pause, and then a thought struck him. "Yes, I just read one. . . . *The Labor Union Racket.* That is the last one I read." But he did not know by whom it was written, except that the author was a newspaperman.

To Mr. Thomas's query whether the author was an authority on the subject, Ross replied lamely that he considered that anyone "who wrote on the subject would be an authority." It might be added that *The Labor Union Racket* is considered among students an irresponsible contribution to the subject and that, so far as is known, there is no Bassett in the field.

Despite all this hocus-pocus about Labor Psychologists, Corporations Auxiliary has been revealed through its own testimony before the La Follette Committee as a fabricator of reports, a provoker of discontent among workers, and a law-breaker in a despicable traffic. From start to finish its work is to foment labor trouble and then sell espionage to offset that trouble. Spies join unions, seduce officers, get themselves elected to offices, waste union funds, report names to the employer for firing, and demoralize the organizations.

Where trouble explodes into strikes, Auxiliary appears with another service to sell: guards for strikebreaking. These "guards," a wretched crew, are picked up from gutters, in New York around Times Square, in Chicago around Halsted Street. Drawn from the underworld, they usually have police records.* Their interest and that of the Auxiliary is the prolongation, the intensification of violence, and enhancement of their incomes.

Employers before the Committee told stories of equipping these thugs with weapons, from hatchet handles to machine guns. They make sober reading. Even more disquieting are the tales of the deputization of such men by city and county police—privateers invested with the power of the law to attack workers on strike. With such collusion, all pretense of a "public" law is abandoned: employer and the Auxiliary become the law.

Auxiliary is one of the concerns whose service since 1933 has been enjoyed by Chrysler, by fifteen plants of General Motors, by Quaker Oats Company, Wheeling Steel, Great Lakes Steel, Firestone Tire and Rubber Company, Postal Telegraph and Cable Company,

* As several hundred of such guards were being hired in a New York "fink" agency during the 1936 elevator strike, word was whispered among the waiting horde of applicants that each man was to be fingerprinted. In the stampede for the door, two men were severely injured.

R. C. A., and many others. A partial list of the clients of other agencies includes Bethlehem Steel, Campbell Soup Company, Curtis Publishing Company, Baldwin Locomotive Works, Montgomery Ward and Company, Pennsylvania Railroad, Goodrich Rubber Company, Aluminum Company of America, Consolidated Gas Company of N. Y., Frigidaire Corporation, Carnegie Steel, National Dairy Products, and Western Union.

One list known to be incomplete gives the kinds of employers known to hire spies: thirty-six employers' associations, fourteen corporations of nation-wide scope, twenty-seven railroads, twenty-nine traction, utilities, and bus companies, fifty-two metallurgical and machinery companies, thirty-two mining companies, twenty-eight employers in the auto industry, twenty steamship lines, and twenty-eight food companies.

In a preliminary report to the Senate in February of this year, Mr. La Follette concludes that these agencies constitute a "colossal daily drive in every part of the country to frustrate enunciated labor policy and to neutralize American Labor laws." Words will not break up this racket. Senate publicity may temporarily place its use under a cloud.

4.

On April 20, 1914, the gruesome burning of eleven children and two women in a tent colony of Ludlow strikers brought the nation's attention to one of the most complete breakdowns of industrial relations in our history. It also brought Mr. J. D. Rockefeller, Jr., financially interested in the company, to Colorado. He began a study of labor problems, which has persisted to this day.

The result was one of the first company unions in the United States. Under the name Employee Representation Plan, it started a movement that rose to a peak among employers during and immediately after the World War. Its impulse was twofold: (a) to improve employer-employee relationships through a form of government under which workers and management might discuss questions of mutual interest, and (b) to offset any tendency for workers to build up unions of their own.

Under the better Plans, industrial relationships have been enormously improved, workers have benefited by countless small and large concessions, and a revolution in the psychology of management officials set in motion. But even in the best Plans, a small minority of the total, the anti-union purpose has remained strongly to the fore.

After their extension to other Rockefeller companies during the War, the Plans grew quickly. In 1922, the National Industrial Conference Board reported 725 of them, for the most part in large concerns—Eastman Kodak, International Harvester, General Electric, Swift and Company, Bethlehem Steel, and the Pennsylvania Railroad among them. Many disappeared in the ensuing decade, until, according to the same research organization, only two hundred were active in 1932, in plants employing about one million workers.

The passage of the National Recovery Act with its enunciation of public policy favorable to unions reversed the trend. In November, 1933, 653 plans were reported, two-thirds of them born out of the N. R. A. matrix. Most of them were shams, designed to kill unionism in the bud—to satisfy the letter of the law, but nullify its spirit.

The National Labor Relations Act obliged the Labor Board to correct this situation, wherever workers made an appeal. Out of many company union cases, the most important, perhaps, was that of International Harvester.

The Employer Fights Back   209

The company affected was a large one. Its Plan was established years ago. Administration was good. Yet Labor Board ordered its dissolution. Why?

The Plan provided a typical central institution—the Works Council, an equal number of workers and management representatives, the latter appointed by the company and the former elected by employees in secret ballot. It was the duty of these representatives to discuss and debate all matters of mutual concern. No questions, presumably, were excepted from their attention. But the Plan, like all of the company unions, had serious drawbacks as a workers' agency. The employees themselves had little contact with the Plan. Annually they elected their representatives. Thereupon they ceased to have any direct concern with its functioning—until the following year. They never voted on substantive questions, or on changes of the Plan. At election time they voted perforce on personalities, never on issues. The candidates had no platform. The workers themselves never met as a body. The Council resolved all questions by a vote. Each side had the same number of ballots. "Obviously," said the Labor Board, "the management representatives did not exercise a judgment independent of that of their superior, the Superintendent. His decision was their decision, so that a conception of the Works Council as a deliberative body possessing power is false."

In this, as in most other Plans, if the superintendent agreed with the decision it would be carried out; if not, there was an end to the matter. The machinery of appeal to the president, the convocation of a General Council, resort to outside arbitration, served only further to create the illusion of equality. As a matter of record, the General Council and arbitration devices never were utilized. "At every step it was merely a question of whether management, subject only to self-restraint and the dictates of conscience, says 'yes' or 'no.' "

The philosophy of the Plan was based on free discussion, which presupposed well-informed representatives. But in this the employee representatives were at a hopeless disadvantage. They never had the aid of experts on intricate questions—wages, hours, and the like. Management, of course, was assisted by a staff of accountants, statisticians, lawyers. In the circumstances, *intelligent* discussion was impossible. If deadlock was reached, the employees were helpless, for they had nothing to fall back upon—no funds, no organization, no mass support.

The representatives of the workers were at all times employees of the management. Even their work as delegates to the Council was paid for by the company. It could produce but a dubious kind of "independence." Inevitably the representative tended to act and talk in terms of loyalty to the company which paid him, rather than the workers for whose interests ostensibly he was there. Since the organization cost the workers nothing, it was "a subtle device to make difficult a fair consideration of the advantages of an outside labor organization through the persuasion of the 'something for nothing' argument." Finally, of course, were the management to withdraw its support, the whole edifice would fall. It had no other base.

This particular company union, conceived by the company, confined to the company, supported by the company, and dominated by the company, was a good organization of its kind. It was informed by a measure of idealism. It did many things to improve conditions of work. But it could be of no use in protecting workers in crises, or assisting them in the major questions of their industrial life. Inevitably the Board concluded that it was an agency contrary to the spirit of the Labor

Relations Act, the creature of the company rather than of the workers.

If this was true of the Harvester Plan, an old and seasoned institution, how much more so was it true of the makeshift organizations set up in Steel, in Autos, and in manufacturing generally since 1933. In the words of fifty-three employee representatives of the Carnegie-Illinois Steel Corporation in 1936, they have been "a sham, a farce, and an insult to the workers."

Action by the National Labor Relations Board in the above and other cases has been a major defeat for the anti-union employer. It seems likely that the company union has passed its heyday. Some interesting shifting, however, is going on.

5.

On July 30 eighty persons from a dozen states and "every industry except mining" gathered behind closed doors at Hershey, Pennsylvania, at the call of the Independent Chocolate Workers of Hershey. For two days the meeting labored and brought forth a new organization in labor ranks: the Independent Federation of Independent Unions. It proclaimed itself as unassociated with either the A. F. of L. or the C. I. O. Upon both of these it declared war.

The extent to which the Federation is a bona fide movement remains to be seen. But it is worth noting: (1) that many of its officers were officials of old company unions, which they never failed to approve and support. (2) Some if not all of the Federation leaders are men whose closeness to the employers in the past has given rise to doubt of their integrity. Among them, for example, is Reginald Boote of Remington Rand fame, whose work we shall examine in detail later in this chapter. (3) The honorary president of the Federation is a U. S. Representative from Michigan, Mr. Hoffman, whose utterances since the automobile and steel strikes mark him as an outstanding foe of unionism. (4) The Federation Constitution abjures all strikes, walk-outs, slowups and especially denounces the sit-down strike as "unAmerican." (5) Affiliates must confine their memberships to those actually employed in the industry. This would seem to eliminate all full-time paid officials —i.e., efficient representatives. (6) There was much discussion of the need in this country for "respect for law and order," an appeal natural to individuals and groups who profess approval of unions in principle but disapprove them in practice.

It is safe to conclude that the Federation is not free from the influence of the old employer-devotees of the company union. It is almost as safe to conclude that it will gradually die of its own ineptitude.

6.

During a bitter strike in the summer of 1935, called by the A. F. of L. Mine, Mill, and Smelter Workers for recognition of their union—in Kansas, Missouri and Oklahoma—the mine operators set up, under the guns of the militia, a company union known locally as the "Blue-Card Union." At its head were a mine official and a personnel manager contributed by the dominant company in the area. The latter testified later that workers were paid ten dollars a head for deserting the A. F. of L., and joining the bogus outfit, with a promise to remain out of the A. F. of L. as long as they were employed. The company instituted a closed shop by which no workers except those in the Blue-Card Union might have jobs. By these tactics and with the assistance of troops, the strike was broken. Five thousand miners were left without jobs. What happened to this pretty

The Employer Fights Back

organization? One year ago, the old Blue-Card Union was granted a charter by the A. F. of L. and baptized with the resounding title of the Tri-State Metal, Mine, and Smelter Workers. Why? To keep the C. I. O. from organizing that territory.

Toledo offers a curious case. Here the local C. I. O. Council started a campaign for members in the Interlake Iron Corporation about March 30 of this year. Sufficient success crowned their efforts to warrant the S. W. O. C.'s granting them a charter on April 25.

Prior to April 20, 1937, a company union had existed in the plant. About that date, as a result of the Supreme Court's upholding the constitutionality of the National Labor Relations Act, the corporation notified the company union that it was no longer legal. Dissolved, it at once voted to organize as a new union and apply for an A. F. of L. charter. Under date of April 23, the A. F. of L. issued a charter to the organization, designating it as a Blast Furnace and Coke Oven Workers Union Local. Three days later the management—refusing to meet with the C. I. O. men—gave the A. F. of L. union sole bargaining rights for the whole plant.

Why did the A. F. of L. grant a charter to this company union in masquerade? The A. F. of L. could not but have known its antecedents and could not but have understood the alacrity of the corporation in signing a contract. White-washing this organization would have been repugnant to the Federation two years ago. But now the C. I. O. is Anti-Christ and the A. F. of L. seems content, for the time at least, to help the employer do his union-fighting.

There are other such cases in various industries and various parts of the country. There is an elaborate case before the National Labor Relations Board, the outgrowth of a charge that the Consolidated Edison Company of New York has entered into invalid closed-shop agreements with A. F. of L. unions to prevent C. I. O. unions from functioning. There are a few alleged instances where similar collusion has been used by C. I. O. unions against the A. F. of L., notably in the Ladies Garment and the Oil industries.

It is the use of the A. F. of L., however, that appeals to the anti-union employer. For the C. I. O. represents in his mind his gravest threat. He sees the C. I. O. as militant, radically, genuinely pro-labor. By comparison the A. F. of L. is not only the lesser of two evils, but a possible ally against the labor movement. In this he calculates shrewdly—for the personal hatreds engendered among the A. F. of L. leaders toward their late associates of the C. I. O. have become in many cases more important to them than devotion to the workers' cause.

The curious picture of the A. F. of L. doing the union-baiting employer's work would be incomplete were the Red cry not mentioned. This familiar technique is now widely pursued by Federation officials, appealing for employer support on the ground that the C. I. O. men are Communists, radicals, Moscow-paid. No better illustration of this can be found than the following amazing letter from the international president of the Machinists Union to his staff. This union, it may be remarked, has grown by one hundred thousand since the C. I. O. was launched. Its efforts have been tireless, its success in numbers impressive. Its methods have been predicated upon the instructions noted in Mr. Wharton's communication.

The Employer Fights Back

INTERNATIONAL ASSOCIATION
OF MACHINISTS
Washington, D.C.
April 20, 1937.

GENERAL VICE PRESIDENTS,
GRAND LODGE REPRESENTATIVES,
BUSINESS AGENTS AND GENERAL CHAIRMEN.

Dear Sirs and Brothers:

GENERAL

Since the Supreme Court decision upholding the Wagner Labor Act many employers now realize that it is the Law of our Country and they are prepared to deal with labor organizations. These employers have expressed a preference to deal with A. F. of L. organizations rather than Lewis, Hillman, Dubinsky, Howard and their gang of sluggers, communists, radicals and soap box artists, professional bums, expelled members of labor unions, outright scabs and the Jewish organizations with all their red affiliates.

We have conferred with several such employers and arranged for conferences later when we get the plants organized. The purpose of this is to direct all officers and all representatives to contact employers in your locality as a preliminary to organizing the shops and factories.

With best wishes, I am fraternally yours,
A. O. Wharton,
INTERNATIONAL PRESIDENT.

Mr. Wharton has not been alone in his attempt to discredit the C. I. O. as a Communist organization. His chief, Mr. Green, has strolled along beside him, arm in arm with Dr. John Frey, secretary of the Metal Trades Department and prosecutor extraordinary of the C. I. O. Recurrently Dr. Frey feels called upon to inform the public that the C. I. O. policy was determined in the "headquarters of the Communist party in Moscow," that the C. I. O. is being used to build up that party, and that the officials of the C. I. O. are in many cases radical plotters against American institutions.

In the words of the secretary of the C. I. O., Mr. Charles Howard, "those whom the gods would destroy they first make mad—*and make them see red.*"

7.

Employers have duly appreciated these handy methods of sabotaging the C. I. O., but one other technique dwarfs them all, in preference and importance: the Citizens' Committee. Far from new in American history, it was never used more baldly than during the early years of the present century, when an embryonic type of Fascism swept through the western mining towns and left liberties prostrate in its wake.

But within the last year the Citizens' Committee has made a dramatic reappearance. Found wherever the steel and auto unions have carried on important strikes, the instrument has been utilized in substantially the same way and to the same ends.

Now the foremost contemporary authority on union-busting is Mr. James Rand of Remington Rand. It is not altogether surprising, then, to discover in this new wave of vigilante groups his own fine handiwork and to trace in their structure the outline of his famous recipe for strike-breaking—the Mohawk Valley Formula. No development in the field of industrial relations is more deserving of study, for none is fraught with greater consequences for the future of the labor movement, and the society in which the labor movement is struggling for its right to exist. Nowhere can the machinery of this formula be more clearly seen than in the company where it was hammered out of the fires of industrial stress.

Remington Rand has plants in Ilion, Syracuse, North

The Employer Fights Back 217

Tonawanda, and Tonawanda, New York, Middletown, Connecticut, and Norwood and Marietta, Ohio. All told these plants employ about 6,000-6,500 production and maintenance employees—of whom 5,306 were A. F. of L. members in 1936. In the fall of 1935 trouble came to Ilion, in the form of rumors that Remington Rand had acquired a plant at Elmira, New York, that units from existing plants would be transferred there, and especially that the plant at Ilion would be closed down as a result of the Elmira undertaking.

Further it was bruited about that the factory had been bought by Elmira citizens and given to Rand with the understanding that Elmira workers would be preferred in employment. The rumors were disturbing to employees, union officials, business men, city officials, owners of real estate, bankers and newspaper editors of all the towns, notably Ilion, which might lose thereby. All these groups turned to Rand for definite information on a matter affecting their very existence. They got little. The union received none, though it tried repeatedly to get in touch with Rand or some responsible subordinate—and though, as the Securities Exchange Commission reported subsequently, Remington Rand had filed notice two months previously of its purchase of the Elmira plant.

The union wanted also to discuss shifts in the wage and hour schedules. Mr. Rand was not in. Apparently he would never be in until they knocked loud enough on the door. In all seven plants they called for a strike.

The vote on the call showed 3,200 in favor of a walkout, to 568 opposed. But still the union gave Rand another chance to confer. And they requested the mediatory aid of the Federal Conciliation Service.

Instead Rand conducted a highly prejudicial strike poll of his own, the ballots containing the threat that if the employees voted to oppose him, the plant would

218   C. I. O. Industrial Unionism in Action

never open again. Rand never gave out the total returns, but manipulated percentages to make out a case for the company. The percentages had no relevance: almost all the unionists had boycotted the balloting.

And still the unions tried to get Rand to negotiate with them—both directly and through the State Labor Department. Rand adamantly refused: "I am getting sick and tired of these men dictating to me how, when and where they will work," he said to the State Mediator. As a last resort, the union's Joint Board wired Rand a quite remarkably rational and patient request that he lay aside anger and meet with them.

No reply. On the morning of May 26, the strike became effective, with all but a handful of employees remaining out of the seven plants. Production ceased.

Rand, however, was not unprepared. Days before he had planned not to bargain with the union and to transfer the affair to the plane of force, on which he would use a combination of weapons. He had associated with himself four individuals, experts in their trade. Pearl Bergoff was the first. His business for thirty years had been strike-breaking. Captain Robert J. Foster was the second. He was the head of an Industrial and Detective Bureau, and had been in the business for twenty-five years. A third member of the party was Raymond J. Burns, president of the William J. Burns Detective Agency. Finally there was added Captain Nathaniel S. Shaw, whose business was "Confidential Industrial Missions." For twenty-seven years he had been what he called a "Radical Investigator."

To these "experts" Rand added the invaluable device of a skillful publicity campaign, to mold public opinion as yet unacquainted with the issues involved or the forces at play, and the services of a canny attorney. With these men and instruments Rand operated

The Employer Fights Back 219

on all fronts at once. In Ilion he was particularly successful.

Ilion is a village of ten thousand persons, altogether supported by two plants, Remington Rand and Remington Arms. In addition the surrounding villages of the valley—Herkimer, Mohawk and Frankfort—depend in large part upon the payrolls of these two concerns. There are two banks in the town, both correspondents and possibly owned by the Marine Trust Company of Buffalo, an affiliate of the Marine Midland Corporation—on which sit four Remington Rand directors.

The business men of the town, concerned about the possible loss of the Rand Company to Elmira, tried for months to get in touch with Mr. Rand and find out the facts. Failure had dogged their steps as it had the union's.

Then suddenly on May 19, Rand invited a group of these business men under the leadership of a merchant, Barney Allen, to his New York office for a conference. Rand told them that he was uncertain whether he would remain in business in Ilion or not, that he was convinced that the town was against him, that quite clearly the newspaper had been antagonistic, that he had met with the union representatives many times only to have his remarks misrepresented to the Ilion public, and that Ilion had ceased to be a good manufacturing town since Mr. Bowen (the international vice-president of the Machinists Union) had come to town.

The business men protested that his opinion of the town's attitude toward the company was not correct. Thereupon Rand called from another room a group of employees from the Ilion plant, headed by one Reginald Boote. It was obviously prearranged that these groups should meet. Mr. Boote was at pains to assure Rand and the business men that he represented the majority of the Ilion workers, and that they were against the strike and were satisfied with the conditions obtaining there. He voiced open disapproval of the union, charged that it was led by "outside agitators," and that even the members were largely dissatisfied with the union tactics.

It is interesting that no one of the business men stopped to question Boote's assertion that his opinion represented the majority of the employees. They left the meeting with two impressions: namely, that the future of their town and their businesses depended upon what the employees did, and that if a strike occurred Rand would refuse to meet with the union and a drawn-out conflict would ensue.

On the twenty-sixth, eighteen hundred workers went on strike, and peaceful picketing was established. In spite of the absence of disorder, fifty guards appeared at once from the Foster Industrial and Detective Bureau. Armed with clubs, and wearing badges, they patrolled the plant. In a few days their number reached a hundred. Next day fifty more men arrived, donned Burns Detective Agency uniforms, and began prowling the streets around the plant, armed with clubs and guns.

Not unnaturally the reputation and presence of these men created high tension. The employees were incensed at the importation of police into a peaceful situation. The sheriff felt the same way. The mayor, urged by the company attorney to allow the Burns men to be deputized, refused on the grounds that non-residents might not be deputized. So the Burns men were withdrawn, the company lawyer uttering dour predictions in the light of what he considered inadequate police protection.

Then the company put up a large "For Sale" sign on the plant. The business community, viewing this as a physical embodiment of their worst apprehensions,

The Employer Fights Back

telephoned Rand, who insisted that more police protection be provided. A mass meeting from the valley towns was called. Boote was invited to tell the citizens that the employees were opposed to the strike. (Again no one stopped to question his authority.) A hint was dropped by the local Rand management that the removal of the plant was "out of their hands," and that "someone higher up would have to be contacted."

The hint worked. The Joint Valley Board, consisting of the officials of the valley towns, met again on June 1, under the shadow of the pressure symbolized in the "For Sale" sign. They called Rand, and asked for a week in which to work out a solution satisfactory to him.

Meanwhile Boote had become the head of what came to be known as the Ilion Typewriter Employees Protective Association. Demonstrably a creature of the company, as were all its duplicates in the other towns, this group worked closely with the business committee, Boote transmitting to Allen and his associates Rand's emphasis on getting the men back to work by providing adequate police protection.

Rand's first move had succeeded. He had forced the business men into alliance with the hired thugs and the subsidized workers to break the strike. The second step, securing police protection in such volume as to reopen the plant, was now undertaken. The governor was asked for state police, which he refused. The business committee then went to the sheriff, and demanded protection for Boote's loyal employees to go back to work. With him they formulated plans for the appointment of three hundred special deputies to be drawn from four villages in the region. The sheriff also promised to order tear gas and ammunition.

On June 8, the business men, now automatons in the hands of the company, ordered a showdown from the authorities. They agreed with Mr. Rand that his devoted employees wanted to go back to work and they demanded police protection for that right, which was to include clearing the streets of all persons and ordering union representatives out of Ilion. When the chief of police timidly called attention to the fact that people had the right to use the streets, the business men's committee called upon him and the mayor to resign if they felt they could not co-operate.

The mayor agreed to "co-operate" and permit more deputies to be sworn in. That same evening he explained tearfully to two union leaders that he was "being compelled to do things that he didn't want to do, because these particular interests had and could wield an influence which would ruin him." The mayor, being a large property-owner in Ilion, was afraid that the bankers on the Citizens' Committee would punish him and leave him "nothing but his coat, hat and pants." Similarly other merchants informed the union leaders that they feared retaliation unless they strung along with the committee.

At the same time, the Joint Valley Board showed where it stood when it issued a resolution sent to the Commissioner of Labor of the State. The resolution stated that the Board was convinced no agreement could be reached between Rand and the union, that the company was determined to "reduce its operation," and would be guided in its decision by the attitude of the communities toward the enforcement of law, that the Board, "as public officials, owe a duty to the industries in our community ... to suppress unlawful practices by the arrest and the prosecution of violators of law," and finally that "if the plants at Ilion are not to be lost to our community for the benefit of some other, prompt decision and action ... must be taken."

No mention here of the fact that law *was* being enforced; that no violence had occurred; *that the only rea-*

The Employer Fights Back   223

son settlement of the dispute was not possible was the refusal of Rand to confer with the union. No recommendation, however tentative, was extended to Rand to take the steps within his power to settle the strike: only an injunction to the strikers to give up their objectives and return to work in defeat.

At this point Rand's company union, The Employees Protective Association, actively re-entered the picture. Advertising in the Ilion *Sentinel* for applications of workers who wished to return to work, it stated that the company would resume operations if the men acted quickly.

No report was ever made as to the number of such applications turned in. The company, however, stated that it was satisfied and the opening was announced for June 10. The grounds were roped off. Police and deputies were present in great numbers, and strutted their authority. After a crowd that was attracted by some slight argument had retired behind the ropes, police dispersed it with tear gas, one bomb coming from a plant window.

The opening was a great success as a party; less so as an opening. About five hundred employees entered the plant, the "For Sale" sign was spectacularly removed, a flag went up, and Rand gave a speech of congratulation to the workers. But thirteen hundred of them were not there to hear him. They were still out.

The following day the plant was to be opened for work. That night final preparations were made. They began with the dissemination of a rumor, subsequently discovered to be false, that five hundred strikers were marching from Syracuse at that very moment. The Citizens' Committee at once asked for state police, and were again refused.

Obedient to pressure, the Board of Trustees of Ilion met and authorized the mayor to declare "a state of emergency in the Village... and that all roads and entrances be blocked and nobody allowed to enter the village unless they have lawful business in the village." The mayor obliged at midnight, and as the Labor Board puts it, "law and order broke loose and Ilion became an armed camp, separated from the outside world." Deputies erected barricades, patrolled all the streets with shotguns, and padlocked the union headquarters. Answering union protests the chief of police tried to convince them that martial law had been declared by the lieutenant governor of the state. This, of course, was utterly untrue.

An investigator from the State Department of Labor visited the town. Questioning the necessity for these militant steps, he was told by the Valley Board that Mr. Rand had threatened to move away from Ilion and that "it was absolutely necessary that the strikers were shown that they were in the wrong and have them return to work." The village became a military pen. Foremen of the plant visited homes of workers on June 11, with offers of five dollars in cash if they would return to work. The bid was later raised to ten dollars a head. Eight hundred five-dollar bills were distributed on one day.

The end of all this was inevitable. The union ranks were broken. Afraid of permanently losing their jobs, men began to seep back into the plant in large numbers. A celebration on July 13 heard speeches by representatives of the company and of the Citizens' Committee. Pictures were taken of this happy reunion.

The strike was over. It meant death for the union, triumph for Rand, and a profound defeat for civil rights. Practically identical plans in the other towns brought identical results. Rand's victory was comprehensive, the collapse of the union complete.

Proud of his achievement, Mr. Rand, with the artist's

The Employer Fights Back

impulse to share, gave to fellow-employers everywhere his invention, the so-called Mohawk Valley Formula. Equally proud of it, the National Association of Manufacturers reprinted it in narrative form in a bulletin headed a "real contribution to civic dignity." Summarized as the Labor Board has done, the Formula reads about as follows:

First: When a strike is threatened, discredit the union leaders in the eyes of their followers and the townspeople by calling them "agitators." Conduct a plant-supervised election to discover the union's strength, and correctly or falsely represent the strike as the movement of a minority group. Employ the press, advertisements, and missionaries to the homes of workers and other citizens to state the issues of the strike so as to make it seem that the union demands are arbitrary. Conceal behind a cloud of confusion that the employer is refusing to bargain collectively. At the same time, bring all economic pressure possible upon the community by threats to move the plant. Particularly exert such pressure upon real-estate owners, merchants, bankers and those most sensitive to such intimidation because of its effect on the value of their investments in the community. Induce the formation of a *Citizens' Committee.*

Second: After the strike is called, emphasize the slogan, *"Law and Order."* Maneuver a massing of police against an imaginary violence. This will induce general forgetfulness that workers and strikers have civil rights too which the authorities are supposed to protect.

Third: Have the Citizens' Committee call a "mass meeting" of citizens to consolidate sentiment against the strike. This will give the committee an apparent popular strength with which to force public officials to approve and collaborate with vigilante activities in favor of the company.

Fourth: Encourage the formation of large armed forces, with local police, state police if possible, and special deputies—preferably from other towns so that they will not be affected by personal ties with the strikers. Teach these men about the law of inciting to riot, unlawful assembly, disorderly conduct. Avoid mention of civil rights of the workers, that they may use their new power to the limit without the confusion of impartiality. This force should effectively intimidate the strikers, as well as cultivate a useful psychological atmosphere in the town.

Fifth: Strengthen all these steps, and focus them in a "back-to-work" movement. For this purpose arrange the setting-up of a dummy association, ostensibly made up of "loyal employees." Use this association through advertisements under its own name, and visits to workers' homes. This movement will greatly assist the employer by informing him day after day of the strength of the union, information which of course he will not share with the public or workers. Censorship will always work toward weakening the strikers' morale. Further, the movement will reinforce the idea among citizens that the strike *is* a minority affair, and that the city is justified in spending money on whatever police force is required to protect the "majority" of the workers who by inference want to go back to work. Finally, the movement will aid the employer later in operating the plant with strike-breakers if necessary, and continuing his refusal to have anything to do with the union.

Sixth: When a number of back-to-work applications are received (from whatever sources), set a date for the reopening of the plant, by having the association request it. Make the occasion one for an impressive display of force and company power. Thus the company will find out if a sufficient number of employees wish to return. In any event the demonstration will weaken others into deciding to come back to work. If the numbers returning are relatively few, clever pictures and newsreels will persuade the public that the opening was a success.

Seventh: Continue the show of police force further to demoralize the strikers. If necessary, by bringing pressure on the Citizens' Committee and the public officials, turn the community into an armed camp, insulated from the outside world, that nothing may interfere with the successful prosecution of the Formula. Eventually the union will realize the futility of its holding out.

Eighth: Continue the publicity campaign to a close on the theme that the plant is again in full operation, that the strike was a minority outrage. Thus get the stamp of moral approval from a public which wishes to believe that it has done the right thing. The strike is now broken, the union gutted, the employer free to run his business as he will.

8.

The importance of the incidents narrated above lies in the wider application of the Mohawk Valley Formula to the labor movement in other communities. The automobile towns experienced its use. The Steel towns, where Republic and Bethlehem refused to deal with the Steel Workers Organization Committee and thus precipitated a strike, saw the Formula filled out to the last dram.

From local eruptions the vigilante reaction inevitably coagulated into a national organization. It was natural, too, that its capital should be Johnstown, Pennsylvania, where the Citizens' Committee of merchants and bankers had just whipped the Steel strike with a frenetic

228 C. I. O. Industrial Unionism in Action

back-to-work movement and were still calling themselves defenders of America.

On July 15, representatives from a dozen states answered Johnstown's call for a conference, cheered and whistled when some speaker yelled "Thank God for Tom Girdler," and elected a National Committee. Key men on it were three Johnstown patriots from the town's own Citizens' Committee—the Rev. John M. Stanton, chairman; Lawrence W. Campbell, secretary; and George C. Rutledge, treasurer.

With the subsiding of the strike against Little Steel, the vigilantes have been somewhat at loose ends. But the skeleton organization is now there, and on a national scale. It will need only another aggressive push by the C. I. O. in these regions to bring the patriots tumbling from their offices and stores, weapons in hand. The C. I. O. means business. So do they.

VIII. THE ECONOMICS OF THE C. I. O.

1.

WILL unionism decrease the national income?

That is the question in which are contained all other questions making up the economic criticism of the new labor movement. That is the question nestling in the minds of many a business man and many a banker. For the C. I. O. has made the question immediately pertinent. The C. I. O. aims to be a national movement, aims at enlisting twenty-five million workers. If it corrals only ten million in the next few years, which is more likely, it will yet be a national force exerting a tremendous pressure, for good or ill, upon the levers of the national economy.

It is not, of course, solely an economic issue, since no economic factor operates independently of society or without interrelating causation. If the C. I. O. has disastrous consequences upon the functioning of the economic machine, political repercussions will follow inevitably as the movement's enemies attempt to hobble the C. I. O. and as the C. I. O. attempts to kick back. But it is perhaps more convenient to isolate the economic problems and consider them before we explore their wider political resultants.

What we are concerned with is the national income—our annual production of food, clothes, houses, cars, pianos, roads, beds, concerts, factories. Our national income is what we live on today, and save from for to-

230   C. I. O. Industrial Unionism in Action

morrow, and that income has not been over-large up to now. Never has it amounted annually to more than twenty-five hundred dollars a family. Only four years ago, it meant fifteen hundred dollars a family. And that was the national average. Consider the enormous disparities in the distribution of this income, and one can gather that many millions of families live at a bare subsistence level.

But the national income is just another name for the national production. Our question can be somewhat rephrased, then: will the C. I. O. inhibit production and raise its costs so that our collective income shrinks? Let's examine the criticism as it applies to two periods which the economists term the secular and the cyclical—which mean simply the long-run period of economic progression, and the inner shorter period of boom and depression.

First, the secular.

In this period certain labor practices operate which employers find restrictive to production. Some of these union rules are direct curbs on output—such as the bricklayers' maximum number of bricks that may be laid in one day, or the railroad trainmen's insistence on setting the daily run by miles and not hours. Then there is out-and-out opposition by unions to labor-saving devices. The long march of technology is dotted with unsuccessful attempts by labor's rear guard to hold up the advance. The cigar-makers fought the "mold," the Knights of St. Crispin the shoe machines, the Chicago stone-cutters resisted the planers, the Electric Railway employees the one-man cars, the painters the spray, the plumbers the anti-siphon trap, the miners the one-man drill, the silk-workers the four-loom hook-up.

From the employer's viewpoint, these practices all appear attempts to retard maximum productive efficiency, and into this category he also lumps a union's insistence upon seniority. The C. I. O. is particularly interested in this rule. Its principle is simple: protect service on the job by restraining the management's right to hire and fire; make discharges a matter of precisely defined rules; in lay-offs, let the last man hired be the first to go, and the last to go be the first returned to work, thus putting a preferment upon length of service.

The management's opposition generally runs along these lines: recognition of seniority as the first factor in promotion and retention makes the foreman a mere clerk: he is no longer free to discriminate between excellence and mere competence, and the result is reduced efficiency, higher costs, and smaller output.

2.

These are the most important types of restrictive union policy, of which seniority, at least, is a deliberate objective of the C. I. O. Their total effect on national production is quite impossible to estimate, but it may well be rather large. Why then have unions indulged in these apparently anti-social acts?

They have their reasons. Workers haunted by the fear of want not unnaturally try to make their jobs last as long as they can. Wherever one finds an industry with a highly irregular employment, such as the building trades, one finds as well that the unions have concocted a great many rules to prevent the several crafts from stealing each other's limited work, and to prolong the jobs of their members.

Related to this fear of unemployment is the fear of the speed-up. Processes change, new machinery and scientific management are introduced. Piece-rates and bonus systems are imposed. Against any such pressure to get him moving faster the worker balks: it is his only answer in a situation open to exploitation. For the labor contract has this curious characteristic, that labor is hired without any precise definition of just what is being bought. A man is hired by the day. But exactly what he shall do in that day, how quickly he shall work, how much he shall produce—these are questions left to a tussle between himself and his foreman. So clumsy an arrangement naturally provokes the worker to conceal what he could do if driven, and management to try and find out.

Even when the worker's task is set definitely in terms of piece-work, he is apt not to work as fast as he might, for fear that the employer will decide his wages are mounting too high and cut the rate. Managements competing with each other to reduce costs and thus prices will always be tempted to slash piece-rates; and the worker's natural defense is a studied slow-down.

Social or asocial, these union rules have their origin in real threats to the workers' welfare. In the circumstances, they are pragmatic, reasonable. The economist may demonstrate debonairly that these union policies do not actually increase *total* work and employment. It is still true that they do increase the amount of work won by the union men themselves.

Beneath all the specific and particular arguments which labor summons to its defense there lies one fundamental plea: that there are things more important than efficiency, that human costs must be reckoned above money costs. The final end of production is not cheap goods, but a life worth living. If cheapness can only be secured at the price of human values, then cheapness and not life must go. The owner of a granite quarry may try to keep expenses down by neglecting to provide masks to protect workers' lungs from rock-dust; that policy cannot be condoned no matter how much cheaper it may make the granite tombstones which will decorate the graves of the laborers whose lungs were infected.

So with the principle of seniority. The employer wants freedom to hire the best available man when times are good, and to fire the least efficient man when times are bad, thus keeping his costs at a minimum. But it's a policy which places the burden of unemployment on the weak, the least capable, and refuses to protect the older man whose very loyalty of service may have rendered him least prepared to change occupations. Human costs or money costs?

There is a further consideration. There are national costs as well as plant and firm costs. The auto industry is able to produce cheap cars because it weeds out men over forty by the bitter driving tempo of the belt-lines. The auto industry, in short, is wearing out a part of the nation's resources—labor—and sloughing it off when no longer useful, for the nation to support. This may be "economic" for the auto industry over the short run. It is disastrously uneconomic for the nation over the long run.

3.

We have scanned the negative side of labor's ledger. But what has it positively to contribute to industrial efficiency? As we indicated above, unionism can lower the *national* costs of production if it preserves the health and long-run usefulness of labor by preventing its premature, wasteful exploitation. The life-product of each worker will thus tend to increase, even though in some instances his day-to-day product will be smaller.

Unionism will serve, too, to puncture a kindly fiction perpetrated by economists and business men alike: that the incentives of competition and of the profit-motive assure the 100 per cent efficiency of employers. Strictly speaking, of course, the profit-motive is confined

234   C. I. O. Industrial Unionism in Action

to small concerns run by their owners, comprising an ever smaller fraction of the country's enterprise. Management is now delegated to hired executives who do not receive profits. They get salaries, and if those salaries are basically dependent upon their success in getting profits for the stockholders, so are the wages of the workers. In any event, the profit-motive, if present, exerts only a tenuous and uncertain influence.

At that, American management is efficient. But is it as efficient as it might be if it were more effectively prodded from below? The experience of industry during the early twenties is instructive. From 1920-23 non-agricultural prices fell 29 per cent—a potentially catastrophic decline unaccompanied by comparable wage reductions. One would have expected that, with employers already working at their famous 100 per cent competitive efficiency, there would have been no room for improvement, and business would have been badly pinched between high wage rates and fallen prices. What actually happened was that management found it could increase industrial efficiency by 23 per cent. That was not all. Prices continued their downward drift, while wages actually rose (though not sufficiently to avert the subsequent depression). Again management was pushed into finding better ways of running its plants—and shoved labor productivity up 25 per cent.

Unionism has within it inherent possibilities of vastly increasing the national income, but in ways so intangible and impossible to calculate that the practical, hard-headed business men will stoutly deny their existence. Labor's resentment, apathy, disinterest in production means the slow-down. And the slow-down in turn means a drop in productivity as huge as it is inestimable. It will be unionism's contribution to the economy to reduce the slow-down by enforcing wages and conditions of work that will moderate the sullenness and fear that now poison the relationships of employers and employees. But it is a contribution which unionism can make only if accepted, encouraged, and understood. It takes two to co-operate.

4.

There is another way in which, during the secular run of events, unionism will affect the national economy, and that is through its influence on savings.

What are these savings? An individual may invest part of his annual income by "saving" it, which doesn't mean hoarding but rather lending it to farmers, buying stock in shoe factories, automobile concerns, rubber plantations. The lender gets paid for the use of these savings because—typically—the borrowers use them to increase their production, fertilizing land, building barns, making machinery, erecting factories, buying plantation equipment. All these paraphernalia are tools with which the workers in the shops and fields can do their work faster and better. Tools which the economist calls capital. If we added up all the savings of all the individuals in the country, we would have the national savings. Embodied in wealth they are the national capital.

A nation growing in capital—the United States, shall we say—is a nation growing in the ability to produce wealth. A nation stripped of capital—such as Germany after the War or China today—is a nation impoverished. Therefore nothing could be more relevant than the question: will a strong C. I. O. slow down the formation of capital by reducing the national savings?

One might say yes on the face of it. For unionism's aim is to push up the wages of its own class inevitably at the expense of owners, high-salaried executives, and company surpluses. And savings are made principally from these large incomes, the twenty-dollar-a-week laborer hardly being in a position to invest in General Motors stock. If savings then are reduced by taking it from this investing class and distributing it among the non-savers, capital will be accumulated less rapidly, the national income will grow more slowly, and wages in the future will be less than they might otherwise have been.

On the face of it. But against this tendency we must set the long-run increase in the productivity of labor freed from the drastic exploitation of shortsighted management. We must set also unionism's goad to management to discover more improvements, better internal organization. And insofar as the C. I. O. makes unionization a national fact, it will cut down the wastes of duplication indulged in by firms (as in the textile industry) which sprout up in non-union areas and demoralize the market. Successful unionization too would rid the nation of the necessity of spending millions annually on industrial spies, munitions, company guards, strike-breakers, and the terrific strike losses under which our economy repeatedly reels.

All these factors would tend to lower costs in the end, increase the profit margin, and thus give larger incomes back to the saving-class responsible for maintaining the national capital.

5.

So much for the secular period. We have seen that in it unionism's effect upon our economy's productivity and hence upon our national income may be on balance positive and beneficial. But what of the cyclical period? Will the C. I. O. increase the instability of capitalism as it is exhibited in these recurrent booms and slumps?

Unionism, of course, cannot be held responsible for that basic instability itself, for cycles are as old as capi-

The Economics of the C. I. O.

talism and antedate the union movement. But would strong pressure by the C. I. O. to boost wages in prosperity and maintain them in depression intensify the extreme oscillations of those cycles?

Take first the depression phase. The academic economists, with only a scattering of heretics heckling them, have somberly agreed that any attempt by unions to maintain wages during a slump will increase unemployment and postpone recovery. Let us consult briefly one of the ablest presentations of the case—that of Professor Sumner Slichter of Harvard University.

In depression, says Professor Slichter, the relationship between the prices at which goods sell and the costs of their production is unfavorable to profits. Prices are too low, costs too high; for during the collapse the former have fallen further than the latter. Driven by mounting losses, business men try to reduce expenses by diminishing the scale of their operations. They dismiss men, close plants, decrease purchases, postpone improvements. And they will persist in this retrenchment until selling prices rise or costs fall sufficiently to restore the necessary margin of profits. This is the very essence of the Profit System.

What steps should be taken to restore that margin? Professor Slichter says: cut wage rates, because wages are a large element in the cost of making goods. Then with lowered costs, more goods will be made, more sold, more people employed, and the dust of depression may be shaken from our feet. The happy employer, he believes, once he has been able to get his costs below his prices, will rehire some of his men, buy more materials —which will in turn lead other business men to rehire and buy. He will spend money on plant improvements, and if costs and prices in other industries have fallen, he may even buy new machines, new gadgets, and make other purchases heretofore postponed because of the general gloom and excessive cost. All of the money spent by this entrepreneur will go to feed the demand for the products of other business men, and they will spend likewise. Thus the circle of employment, production, and recovery will widen until the halcyon days are here again.

What started the ball rolling? asks Slichter, and answers—wage cuts.

Or put it in more general terms. Depression is a time of underproduction. All the resources of men and matter are used at less than capacity. Some erroneous people, says Professor Slichter, will call this condition underconsumption: that is, inadequate consumers' purchasing power: the public cannot buy all the goods that can be produced, at a price profitable to the producers. This is true enough, according to Professor Slichter, but it's putting the cart well in front of the horse. Of course consumption is low, since consumers' incomes are low. But consumers' incomes are low because many consumers are unemployed.

They are unemployed because business men are not producing enough. This is the case, because it is not profitable for them to produce at the prevailing prices, and with the prevailing costs. Therefore, this underconsumption is caused by underproduction. To increase consumers' purchasing power we must first increase production itself.

Wage cuts, then, are imperative. They are the best way to cut production costs because they are, presumably, the larger element in general costs, and because lower wage rates may lead manufacturers to substitute less expensive labor for machines, thus further aiding employment and swelling consumers' purchasing power.

6.

There are a few practical deterrents to adopting this policy of wage cuts that may well be considered before we peer into its theoretical shortcomings. One is that in many great industries wages are *not* the largest element in costs. They are 60 per cent of the total costs in mining but less than 5 per cent in meat-packing. They are nearly 50 per cent in the manufacture of office equipment, but under 10 per cent in the making of foods. The cost of the ship on which we travel is 40 per cent wages, but that of the cigarette we smoke is only 3 per cent. Reduce wage rates 10 per cent on gray-iron steel, and total cost of its production is diminished five cents on the dollar. Cut wage rates on tobacco by 100 per cent and only eight-tenths of a cent is saved on a fifteen-cent pack. Wage reductions save some employers a great deal, others little at all.

Another objection to cutting wages is that the people whose wages are being cut usually don't like it. In fact they are frequently impertinent enough to ask why executive salaries so often stay the same, why interest on old debts is maintained, why light, power, and heat charges remain so high. They are not even perceptibly moved by the argument that the courts uphold the strict payment of such fixed costs, and they suggest that the judges are simply legalizing a "right" that is set more by power than by any conceivable standard of justice. From 1929 to the pit of the depression, total income fell 40 per cent, wages fell 60 per cent, and interest fell by but 3.2 per cent. Why should not all classes suffer alike? they ask, and there is no very good answer.

But let's turn to the central and not the peripheral weaknesses of the economists' doctrine. Professor Slichter's theory suffers from the implication that there is only a one-way connection between business spending (the buying of materials, hiring of men, purchase of new equipment) and consumers' spending (the purchase of clothes to wear, food to eat, cars to drive in, pianos to play). Business spending, he suggests, feeds consumers' spending, but not the reverse.* The only way to stimulate the economic machinery is to prime the business man's pump.

Actually, the relationship is not so simple. These types of spending interact upon each other and their interactions are different in various phases of the cycle. The harder-headed economists have been almost unanimous in forgetting this, and almost the only men who have remembered are the good-natured cranks whose reasoning has usually been so naïve and ill-jointed that they've been laughed out of the academic courts.

The critical point at issue lies here: if the economists' recommendations are followed and wage rates are cut, employers will have more money than before—by the amount of their saving on reduced payrolls. They must at once spend this on more employment, more purchases of materials, new improvements. For if they hold any of the money, if they put it in idle bank accounts, pay off old debts with it, or hide it in their socks, the result is disastrous. The total demand for goods will be reduced by the amount of that lost payroll. Fewer goods will need to be produced to meet that lessened demand, unemployment will increase, and the depression will deepen.

Here we have underproduction, caused by underconsumption.

---

* This does some injustice to Professor Slichter's argument, which is very carefully qualified. However, the qualifications are given little weight when his theory materializes into advice on public policy. I therefore ignore some of the niceties.

The Economics of the C. I. O.

Professor Slichter sees this possibility. Many economists who have arrived at his conclusions do not. But even he sees it as a possibility. He doubts that it will really occur. Wishfully, he concludes that the business man will do the necessary thing, will spend his gains as rapidly as he makes them.

Has Professor Slichter read aright the psychology of the business man? Do wage cuts have this cheerful effect upon confidence? Remember that this business man is in depression. He is burdened by pessimism concerning his chances of making money in the months ahead. The future dictates to him, and the future is dark with the shadows cast by the unused machines, factories, ships, railroads, materials that stand around him. He reads this as evidence of surplus, of excess (excessive from his own point of view, not the nation's). These "excessive" instruments and goods are yielding him losses or at the most slim profits. To add to the excess would drive the values of those capital goods still lower.

In short, the business man sees all about him the evidence of low demand, of falling prices—among them his own. His fear is that demand and prices will fall yet further. Now how will he react at this point to a wave of wage-cutting? He will expect prices to fall some more as costs are lowered. He will expect, too, that his own demand will be cut as the national payroll is sliced. To him that will mean simply another circle of the downward spiral, an accentuation of the depression. He will be discouraged. Whatever he saves from his own wage-cutting, he will not spend. He will retrench, cling more tightly to that which he has.

If wage-cutting, then, will only drive the employing class to murkier gloom and deflationary action, what other means have we to recovery? In depression, the demand for goods needs to be encouraged along two fronts at the same time: maintain the demand for con-

242 C. I. O. Industrial Unionism in Action

sumers' goods by maintaining and supplementing payrolls; and maintain the demand for capital goods by lowering the cost of borrowed money with which to buy them—i.e., the rate of interest.

The unions can help take care of the first step if they are allowed to do so. They will put a floor under wages, give employers the assurance that at least one item in their business calculations will be a certainty, and bring them to feel that the depression has touched bottom.

A union policy of wage-maintenance, too, will compel a search to control the cycle along more important lines: the improvement of our violently unstable and rickety banking system; a closer check and possibly governmental control of the investment market; an overhauling of our accounting methods, which now make profits appear larger than they are in prosperity, and losses seem worse than they are in depression. We have not undertaken seriously to effect these changes because we have had always at our side the patent medicine of wage-reductions, and doctors to advise strong and immediate doses to cure all that ails us. Actually, of course, the case history of cycles points to the belief that the patient has cured himself despite these medicines. Nobody knows with any exactitude what has pulled us out of one depression after another; it may be the sudden appearance of a new industry, a new market, a gold influx, or a war. It is impossible, indeed, to point to any instance of wage-deflation as the cause of a recovery, and wage-maintenance has never been tried as a deliberate policy on a large scale. There are innumerable evidences of the disastrous results of cutting pay-checks.

Some qualifications: (1) Only strong unionism can enforce wage-maintenance: the government would never do it without pressure from a powerful labor movement. And strong unionism depends now almost wholly on the success or failure of the C. I. O., and on the degree of encouragement that it receives from the industrialists. (2) Monetary authorities must be induced or forced to co-operate. Wage deflation cannot be accompanied by monetary deflation, or business confidence will be hopelessly injured. During the early days of a depression, the banks must follow a policy of controlled price-raising.

7.

We turn now to the second part of our question: the effect of unionism's wage-boosting upon recovery, once achieved.

All economists give at least a qualified approval to this pushing up of wage rates. In the recovery period there is a pronounced tendency for the costs of production to rise more slowly than prices. In consequence, profits of employers rise relative to wages. From these increased profits come greater savings. The profitableness of current business makes employers optimistic about the future and stimulates the investment of these augmented savings in new and improved plants, extensions of old ones, and the bewildering variety of additions to capital so familiar in the upward phase of the cycle. The profit-seeking employers are assisted by the profit-seeking banks. Expanded credit goes to expanding enterprise.

Naturally there is latent danger in this. Inevitably, through the glasses of a prosperous present, the future looks more favorable than it turns out to be. For costs in the end *do* rise. They are bid up by the enthusiasts themselves. As factories, machines, shops, office buildings, apartments are multiplied, their value declines because of their very increase. An investment that first excited confidence by a promised yield of 10 per cent is subsequently discovered to yield a modest 4 per cent. With costs mounting—costs of labor, materials, and money—investments initiated at one level of costs must be completed at another and higher level. On this account the yield will be less than expected. The future persistently betrays the hopes of a confident, bullish present.

This disillusion saps business optimism in the later stages of the cycle. To make the turn even more emphatic, the highly organized and mercurial stock market sheltering the invested savings of the country reflects with absurd intensity the revised reading of future values. Market prices of shares fall like rocks. A stock-minded public, told crudely and brutally in this way that its wealth is less than it had thought, concludes that it has actually lost cash.

That the losses are as yet but paper losses doesn't matter. Every stock-owner will pull in his belt, spend less of his income, keep more cash or savings idle in the bank. So the demand for consumers' goods falls. Merchants and manufacturers find themselves with unsalable stocks of shoes, clothes, phonographs, toothbrushes. Further losses occur in the value of the capital with which these goods have been made. The future begins to look worse and worse to enterprisers, who will shove their savings deeper into their strong boxes. The spiral of deflation will be well on its way down again.

What can unionism do to check these mad fluctuations? This. The boom is riddled with misplaced expectations, inaccurate readings of the future, cheerful decisions built on the mirage of the green months ahead. Recovery's first crop of profits causes the economy to break out in a rash of optimism; it is champagne on an empty stomach. Unionism will put the economy on a saner diet. The rise of wages will retard the increase of profits, and the future will seem a little less attrac-

The Economics of the C. I. O.

tive to additional investments. The larger incomes from which savings are made will be smaller, thus also helping to reduce investment to a more moderate and sensible pace. The whole period of recovery will proceed more cautiously, more circumspectly—and will last a good deal longer.

Of course, if employers use wage increases as an excuse for more than proportional price increases—as Carnegie-Illinois did when it signed its C. I. O. contract—then a spiral of wage-price increases will be induced which will restrict production, diminish the absorption of the unemployed, maintain a dangerous distribution of income, a tardy rise in the standard of living, necessitate continued government relief for the poor, and hasten the reappearance of depression.

This is not a problem of unionism but of monopoly control of prices. Unionism cannot be held responsible for it. Nor can unions do anything directly about it. That must be the task of the government, undertaken with the determined support of groups interested in the social welfare. Labor unions will be among them.

8.

Now to turn back for a quick glance at some pertinent comments of Professor Slichter's concerning growth, change, and discovery in our economy. He observes that a substantial part of our industry depends upon discovery by employers of new ways of making money, for which new machinery must be built, new buildings added, more extensive processing of materials secured, and the like. He believes further that the rate of change and discovery of new methods is irregular: that it betrays ebb and flow. Industry dependent on this stimulus is correspondingly unstable. When discovery is rife, all business is stimulated. When discovery is slack, all business is depressed.

To offset the decline of the rate of discovery, he feels, costs must be adjusted downward, thus enticing business men to exploit the less profitable but more modest improvements that are available. And what costs does Professor Slichter want to "adjust downward"? Wages. Here again we have the attack upon the rationale of unionism.

But is the rate of discovery as irregular as he thinks? There is good reason to believe it is continuous. Industrial research, so generously subsidized by American business, has moved far toward regularizing invention and change in industrial process.

Actually, what is needed is not changes in wage rates to offset changes in the rate of discovery, but an attempt to smooth the tempo at which discoveries are put into effect. Unionism will help by shaving off exuberant profits and retarding rash investments in new gadgets. The banks and the government will help by raising somewhat the interest rates at which men can borrow to exploit new ideas, preventing premature expansion.

Unionism will compel other and necessary investments. The United States has pretty well completed its physical self-discovery. Its frontiers are gone, its resources brought into prospective if not actual use. Its future growth will be slower than in the past. Immigration laws and birth rates are seeing to that. Within a generation the population may have reached its maximum.

But much of the country's industry is still geared to a high rate of growth, as well as change. A serious disparity. For more of the country's resources must now go into the production of goods for consumers' use, and less into capital equipment, demand for which depends upon growth and change.

And this readjustment is going to be resisted, strenuously. One factor, however, will speed it. A strong unionism led by the C. I. O. will accomplish a shift in income from savers to consumers, from owners to workers, from investors to spenders. The demand for capital goods will shade off, the demand for consumers' goods will increase; and the allocation of capital will follow those shifts in demand. More, if investors expect present wage increases to be followed by others, they will foresee a fall in the future rate of profit, and tend to put their money in short-term investments, rather than long-term capital. Which will help modify the economic structure of the nation in the direction required by a diminishing rate of growth and change.

Another point. If union wage increases cause American prices to become high, relative to prices in other countries, this may induce Americans to invest more of their savings abroad and less here. Insofar as domestic investment during recovery tends to be too rapid, this might have a stabilizing effect. The rise in the interest rate might work to the same end.

9.

We have run through quite a number of tangled considerations. Enough at any rate to show that those who oppose the C. I. O. because of its threat to economic stability by boosting wages must be asked to reconsider their case. The burden of proof rests squarely upon them. For unionism is here to stay and will not be exorcised by any such arguments as have yet been waved at it. If the critics hope to make any impression, they will have to do a more convincing job of proving that wage cuts in depression do not scuttle the ship, and that wage-maintenance might not help bring both crew and officers back safe to port.

IX. THE POLITICS OF THE C. I. O.

1.

AMERICANS fear and distrust John Lewis, or applaud and support him, chiefly on political grounds. The man is an "agitator," a "would-be dictator," a "Communist"; or contrariwise, he leads a movement destined to enhance and preserve our democracy.

Future events may belie all these contentions, for the C. I. O. is young and John Lewis a mysterious figure. The political consequences of the C. I. O. lie with the future rather than with the present. However, popular instinct makes no mistake in examining political potentialities as the basic test of the C. I. O.'s desirability. If its organization drive attains reasonable success, political changes of some kind will follow.

Men united by similar economic experiences and interests inevitably seek to give them political expression. Individuals gain their livings within a framework of law and government. Its influence upon food, clothing, and shelter problems grows as the economy becomes more and more a matter of common, collective effort. In consequence, political movements grow out of important currents in economic affairs.

The rise of the C. I. O. is an economic event of the first magnitude. What changes will it effect in American political life? Will it cause the collapse of the two-party system? Are the Democrats to be split on the rock that is Lewis? What does he want that the New Deal cannot

The Politics of the C. I. O.

give him? Will he lead a labor or farmer-labor party? May either Fascism or Communism replace American democracy?

2.

The relations between Franklin Roosevelt and John Lewis symbolize the C. I. O.'s present status in American politics. To the degree that they pull together, mutual necessity is responsible.

The press has dwelt upon superficial and transient aspects of their friendship, in part to sell papers, in part to discredit both men. Does the President speak and act in support of the labor leader? Then he is partisan and headed leftward. Do the two of them "rebuke" each other publicly? The C. I. O. is slipping from public favor.

The facts of their co-operation lie much deeper than this gossip would lead us to appreciate. Essentially the New Deal and the C. I. O. are politico-economic twins, with a common heritage but different temperaments. The one had to come before the other could win its right to exist; both issued from the womb of an unhappy, unbalanced capitalistic democracy.

Unionism needed the New Deal because powerful forces had for decades postponed its full emergence. Free land and a labor shortage until the turn of the century kept alive certain outmoded traditions: "equality of opportunity"; the identity of individual and social welfare; reliance on individual abilities to solve the maldistribution of income, dominant among causes of the business cycle. The A. F. of L. built a fairly successful profiteering brotherhood for skilled workers only by refusing to organize the unskilled millions pouring into the labor market from Europe and subsequently from American farms. Finally, industrial ownership and control—rabidly anti-union—wrote and enforced the law through the medium of the Grand Old Party.

After the World War a "New Era" marked the triumphant climax of twentieth-century capitalism. But behind the gaudy backdrops of this spectacle a great shifting and changing was going on, constituting a veritable revolution. Technological advance, a declining birth rate, concentration of industrial and financial control, and the rise of the wage-earning middle class—these and other developments were setting the stage for a truly new era. Not until the collapse of the boom did the country begin to recognize it, or sense the hopeless incapacity of our economic and political leadership to keep step.

By contrast, Roosevelt's impressionistic sketch of a "New Deal" for the forgotten man seemed the epitome of statesmanship. However, neither the Democratic candidate nor platform in 1932 gave more than the routine vague attention to collective bargaining and organized labor. John Lewis supported the Republican ticket.

3.

How then did the New Deal come to champion the cause of unionism more forcefully than any previous administration? The answer lies in the nature of Mr. Roosevelt's major objectives for American society: a greater degree of economic and political democracy, mitigation of the business cycle, and security for the individual. Direct legislation alone could not realize these aims. Although the President did not understand it during his first term, and seems not to grasp it yet in a practical way, a mature and equalitarian relationship between capital and labor forms the keystone of the arch he seeks to build. In other words, the New Deal's ultimate program cannot advance without large,

The Politics of the C. I. O.

powerful labor unions. In themselves unions are not the end; they are the most essential, most democratic means toward the end.

Unionism revived under the New Deal, but the policies which stimulated its recovery were only half-deliberate. The administration inserted Section 7A into the N. R. A. to obtain labor support for the price-fixing machinery which industrialists wanted. But the workers didn't worry about Roosevelt's motives. They accepted 7A as a guarantee of collective bargaining and signed their union cards. This organization of workers, chiefly in industrial and quasi-industrial unions, has proved an integral and perhaps the most important single result of the New Deal. First it showed the administration that unions could do the best job of increasing consumer spending—thereby aiding general economic recovery—through boosting wages. This in turn led to a realization that labor unions can be very useful to a program designed to help laboring men, and that they ought to be encouraged. As 1936 election-time drew near the President saw clearly that organized labor was fundamental to his plans in more than a purely economic way.

Evidence of this new philosophy came after the Supreme Court killed the Blue Eagle. In its National Labor Relations Act the New Deal stated in precise language that collective bargaining through unions was desirable for the country. Presumably there would be no pretense at "neutrality" as between anti-union employers and pro-union workers. That concept belonged to the past, to the adolescent pre-depression days of Republican administrations. On the statute books as well as in the logic of his entire program, Roosevelt stood committed to *encouragement* of unions and a labor movement as "the policy of the United States."

Despite the weakness of 7A's administration, the implications of its doctrine were not lost upon labor. Workers as well as union leaders sensed the potentialities of White House support. By November, 1935, the impetus toward a genuine labor movement burst the bonds of A. F. of L. policy and called forth the C. I. O. to play a part in the New Deal and in the whole range of American economic and political life which the Federation could never hope to encompass.

4.

Ever since its inception the A. F. of L. had chosen to remain a "pure" economic enterprise, a special interest whose sole political activity had taken the form of lobbying, and helping in a random way to elect or defeat particular congressmen and local candidates. Its political activities resembled those of public utilities, employers' associations, and other vested interests in the economy—except that they were less bold, less unscrupulous, and less successful.

In defense of its policy the Federation pointed to the history of the failure of unions, like the Knights of Labor, which had flirted with third parties; and it emphasized that abstention from independent tickets proved the Federation's loyalty to capitalism and democracy.

In any event the A. F. of L. was essentially a business, not a social, organization. Gompers didn't want to build a labor movement; he wanted to win certain immediate gains in wages and hours for a limited and unimaginative group of workers—by standing on the backs of all the others. Active participation in politics would have endangered such a monopoly, for a labor party must include workers as a class, on equal footing with each other.

Gompers' doctrine was well adapted to the shaky beginnings of unionism, when the Federation needed all its strength merely to survive. But this could not long suffice in the face of a growing compulsion for working people to take a hand in solving the problems of capitalism under democracy. So far as labor politics are concerned, the change from A. F. of L. to C. I. O. policy has meant a shifting from special self-interest to concern for the entire social and economic structure. Open political activity on the basis of a national platform requires a program for the country as a whole. Such an undertaking on the part of organized labor signifies that it has arrived at maturity, that it is willing and eager to take part in the formulation of basic policy and administration for all classes, for the nation itself.

No longer, as under the Federation, will unionism make demands upon the body politic as a child makes demands upon its parents. Grown up, labor is willing to assume the social responsibilities which go with adulthood. It is prepared to stand or fall on its own independent conception of American society. Under the C. I. O., labor is willing to enter the political arena and submit its ideas to the entire democracy. It is marshaling its forces against the opposition of our business and political tradition, which will resist to the last labor's effort to take up its mature tasks, just as parents resist the breaking away of children to new values and ideals.

The C. I. O. has indeed adopted an outlook fundamentally uncongenial to both old parties. Consequently it will proceed under their wings only until it achieves its full powers and builds its resources to the point at which it can act independently without fear of calamitous reprisals.

At present the C. I. O. is traveling chiefly with the New Deal, for reasons of necessity and benefit to both. But its needs, ambitions, and outlook exceed anything the New Deal, as such, is capable of supporting. For

254   C. I. O. Industrial Unionism in Action

the New Deal is struggling for life in its own party under the blows of traditionally-minded Democrats who no longer feel compelled to play along with Mr. Roosevelt's program. In this very struggle the New Deal is forced to acknowledge that both parties, notwithstanding progressive elements in each, remain organs of our economy's capital interests. Between them they have ruled this country for industry ever since the Civil War, and there is no chance that either party as such will give the C. I. O. the freedom or sympathy that it will demand, and indeed is already demanding.

Another factor in the C. I. O.'s inevitable refusal to dally along under old banners lies in the abject failure of recent semi-independent action. Labor together with rural and progressive groups has tried repeatedly to mix its wine with old party beverages. In 1908 these elements supported Bryan's Democrats to check the use of the labor injunction and in general to restrict the depredations of Big Business. In 1912 Teddy Roosevelt led the same forces to defeat on progressive issues; and eight years later both Farmer-Laborites and Democrats tasted the bitter dust of a Republican landslide. "Fighting Bob" La Follette's frantically organized campaign in 1924 only served to underscore the growing disillusionment of progressives; for back of that failure lay the predicament responsible for the sterility of all these attempts. The existing parties possessed the political terrain; they had their machines, built up through the years. No effort of a compromising or temporary character could budge the strength of these entrenchments.

Nor has success rewarded attempts to capture the old party set-up at home base, through the primaries. The late Non-Partisan League in the Northwest made the most business-like attack of this kind, enrolling thousands of farmers on a dues-paying basis, supporting a press, nominating full tickets of candidates, and for a

The Politics of the C. I. O.

number of years during the twenties controlling North Dakota and strongly influencing near-by states. But compromise and slim triumphs killed the League, and no such thoroughgoing tactics have since been tried except in Wisconsin. True, the Non-Partisan League's endeavor has borne fruit in Minnesota; but the harvest has been reaped there only by a completely independent machine built up under a Farmer-Labor flag.

Inevitably unionists and liberals, if they make any sort of deal with either party, must give up their identity and make compromises with the old machine. Policies are watered down; popular faith grows dim; and basic purposes which alone can pull a new effort through to lasting strength gradually fade away.

The issue is nothing new. Towards the close of the last century British laborites faced the decision which the C. I. O. faces today. Under the eloquent leadership of Keir Hardie they set up as an independent party rather than remain a Liberal bloc. Saved from innocuousness, they began to exploit their own reserves of strength and initiative and to piece together the machine which brought them control of the government in post-war years.

Because of the determined opposition of its foes, the C. I. O. will have to build its "political home" almost overnight. For although the Democrats have for the time being taken labor to their bosom, events already indicate their repudiation of the intimacy. New York City foreshadows the drift. Here Mayor La Guardia's chief support in the present campaign comes from the American Labor Party, a state affiliate of the C. I. O.-controlled Labor's Non-Partisan League. La Guardia represents the New Deal, the C. I. O., the A. F. of L., and the advocates of "good government." He has split Tammany and the G. O. P. wide open. Conservatives of both houses have joined forces in support of anti-New Deal, anti-labor candidates.

In effect New York has already abandoned the old two-party system for a new one. Eventually such a liberal-conservative pattern will replace the Democratic-Republican duality throughout the country, and the C. I. O. will be chiefly responsible. The only issue in the New Deal which packs enough dynamite to blast Democrats and Republicans into each others' arms is the labor-capital issue—which means, concretely, the C. I. O.

5.

What are the C. I. O.'s own political objectives, and what planks must it offer if it is to win the support of voters outside its constituent unions?

First let us consider the immediate needs of the labor movement itself, for which Lewis is already working through Labor's Non-Partisan League as well as through the New Deal proper.

1. *Social security:* The present Social Security Act must be widened to include many classes now excepted, among which are four million five hundred thousand agricultural workers, three hundred thousand maritime workers, and some six million men and women in domestic and personal service. The Act now represents but a modest step towards a comprehensive elimination of insecurity in employment, old age, and illness; and many of its provisions are highly unsatisfactory if not actually contradictory to its aims. Supplementing such a program a new liberal-labor party will do a real service to the economy at large as well as to thousands of individuals during depression, by calling for a long-range schedule of public works including low-cost housing and a thoroughgoing public employment service.

2. *Wages and hours:* In many chaotic and low-scale

The Politics of the C. I. O. 257

industries such as textiles, water-transportation, and agriculture, only the federal government can effectuate immediate widespread and equitable adjustment of incomes and working days. A bill for this purpose—the Black-Connery wages and hours bill—came before the last session of Congress, and threw into high relief the conservative-progressive division in the old parties. It will almost certainly be presented in the forthcoming session and stands a good chance of passage.

3. *Wagner Act:* As this book goes to press the National Labor Relations Act and its Board are under fire from employers and their legislative representatives. An immediate task for labor in politics is a vigorous defense of the Act, lest it be mangled or destroyed, and strong support of the Board in its effective administration. Further, labor needs desperately to remedy yellow-dog and injunction practices. The Norris-La Guardia Act of 1932 renders void any yellow-dog contract—under which workers agree to quit or stay out of a union—in interstate commerce; but many states still permit the enforcement of such arrangements. The vindictive use of the anti-strike injunction in labor disputes poisons the process of collective bargaining everywhere.

4. *Courts:* To insure the validity of legislation on all these matters, as well as to restore the law-making faculty to Congress and the legislatures, organized labor will probably need to deprive the nation's courts of their ability to kill statutes on grounds of unconstitutionality. At the least, the C. I. O. will press for some such proposal as Mr. Roosevelt's, by which to free the Supreme Court of dangerously outworn economic theories and political prejudices.

There remain those planks for a prospective political platform whereby the C. I. O. could serve the great majority of citizens regardless of their relation to unionism.

1. *Taxation:* In its drive for a redistribution of the nation's wealth, the C. I. O. cannot afford to overlook the tax machinery, which may be controlled for the benefit of the whole economy. Higher levies on larger-than-average incomes, on inheritances, and on land values will be helpful in reducing some of the evils of concentration of wealth.

2. *Public ownership or control:* Private ownership of many vital industries works to the detriment of the entire population. Coal, electric power, banking, railway and marine transportation, telephones—all of these now operate in private hands to squander wealth either through restriction of output, direct wastage of natural resources, or governmental subsidy which goes largely into executive salaries. Hand in hand with this question goes the problem of conservation of natural resources, on which the New Deal has made an excellent beginning in its studies of America's physical wealth. But even such preliminary steps have already met with opposition from Democrats who represent the private interests involved.

Another important phase of this matter of ownership and control over industry has just begun to claim attention in the United States. Consumer co-operation holds considerable promise of relief from monopoly practices in consumers' goods. In England and Scotland, and the Scandinavian countries especially, co-operative ownership of food, clothing, fuel, and power enterprises has yielded a rich return by raising real incomes and educating thousands of citizens in economic and political democracy. Usually co-operators have worked closely with organized labor and progressive political groups to attain common ends. The

C. I. O. furnishes the one solid basis for the growth of consumer co-operation in this country.

3. *Farm relief:* Here again the New Deal has made a more determined and realistic effort than any previous administration. Its attempt to follow out the rather stupendous requirements indicated by Mr. Roosevelt's investigating committee, however, has been stultified at the outset by the prevailing tariff policy.

For generations farmers have swallowed the manufacturers' tale that tariff walls benefit agriculture as well as industry. An examination of the claim reveals its essential falsity. If tariffs on manufactured articles were reduced, prices of goods which farmers buy—textiles, fertilizers, machinery—would fall considerably, and large-scale importations would create buying power abroad for American farm produce. The net effect would be to remedy much of the present disparity between industrial and agricultural prices, and so increase farm incomes and the capacity of farmers to buy processed goods.

It is true that a small sector of agriculture—principally sugar, wool, hard wheat, and long-staple cotton—benefits from our present tariff structure; but the chief and fundamental crops of the American farm such as cotton, corn, eggs, pork, beef, wheat, hay, oats and other grains, need no protection and actually suffer under it. The danger to wage-earners in the few industries which require protection would be offset by the health of the economy as a whole, and by increased productivity in those industries which stand to gain most by tariff reduction: chiefly exporters of metals, and metal products such as automobiles and farm machinery.

Realizing this, Mr. Roosevelt and Secretary Hull have signed a good many reciprocal trade treaties with individual countries involving particular goods. Their efforts have been prodigious and the results encouraging; but such limited reduction fails to achieve a general lowering of commodity prices in this country, and moves little gold abroad.

4. *Good government:* Whether a progressive party built around labor would indulge in political favoritism and log-rolling remains a matter of speculation. Once in power, any group tends to fill appointive offices from its own ranks; but the question can only be considered realistically in terms of degree rather than absolutes. Such practices become venal and vicious in strict proportion with intellectual and moral bankruptcy; and the C. I. O.'s "must" program for the nation includes so many difficult problems that it will not be able to afford that drain upon its energies and reputation which political graft entails. Certainly the cause of good government could not suffer more acutely than at present, under the domination of two parties which find it so convenient to oil their machines with public money.

5. *War:* Finally, increased participation of labor in our national government would constitute the nation's best safeguard against international war. Workers and their organizations stand to lose more than anyone else by going to war. Conversely, those who own and profit from industry stand to gain from war's illimitable demands at the same time that most of them stay safely at home. It is the latter who now dominate the party system which in turn formulates foreign policy.

6.

The objectives here briefly outlined constitute a possible platform from which the C. I. O. can appeal for public support. But a platform presupposes a party organization. How soon will Lewis and his associates get one?

It may come sooner than most people expect. As in the settlement of our vast continent, in the creation of the world's most efficient industrial plant, in the urbanization of a once predominantly rural society, and in the current process of stabilizing industrial relations through collective bargaining, America may telescope into a few noisy, violent years a major social development which European nations took years to encompass.

Less than a year after its birth the C. I. O. assumed a role of decisive importance. In the presidential campaign of 1936, the United Mine Workers contributed a half-million dollars outright to Mr. Roosevelt and supplemented it with a loan of fifty thousand dollars more. Labor's Non-Partisan League—created by Lewis, Hillman, and Major George Berry—became a potent vote-getting organization in the President's behalf as well as in many a state contest.

The stage is set for the C. I. O. to step into a leading part. The quarrel between progressive and conservative elements in the Democratic party has become intense. The President makes no effort to conceal his hostility toward the southern bloc of Democrats and the isolated northern senators who have turned with such ferocity upon his program.

The prospect, then, based on the exigencies of the present political situation, on historical example, and on John Lewis's own ideas in the matter, is for the C. I. O. to step into the shoes of one of the two major parties. The two-party system will remain; but in place of Democrats and Republicans, voters will support either a liberal party in which the C. I. O. forms the central influence, or a conservative party dedicated to the restriction and perhaps the destruction of organized labor.

Rather than form a third party with the aim of working up to the stature required of a participant in a two-party system, Lewis will undoubtedly hold Labor's Non-Partisan League within the Republican-Democratic framework for the next three years. Locally, of course, the C. I. O. will frequently use independent or third-party tactics, because the New Deal has no place in many local Democratic machines. In some communities and states, where farmer-labor coalitions have already gained some strength, the League will fit into an active independent movement.

The League has set its task for 1938: to elect senators and representatives who will support the C. I. O.'s objectives, concentrating this effort on those states in which the unions are strongest. Lewis counts nine states predominantly pro-C. I. O.: New York, Pennsylvania, Ohio, Michigan, Illinois, West Virginia, Kentucky, Indiana and Wisconsin. In each of these except the last, one or more of the big C. I. O. unions form a large and cohesive nucleus. In Wisconsin the La Follette Progressive party will go to bat for Lewis. Further, the League looks for considerable influence in a dozen other states including Minnesota where the Farmer-Labor party is strong.

In these and other states the League is working night and day on permanent organizations "to throw the support of labor into channels where labor will be effective."

The American Labor Party, the League's New York State branch, has gone farther than any other labor group along the road to effective organization. In 1936 the A. L. P. polled three hundred thousand votes for Roosevelt and Governor Lehman, though but newly formed and lacking a party tradition. By July 1937 it

The Politics of the C. I. O. 263

felt strong enough to assume the leadership of Mayor La Guardia's campaign for re-election. The party combines group and individual memberships. Labor unions alone can join as organizational affiliates; and more than three hundred thousand unionists now pay per capita dues through their local units. In New York City the A. L. P. has formed some hundred district "clubs" for membership on a geographical basis, and similar units are being created upstate. A third form of membership has been arranged for sympathizers who do not wish to take active part, but will pay nominal yearly dues and support the party's candidates. In 1936 there were more than seventy thousand of these.

Labor's Non-Partisan League in New York is not a united-front group; it accepts the support but not the affiliation of radical parties, fearing a Communist label. It is not a farmer-labor party, though farmers who care to join through a district organization will of course be accepted. This latter situation varies from state to state. Most New York farmers are well-to-do, and indifferent if not antagonistic to organized labor. But in Minnesota, North Dakota, Washington, and to a lesser degree even in Pennsylvania, there exist groups of poor farmers who will work with League candidates, especially if these include farm-relief planks in their platforms.

The C. I. O. may also receive some votes from agricultural sections through its new affiliate, the United Cannery, Agricultural, Packing and Allied Workers of America—a union for wage-earners engaged in the production and processing of farm produce. Such a union, however, involves the danger of antagonizing farmers who employ even one "hand" during harvest season.

If Labor's Non-Partisan League attains reasonable success in municipal elections this autumn—as it has already in the Democratic primaries in Akron and

Canton, Ohio—and lives up to its possibilities in critical congressional contests a year hence, there can be little doubt that the Democratic party will split into conservative and liberal camps before the presidential race of 1940. Already Mr. Roosevelt has been freely quoted as hopeful of bringing Senator La Follette ("Young Bob") to the White House as his successor. If this idea alone does not suffice to drive conservative machine-Democrats over to the Republicans, John Lewis's strong insistence that Roosevelt revive the Supreme Court proposal and the Black-Connery wage and hours bill will almost surely turn the trick. Thus men and issues alike contrive to bring the C. I. O. to the center of the progressive movement in American politics.

The C. I. O. needs the strength and loyalty which the President commands. In turn, Mr. Roosevelt has no political friend as determined, bold, and powerful as John Lewis. Though the C. I. O. is straining for more speed ahead, Roosevelt and Lewis—if they maintain their respective directions—must travel the same road for some time to come.

The Labor Day pronouncements of the two men show the stresses placed upon this "alliance" by the recent steel strikes. The President poised himself on wings of lofty neutrality. "I am for you both if you'll be good" was the gist of his message to capital and labor, to Little Steel and the C. I. O., to Girdler and Lewis. It makes no sense in the context of his New Deal. It is remarkably blind to the brutality and illegality of the companies during this battle.

In trenchant words Lewis warned the President that he was forsaking his own program and betraying his own people: "Labor, like Israel, has many sorrows. Its women weep for their fallen and they lament for the future of the race. It ill behooves one who has supped at labor's table and who has been sheltered in labor's house to curse with equal fervor and fine impartiality both labor and its adversaries when they become locked in deadly embrace."

Yet it is premature to conclude that a break has come. The President, primarily a politician, may never reach the point of riding only one horse in one direction. He will find it as hard to split with the C. I. O. as to follow it. Lewis, primarily a labor man, may move toward conciliation as his understanding of society grows beyond the confines of the labor movement. The crucial factor, however, is the hardest to estimate: the instability of capitalism. An economic crisis within the next three years would render these differences of personality and inclination decisive, hastening the cleavage of classes, hastening the necessity to choose one road or another. Meanwhile Roosevelt and Lewis stand companionably undecided, waiting for history to make up their minds. And in this, be it remembered, they symbolize the tendencies of the American people themselves.

7.

The C. I. O. as a political instrumentality faces innumerable and annoying difficulties. The American tradition requires that candidates for important offices should already have served apprenticeships as county clerks, city prosecutors, or police magistrates. Although organized labor will do its best to fill such positions with friends or sympathizers, its major political effort cannot wait upon the observance of such convention; it must take its chances with voters' traditionalism and plunge ahead.

Getting into office will be one job; holding it another. The temptations incident to public position have often proved overpowering to labor's legislators, mayors, and governors. There is no reason to believe that the C. I. O.

will escape such sell-outs among its representatives. It must rely on the intelligence and loyalty which have so far characterized its leaders, and on an alert democracy within its own ranks.

A far more formidable obstacle than any of these specific considerations looms in its path, an animate force which the C. I. O.'s very successes will arouse to intensified fear and hostility: Fascism.

Fascism will never stem from the C. I. O.; it does not proceed out of labor movements. It arises in periods of economic dissolution and social decay to destroy them. Fascism becomes a possibility in America not because of the C. I. O. but because our society is suffering from a critical malaise whose cure it is the purpose of potential Fascists to resist.

Earlier in this chapter we referred briefly to certain changes which have rumbled for years beneath the surface of our national life. Few persons have given them serious attention, least of all the acknowledged business leaders who control our economy. Yet these changes constitute the revolutionizing of American society.

Technological progress year after year has increased our capacity to produce wealth. The decade of the twenties witnessed a spectacular acceleration of this movement—an acceleration that continued even during the depression. This basic change necessitates an increased rate of adaptation on the part of the whole economy; capital and labor must move more readily from declining to expanding industries; consumers must modify their demands and buy ever increasing amounts of goods; to do this the mass of the people must receive a rapidly augmented purchasing power.

Unfortunately another change—itself induced by technical advance—makes our economy less able to adapt itself in the direction required. Technology has wrought a profound transformation of industrial prop-

The Politics of the C. I. O.

erty, concentrating its control until "less than two hundred men are active in the top control of the big business and banking concerns which are the real center of our system. On what they do or don't do the welfare of forty-eight million others and their families depends." Forcing the enlargement of the scale of enterprise, this centralization of capital has necessitated a spectacular development of borrowed capital as the basis of its functioning, and correspondingly extended the area of fixed costs in industry. As its primary task the management of business protects these capital costs. Two consequences follow.

Both booms and depressions are intensified. Ownership soaks up the gains of our economy during prosperity, thus narrowing the base of consumer demand and making breakdown more certain. After a smash-up, the same ownership under the compulsion to shield fixed-income receivers throws the heaviest burdens upon the weaker and most poorly organized sections of the population: industrial workers through wage cuts and unemployment, and the rest of the consumers (notably small business men, salaried workers, and farmers) through price maintenance as incomes fall. This calamity is quite inevitable; it is not the result of personal malevolence. The logic of our economic system demands protection for the capital claims which have come to characterize our economic life—even though national impoverishment be the consequence.

Of course, such favors to owners eventually come home to roost. Profits and interest cannot forever be paid, unless goods are sold in larger quantities to the persons whom they have made unable to buy. Collapse is the net result. And each time such a collapse occurs, it imposes painful adjustments and arouses sharp social tensions which carry over in some measure to the next debacle.

268 C. I. O. Industrial Unionism in Action

A third revolutionary change, intensifying our growing sickness, is the decline in the rate at which population increases, modifying the nature of the market. Industry can no longer rely on growing numbers of consumers, hordes of immigrant workers, and the exploitation of a rich and empty continent to sustain its own prodigious powers of expansion. It must instead depend upon the enlarged demands of a relatively stable population—from which, however, ownership withholds the necessary rise of income by which such demand becomes effective. The fact that this change in population growth means more older people wanting work, with settled habits of consumption and high resistance to change, does not brighten an otherwise dour picture.

Finally, opportunities for men to become independent through their individual efforts have almost disappeared. Little is left of that American tradition except a blind and ignorant faith. Only ten out of a hundred persons gainfully employed today own their business. Nearly three-fourths of these are farmers who employ no "help," while a slim 3 per cent of the total are retail merchants. The independent proprietor is a vanishing species. As Mr. George Soule observes, "if you do not already own a business and want to engage in private enterprise, your choice is virtually limited nowadays to buying a farm or starting a retail shop in competition with the chain stores, or setting up another filling station or garage or beauty shop on still another corner." When the economic system jams, the individual by himself is able to do very little about it. He is an inseparable part of a distressed whole.

These changes cry out a warning that America has entered upon a revolutionary period, that a profoundly different pattern of life is in process of development.

All our "piety and wit" will not avert its appearance. Resistance to its realization, however, may provoke disaster.

The basic modification required is the progressive socialization of private property in industry, that individual ownership may not prevent (for its parochial interest) the long-range and immediate adjustments by which alone the *general* welfare may be achieved. The real interests of wage-earners, farmers, and middle class demand the necessary adaptations. For they are the people who suffer the fever of the cycle and the bitter chill of prolonged decline.

Resistance to this modification is strong, however, and will increase as economic troubles produce more general discontent. It springs fundamentally from a small group—those whose privileges as owners are substantial, who escape actual personal suffering when the system falters, whose vested interest in unabridged capitalism is such as to provoke them to reaction against change. Without hesitation they move to defend accustomed prerogatives.

Here, then, are irresistible force and immovable object. If the economy buckles more frequently in the future, those who suffer will become increasingly critical. Witless muddling and needless pain will excite a temper of restlessness; teachers, writers, and artists will depict more vividly the stupidities of such a state of affairs; the fundamental sanctions upon which capitalism rests will be called into question. As the impoverished and disillusioned make more insistent demands upon their government for aid, the masters of property and the recipients of large incomes, who pay considerable taxes, will bitterly oppose such inroads. As the workers of all classes grow in their understanding and press toward the modifications necessary to make life tolerable, the capitalists will—at some point—cease to acquiesce. Fearing democracy in the hands of their critics, they will reach out and strangle it. Economic power will arm itself with political despotism.

This is the essence of Fascism.

Despite our old and still vital tradition of democracy, it is not impossible to imagine Fascism appearing in America. The chief ingredients are already with us: large numbers of unemployed, diminishing opportunity for the individual, growing industrialization of the people, diminishing competence of the economy to do its job. The trappings generally affected by Fascism are also at hand in abundance: a bumptious national pride, racial scapegoats, habits of violence (lynching, industrial warfare, vigilante "law"—the Black Legion, Ku Klux Klan, organized criminals). The appropriate moment will select a leader.

Beneath hatreds of color and creed, patriotic slogans, uniforms, talk of Socialism, promises to aid the little man, and pretentious gestures toward industrial reorganization, Fascism always betrays itself—and will here—as a brutal attempt to preserve the privileges of the few major capitalists at the expense of human decency and the spirit and forms of democracy. Its first step to this end is invariably the destruction of all organizations critical of capitalism. Heading the list comes the labor movement, its unions and political parties.

John Lewis and his followers may meet Fascism on their way. The C. I. O. stands ultimately for everything opposed by such reaction, and its triumphs may stir Fascist attempt sooner than otherwise. For this reason some progressives oppose the movement, or at least its militancy.

But a collision of the labor movement and Fascist forces looms inevitable in any event. That rests upon the basic inconsistencies of our decadent economy. It may come soon; it may be postponed a generation or two. But to repeat and emphasize, it is not the labor movement that produces Fascism; it is the increasing inability of capitalism to give men a decent existence, and the consequent necessity for industrial ownership to bolster its interests by force against the efforts of the people to throw off an outworn form of social organization.

The possibility of a Fascist coup, therefore, should not discourage the C. I. O. from pursuing its program militantly and without interruption. But it should inspire a most earnest preparation for trouble ahead. Labor must study and learn. It must discipline itself. It must win the trust and co-operation of those millions who, whether they realize it or not, are riding to the same future.

X. PROBLEMS AHEAD

YES, the C. I. O. is a fact.

Its twenty months of life have witnessed a whirlwind of victories, marked by but one major defeat. No amount of Cassandra prophecies from those who hate or fear it can alter that record. No campaign of alternative vituperation or lofty indifference can change it.

What can be said of its immediate future, of its internal difficulties, or its relationship with the American Federation of Labor? A few short notes, primarily addressed to friends of the movement, may be in order.

The C. I. O.'s success has been the organization of millions. But can it hold them? The A. F. of L. could not: out of three who join two drop out. The C. I. O. can expect a high mortality rate, too: when early enthusiasm dies, the cheering gives way to routine, and employers' concessions or return of prosperity make workers forget the discontent that sent them unionwards. Too, the Lewis organization is particularly vulnerable to this kind of defection—since most of its new recruits comprise the less secure American workers. Semi-skilled or unskilled, they are not as well paid nor are their jobs as regular as those of the craftsmen, who have become the aristocrats of scarcity. Dues will not roll in to support the expensive systems of insurance which help the older unions hold their members. The very size of the great industrial unions will make it seem less imperative to individual members to contribute their share.

Problems Ahead 273

Again the C. I. O. has made at least two serious types of organizational blunders: leaders have at times neglected to consult the rank-and-file; and headquarters has sometimes needlessly ignored workers' prejudices in the selection of organizers. The Textile Workers Organizing Committee in New England casts each of these into high relief.

Recently in the course of a single week ten textile locals—old ones, too—voted to withdraw from the T. W. O. C. Some of these asked for and received A. F. of L. charters. Why this secession from the C. I. O., at the very flush of its drive?

They were piqued at being "pushed around"; and they didn't like the organizers. They had wakened one morning in the spring to find that their United Textile Workers' Union had, without consulting them or the other members throughout the country, handed itself over to the C. I. O., and transferred the membership with it like so much baggage. "High-handed action," they called it; and they resented it to the point of withdrawal.

In some of these communities, the workers bid by the T. W. O. C. were exclusively Gentile. The new textile union was headed by Jews. To the workers came an organizer, a devoted and highly intelligent union man, but a Jew. They viewed his coming stonily; they listened to his talks with suspicion. And finally, in their unreasoned anti-Semitism, they decided not to join. As one worker said, "They don't seem to realize we are Christians." In the same way, Catholic workers in Massachusetts towns have been unnecessarily antagonized when organizers who were known to be political radicals were sent to them. The clergy were quick to label them Communists and tell their congregations to have nothing to do with them—or with the C. I. O. The workers obeyed.

These are deplorable prejudices. A rationally-minded person is strongly tempted to challenge them whenever they arise. But they are dangerous prejudices too, and latent in the entire nation. To provoke them unnecessarily is to invite trouble. For they will not only obstruct specific efforts at organization; they will place the whole labor movement on the defensive for wholly incidental reasons. Already the A. F. of L. has begun waving the red shirt and yelling "Bolshevik!" and in a few localities their less responsible representatives have tried Jew-baiting to stop the C. I. O. They may make a few hits, but they're throwing boomerangs.

The C. I. O., however, is going to have some trouble with its own captains. Disagreements have broken out openly in the United Automobile Workers Union. Dissension smolders in other of the affiliated groups. It is even rumored in the high command itself. For the choice of leaders has not yet crystallized, and there are many candidates for preferment—candidates who differ on more important issues than temperament.

The situation in the Auto Union deserves a word; it's an indication of what may develop elsewhere. President Martin and Vice-President Mortimer oppose each other ostensibly on the question of union government. Martin wants control over the national officers, and a large measure of national control over the local units. Mortimer fights for local autonomy and greater independence of the officers.

It is the familiar political riddle: how much centralization can democracy stand and how much democracy can efficient government tolerate?

Martin thinks the size of the sprawling auto locals demands drastic modifications of the awkward town-meeting structure. What's more, he feels their relative irresponsibility to the national command has embarrassed him when they have broken contracts. It does not help him to realize that many of the violations were provoked by the management; it still looks just as bad in the press. Mortimer, however, wants the furthest possible extension of democracy within and without the locals.

But this is a superficial view of the issue. There is the matter of radicalism. The U. A. W. no more than the Rotary Clubs asks prospective members their political connections—before admitting them. Republicans, Socialists, Democrats, Prohibitionists—they all come in. But what is important in this intra-union conflict is that the Martin contingent believes that the Mortimer group represent the Communist wing and that they are anxious to proselyte. Such education, it appears, would be easier with considerable local autonomy and with friends on the Board.

This situation is nothing new in the labor movement, and there is no reason why one faction should expel the other. The political ideas involved need the freest and fullest discussion: a difficult liberty to administer, nonetheless.

But the Communists have gained in tolerance in the last few years. They are far more sympathetic with the "shortcomings" of the less radical members of the working class, and their determination to co-operate with all groups in resistance to Fascism may prevent them from becoming sufficiently obstreperous to win expulsion.

In Washington and elsewhere there are many stories about a split in Lewis's cabinet. Most of these loudly whispered rumors are merely wishful thinking. But some are not.

After the Steel strike the United Mine Workers, under Mr. Lewis's direction, issued a statement denouncing the local, state, and federal officials who remained silent and inactive during the conflict. Everyone knew that Franklin Roosevelt, although not named, was not omitted from the collective criticism.

It shocked some of the C. I. O. command—Sidney Hillman apparently among them. They found the statement a gratuitous and unwarranted attack upon the President. They feared it might alienate his favor. They believed it would pour fuel upon vigilante flames. In short: unjust, politically risky, socially dangerous. Mr. Lewis disagreed.

No revolt here or threats of secession, but a squall that might precede a bigger storm. For behind this controversy lurk sharp disparities of temperament. Lewis is by nature a fighter, whose punches are vigorous and rarely concealed. Sidney Hillman is a fighter, too. But his flair is for conciliation, negotiation. Lewis is less impressed with the necessity of keeping Roosevelt in good temper. He is more cynical about politicians, and has more confidence perhaps in the unaided strength of the workers he leads. Which makes him less fearful of the groundswell of middle-class hostility. Hillman, however, with a different background, and of a different race, is more sensitive to that incipient menace.

What may prove a dominant factor is that both men are exceedingly able. They're both leaders; but when two men are riding a horse, one of them has to sit behind. Hillman is riding pillion now, but there's no doubt that he—like some of the other first lieutenants—would find the saddle more comfortable. Yet the rumors overreach events. The strains between these men are far from sufficient to break the bond that holds them. They are as yet deeply and loyally attached to their original program.

More serious than leadership wrangles are certain specific deficiencies of organization. Money is short, far too short to do the things a full-fledged labor movement must do. But even were there adequate money, there is no assurance that the right things would be done. There is too little perception of their importance.

Local leaders are insufficiently trained. From every town comes that complaint. And training facilities are still pathetically inadequate. The C. I. O.'s publicity, with the distinguished exception of the Union News Service, is dangerously meager and poorly presented. For nothing was clearer in the recent strikes in Steel than the critical role played by the "neutral" public. The public can defeat strikes, twist government officials into partisans, effect the destruction of civil liberties. And as the Steel towns demonstrated, the "public" can be led to do all of these things if told that it is necessary and in the interests of "law and order."

Only accurate information regularly supplied can counteract this education. But the C. I. O. cannot swing it. It is not even equipped to keep its own strikers informed. In spite of strike meetings, bulletins, and editions of *Steel Labor,* Little Steel's workers proved easy targets for the barrage of propaganda that poured from the regular papers, and the town's orators. Communities became so thick with rumors that the workers did not know whether they were winning the strike or not. They were demoralized.

If this was true about the strikers, how much more true was it of people presumably not involved in the conflict. Effective "education" got them involved quickly enough.

The C. I. O. must somehow mend this gap in its armor. It must acquire a national newspaper of its own, to connect the worker not only with the labor movement but with the outside world of events. Such a paper must have a wide circulation among the middle classes and farmers, who are prepared to be sympathetic with the labor movement if they are but given an understanding of it. As matters stand now their knowledge comes from anti-labor sources. And that tells in the crises.

The C. I. O. needs a good many things, but few more than workers' education: not only to train workers how to manage their organizations, but to inform them of the kind of world they live in. They need to learn what their labor movement is, why it has existed in all capitalistic countries, where it is going, what the hurdles in its path will be. A few of the C. I. O. unions have always maintained ambitious programs, and notably the garment union. The U. A. W. has also initiated an extensive project. But the C. I. O. as a whole has given little evidence of concern for these activities. No exploration of educational needs has been made.

If publicity and educational arms are needed, so too is research. It is a shock to discover that the labor movement still retains so few economists, statisticians, and lawyers. It was understandable enough in the past. Unions lived a hand-to-mouth existence. They muddled along. But now they need the aid of specialists if they are to negotiate intricate questions with the best brains industry has to offer. They can no longer rely on a rule-of-thumb knowledge and a flair for bargaining.

What the C. I. O. needs is a research organization, with regional offices and staffs to assemble and analyze regularly the relevant facts about the companies and industries with which it deals, to explore the industrial make-up of the country, the conditions of the working class, the nature of the secular influences that are molding their lives. Section by section, the nation should be drawn under its microscope. And particularly if the C. I. O. plans extensive political forays, they must be fortified with studies of taxation, money and banking, social insurance, technological change, investment—all of them intricate problems, whose solution is critical for the workers and for the nation. The C. I. O. needs its own Fabians to blueprint the future. Without them the whole movement is wrapped in blinders.

Among the C. I. O. adherents there is a disposition to dismiss the A. F. of L. as of little further significance in the labor movement. Nothing could be more foolish or more fatal. The Federation has great survival powers. Its center is sturdy. Its well-paid craft members are loyal. They have the advantage of long experience in collective bargaining and union discipline. In many cities and states they *are* the labor movement. They have working agreements with government officials. They control machinery by which labor opinion is expressed. Their Washington lobby is one of the strongest. And under the stimulation of the C. I. O. drive, the Federation has found a vitality of its own.

In short, the A. F. of L. can still put up a magnificent fight against the C. I. O. and is prepared to. But why should they? It would be foolish of course to say that the issue that split the Federation was not a real one. The antagonism of many craftsmen to industrial unionism is built upon deep conviction.

Yet the basic character of the division should not obscure the unity of interest which comprehends all workers, industrialist and craft alike. Less obvious than the bond between craftsmen, it is more fundamental. All workers stand in the same relation to income-producing property: they have none. They earn their living on the job. They are the defenseless victims of business depressions. They are defrauded by legislation protecting industrial and financial monopoly, and by the inadequacy of laws providing security for the poor. They all need the guarantee of civil liberties. And they all face the same foes. The forces that attack the C. I. O. today with its unskilled workers will tomorrow attack the A. F. of L. with its skilled, whenever the tensions in our society drive property to defend its profits at the expense of democracy.

In all fairness the Federation must bear the chief brunt for bisecting the labor movement. At no point did it show capacity for intelligent compromise, and since its suspension order, it has added bitterness to stupidity. It has ordered its city and state affiliates to expel the C. I. O. unions. Some of its units have boycotted products made by the Lewis followers. Others have broken all jurisdiction restraints to prevent the C. I. O.'s gaining adherents. They have even entered into collusive contracts with employers to close out their rivals, when it meant the essential defeat of unionism of any kind. They have attacked their recent associates as Communists, as racketeers, as members of an alien race. Most recently without warrant they have officially criticized the National Labor Relations Board as partisan to the C. I. O.; can it be said that the grapes they expected have turned sour?

Inevitably the C. I. O. has retaliated; chiefly with verbal blows aimed at the ineptitude and hypocrisy of their opponents. They have whipped out in anger words that will continue to rankle, give old suspicions new life, and form fresh hatreds. A tragic waste, a pitiful deflection of men from the purposes for which their organizations exist.

But it is not too late. If the ground were carefully prepared the C. I. O. could still be admitted to the Federation, *with full freedom to carry on the work it has begun.* Naturally such a move would be fought by strong groups and a few influential leaders of the Federation, by all those who fear loss of power, loss of jobs,

Problems Ahead 281

loss of dues-paying members. Nor would the opposition parade in its true dress. It would probably muster an old one for the occasion: the uniform of the Defenders of American Institutions from the depredations of Lewis-led Communists. The drums would beat a music congenial to the ears of Dr. Frey.

Yet compromise would have its friends. There are still a great many in the A. F. of L. who consider the present duality an absurd and dangerous state of affairs. And there are C. I. O. leaders and members who agree.

Some, of course, consider any effort at reunion hopeless from the start and still others fear that its price would be concessions that would alienate the newly-enrolled millions. Perhaps the most powerful factor in the situation is Lewis himself. He has opposed such an overture, and with much reason. But behind his logic may lurk a rather human determination no longer to be subordinate to men whom he has come to despise. And these men would not enjoy serving under Lewis, now that so much muddy water has flowed under the bridge.

But the issue at stake warrants a degree of effort not hitherto expended by either side. If some measure of peace is not soon achieved *A. F. of L.* hostility will become crystallized. Expulsion of the now suspended unions may follow. Which means war on all fronts. And dog will eat dog to no one's benefit but that of their mutual enemies.

If the A. F. of L. will not stretch out a conciliatory hand, the C. I. O. must. It would be a gesture not without dignity and in no sense disloyal to its recent achievements. Already it has brought American unionism to the threshold of a new maturity, and its emergence as a democratic force has heartened the liberal movements of all Europe. Now it has the opportunity to draw upon that maturity and that democracy to weld the trade unions of the United States into a unity once more.

Is it too much to ask the C. I. O., with so many distinguished victories won, to muster a pride too big for rancor and a statesmanship equal to the attainment of peace within the labor movement?

NOTES ON SOURCES

The facts concerning the conflict at the South Chicago Republic Steel plant were taken from the *Report* of the Senate Committee prepared under the chairmanship of Mr. Robert La Follette, and published in the New York *Times* for July 22, 1937. All direct quotations are from this document. An extraordinarily vivid account of the affair, as registered by the Paramount News camera, appeared in the St. Louis *Post Dispatch* on June 16.

* * *

The historical review in Chapter II is based on well-known materials: Commons, John R., and Associates, *History of Labor in the United States*, Vols. I and II; Perlman, Selig, and Taft, Philip, *History of Labor in the United States, 1896-1936*; Ware, Norman, *Labor Movement in the United States, 1860-95;* Ware, N., *Labor in Modern Industrial Society;* Wolman, Leo, *Ebb and Flow in Trade Unionism;* Lorwin, Louis, and Wubnig, A., *Labor Relations Boards;* Taft, Philip, "The Problem of Structure in American Labor Unions," *American Economic Review*, March 1937; *International Juridical Association Monthly Bulletin*, August 1936; American Federation of Labor, *Proceedings* of the annual conventions; A. F. of L., *Executive Council in the Matter of Charges Filed by the Metal Trades Department against the Committee for Industrial Organization*, and *Conference of Representatives of National and International Unions*, Cincinnati, May 24-25, 1937. The schism between the A. F. of L. and the C. I O. was well reported in the N. Y. *Times, The New Republic,* and *The Nation.*

* * *

The descriptive material on the steel industry was drawn largely from Mr. Harvey O'Connor's well-packed book, *Steel Dictator,* and *Economics of the Iron and Steel Indus-*

try by Professor Carroll Daugherty and others. The strike of 1919 is ably reported in the former and in Yellen, Samuel, *American Labor Struggles.* For the C. I. O. organization drive and the strike against Little Steel, the following daily newspapers were consulted: New York *Times,* N. Y. *Herald Tribune, Daily Worker,* Youngstown *Vindicator,* Johnstown *Tribune* and *Democrat.* Mr. Benjamin Stolberg's article in *The Nation,* July 31, 1937, was very helpful. Union publications, especially the C. I. O. *Union News Service,* were useful. Most important were interviews with union leaders and business men in the strike area, during and prior to the strike.

* * *

For material in the first part of Chapter IV I am indebted to Dunn, Robert, *Labor and Automobiles,* and Muste, A. J., *The Automobile Industry and Organized Labor.* The financial and commercial structure of the larger companies was read from their annual reports to stockholders. The N. R. A. report on labor conditions in the industry, prepared under the direction of Mr. Leon Henderson, was useful. For the discussion of the strikes, the New York *Times, Daily Worker,* and the Detroit *Free-Press,* as well as the journal of the United Automobile Workers, were consulted. Many persons throughout the automobile section of the country were interviewed. The United States Bureau of Labor Statistics, *Handbook of Labor Statistics,* provided many of the figures for this and the preceding chapters.

* * *

Chapter V depended on N. Y. *Times* accounts of union activities, interviews with union officials, and official material provided by union offices. I was much assisted, in the discussion on textiles, by an unpublished undergraduate Honors Thesis written by Mr. Joseph Share, Harvard 1937. Pell, Orlie, *The Office Worker—Labor's Side of the Ledger,* proved useful.

* * *

The discussion in Chapter VI on labor and law is based upon the *Decisions* of the National Labor Relations Board,

Notes on Sources 285

the *Annual Reports* of the National Mediation Board, the Senate Committee *Hearings* on the National Labor Relations Act, the decisions of the Supreme Court in the several cases brought before it under this Act, and the *Congressional Record*. Professor C. Magruder's article, "Development of Collective Bargaining," *Harvard Law Review* (50) at page 1071, is excellent. Edwin E. Witte, "British Trade Union Law Since the Trade Dispute and Trade Union Act of 1927," *American Political Science Review* (26), pp. 345-51, is valuable. The sit-down strike as a union tactic is reviewed by Mr. Joel Seidman in a pamphlet entitled "The Sit-Down." Mr. Adamic's article in *The Nation*, December 5, 1936, at page 652, is very suggestive.

* * *

The *Decisions* of the National Labor Relations Board were important in the preparation of Chapter VII, especially those on the Remington Rand and International Harvester cases. "Truth Will Out," a report issued by the Joint Committee of Remington Rand Employees' Association, April 3, 1937, and the *Labor Relations Bulletin* of the National Association of Manufacturers, April 12, 1937 (19), were read on the Remington Rand case. A rich source of information on employers' associations and industrial espionage is the *Hearings* of the Subcommittee of the Committee on Education and Labor of the U. S. Senate, appointed to investigate violations of civil liberties. The Committee has been sitting intermittently during the past year.

* * *

The sources for the discussion in Chapter VIII are many. Primarily the following were used: Slichter, Sumner H., "Notes on Collective Bargaining," in *Explorations in Economics*, "Adjustment to Instability," *American Economic Review Supplement*, March 1936, and his book, *Toward Stability*; Soule, George, "The Maintenance of Wages," *Proceedings, Academy of Political Science*, January 1932; Hansen, A. H., "Capital Goods and the Restoration of Purchasing Power," *Proceedings, Acad. Pol. Science*, April 1934;

Keynes, John M., *General Theory of Employment, Interest, and Money.* Mr. Keynes' book is an important one. With it I find myself largely in agreement. Through its emphasis upon expectations, it provided the theory upon which the all-too-brief discussion of the complicated subject of this chapter rests. Mr. Keynes' book has been subjected to energetic and penetrating criticism in all the standard journals on economics. These articles should be studied by one wishing to go further with the theory.

* * *

Chapter IX is indebted to Mr. George Soule's excellent book, *The Coming American Revolution,* and Mr. Nathan Fine's *Labor and Farmer Parties in the United States.* The literature put out by the various political parties, the would-be parties, and Labor's Non-Partisan League was reviewed.

INDEX

Adamic, Louis, 176
A. F. of L. company unions, 198, 212-213
Aluminum Workers of America, 156
American Federation of Labor, 14-15, 16 ff., 22-23, 24, 25-31, 31-34, 37-40, 41 ff., 45, 47, 51, 96-97, 121, 139, 141-143, 151-152, 154, 155, 157-158, 160, 174, 178, 183, 185, 198, 203, 212-216, 249, 252-253, 272-274, 279 ff.
American Iron and Steel Institute, 63, 68, 75, 199
American Labor Party, 255-256, 262-263
American Labor Union, 24
American Newspaper Guild, 152-153, 157
American Sheet and Tin Plate Company, 51
Andrews, John, 108
Anti-unionism, 69, 74, 77, 78 ff., 82 ff., 96, 109 ff., 113, 134, 136-137, 146, Ch. VII
Architects, Engineers, Chemists, and Technicians, 156
Automobile Industrial Workers Association, 30
Automobile industry, 97; significance, 98; size, 98-99, 102; status of workers, 103-110
Automobile workers, early organization, 97; nature of work, 103; earnings, 103-104; instability of employment, 104-105; speed-up, 105; youth of, 106; incentive pay, 106; espionage, 107
Automobile Workers, Associated, 30

Automobile Workers, United, 45, 76, 97, 114, 116-118, 122, 125-126, 130-131, 133-138, 159, 172, 177, 274-275, 278

"Back to work," 81, 84, 85
Bassham, Pearl, 200
Bennett, Harry, 132
Berry, Major George, 261
Bethlehem Steel Corporation, 60-61, 71, 75, 78 ff., 93
Bittner, Van A., 44, 70, 94, 163
Black, Judge, 112-114
Blast Furnace and Coke Oven Workers Union, 213
"Blue Card" Union, 212
Bookkeepers, Stenographers, and Accountants, 151
Boot and Shoe Workers Union, 157
Boote, Reginald, 211, 219 ff.
Brewery Workmen, United, 24-25, 28, 157
Bridges, Harry, 141, 142, 157, 164
Brophy, John, 37, 94, 160
Broun, Heywood, 152
Browder, Earl, 39
Brown, Thomas, 37
Brubaker, Howard, 153
Building Trades Alliance, 26
Building Trades Department, 26
"Bull's Run," Battle of, 117
Burns Detective Agency, 81
Business cycle, 236 ff.

Calzada, Fulgencio, 89
Campbell, Judge, 127
Campbell, Lawrence, 80, 228
Cannery, Agricultural, Packing and Allied Workers, United, 263

Captive coal mines, 78
Carey, James, 163-164
Carnegie, Andrew, 49
Carnegie-Illinois Corporation, 74, 76, 93
Carnegie Steel Company, 48-50
Carpenters' union, 35, 158
"Chicago Massacre," 11-14, 91
Chrysler Motor Company, 99, 120; size, 102; espionage, 108-110; strike, 126-129
Chrysler, Walter, 126, 127, 128-129
Citizens' Committees, 78 ff., 82 ff., 84 ff., 87 ff., 90, 96, 118, 123, 136-137, 140, 198, 216 ff., 277
Clerks, 148-149, 158
Closed shop, 171-173
Clothing Workers, Amalgamated, 29, 37, 46, 147, 159-160
Collective bargaining, 72, 111, 119, 126, 171, 190, 193
Committee for Industrial Organization, 14, 15, 17 ff., 20, 37-41, 45-46, 67 ff., 73-75, 81-82, 93-94, 97, 112, 114, 120-121, 129, 139 ff., 156 ff., 158 ff., 166 ff., 174, 178, 184-186, 195, 197-199, 213-215, 228, 229, 235-237, 243, 247-248, 252-253, 254 ff., 260 ff., 270-271, 272 ff.
Communications Association, American, 156
Communist Party, 25, 39, 263, 275
Company unions, 65-66, 70, 72, 109, 127, 143, 198, 207 ff., 212 ff.
Conemaugh and Black Lick Railroad, 78
Consolidated Edison Company, 213
Consumer's co-operation, 258-259
Corporations Auxiliary, 55, 108-110, 204 ff.
Cost-of-living, index for wages, 71-72
Cotton Textile Institute, 145
Crawford, E. R., 61
Crawford, George, 61

Curley, Captain Harry, 88
Curran, Joe, 141, 142, 158, 164

Davey, Governor, 83, 85, 92, 95
De Leon, Daniel, 24
Democracy in unions, 274-275
Die Casting League, National, 156
Dualism, 39, 41
Dubinsky, David, 32, 37, 42, 44, 46
Dues-dodgers, 173
Du Pont family, 100

Earle, Governor, 50, 80, 91-92, 171, 185
Economic change, 245-247
Electric Railway and Motor Coach Employees, 142-143
Electrical Workers, Brotherhood, 40, 117
Elser, Sheriff, 83
English unions, 193-194
Espionage, 55, 81, 107-110, 111, 198, 203 ff., 206-207
Evans, Sidney D., 80

Fagan, Patrick, 49
Fairless, Benjamin, 72, 74
Farm relief, 259
Farmer-Labor Party, 254 ff., 263
Fascism, 266 ff.
Fear, 70-71, 166-171
Federal Employees, National Federation, 154
Fiig, George, 79
Finances of unions, 277
Firestone Rubber Company, 140
Fitch, John A., 50
Flat Glass Workers, American, 40, 44, 114, 119, 125
Flint Alliance, 115-116, 118, 119, 121, 122
"Flying Squadron," 135
Ford, Henry, 103, 105, 129, 132-133
Ford Motor Company, 99, 101, 102, 120
Foster, William Z., 24, 28, 51 ff.

Index

Frankensteen, Richard, 107-109, 131-132, 138
Fremming, Harvey C., 37
Frey, John, 32, 33, 45, 117, 215, 281
Frick, Henry, 49, 197-198
Fur Workers Union, 157

Gadola, Judge Paul V., 123
Garment Workers, International Ladies, 29, 32, 37, 159-160
Gary, Judge, 52
Geis, Carl, 79
General Motors Corporation, 73, 77, 93, 99, 100, 101, 109, 110-127
Girdler, Tom, 61, 63, 72, 75 ff., 91-92, 167, 171, 190
Golden, Clinton, 44, 76-77, 163, 166
Gompers, Samuel, 18, 25, 26, 47, 51, 52, 53, 252
Good government, 260
Goodyear Rubber Company, 139-140
Government, and unions, 49, 52, 120, 170, 184 ff.
Government Employees, American Federation, 154
Government workers, 154
Grace, Eugene M., 61, 63, 66, 75-76, 91
Green, Leon, 184
Green, William, 16-17, 26-27, 30, 37-39, 40, 42-45, 96, 125, 139, 160, 178
Guaranty Trust Company, 75
Guffey, Senator, 50
Guffey Coal Bill, 185
"Guild Shop," 153

Hapgood, Powers, 164
Hardie, Keir, 255
Harlan County Coal Operators' Association, 199-200
Harris, T. K., 84
Hatters, Cap, and Millinery Workers, United, 37, 44, 155, 157

Haywood, "Big Bill," 25
Heckman, S. H., 78
Henderson, Leon, 103, 106
Hillman, Sidney, 37, 147, 162 ff., 261, 276
Hoffman, U. S. Representative, 212
Hoffman, Warren, 85
Homestead, steel strike 1892, 27, 48 ff.
Hotel and Restaurant Employees International Alliance, 158
Hours, steel, 59-60
Howard, Charles P., 32, 37, 44, 157, 159, 163, 216
Hughes, Mr. Justice, 184
Hull, Secretary, 259-260
Human costs, 232-233

Independent Federation of Independent Unions, 211
Individualism, 17, 196-198
Industrial Relations Councillors, Inc., 66
Industrial Workers of the World, 24; membership, 25; strikes, 25; character, 25; war and criminal syndicalism, 25, 54
Injunction, 112-114, 123, 127, 194
Inland Steel Corporation, 75, 91
Interchurch World Movement, 54-56
Interlake Iron Corporation, 213
International Harvester Company, 208 ff.
Irvin, President, 63, 75, 76

Jones, C. R., 82
Jones and Laughlin Steel Co., 61, 69, 71, 74, 167-170
Journalists, 152
Jurisdictional disputes, 26

Kennedy, Thomas, 49
Knights of Labor, 20, 21-23, 47, 252

290 C. I. O. Industrial Unionism in Action

Knudsen, William S. 110, 111, 115, 118, 119, 120, 123, 125

Labor Board, Railway, 52
Labor's Non-Partisan League, 261, 262-263
Labor, U. S. Department of, 60
Labor Union Racket, 205
La Follette Committee on Civil Liberties, 13, 107 ff., 186, 199 ff.
La Follette, Senator Robert, 262, 264
La Guardia, Mayor, 255, 263
Lamont, Thomas, 73, 75, 76
Landis, James, 181-182
Leadership, 137-138, 161-164, 274 ff.
League for Industrial Rights, 198
Leather Workers, National, 156
Lehman, Governor, 262
Lever, Jack, 163
Lewis, John L., 17, 29, 32, 33, 36, 37-38, 40-43, 46, 68-69, 72-74, 92, 94, 118-119, 120-121, 123-125, 127-129, 139, 141, 155, 158-162, 248-249, 261 ff., 270, 275-276, 281
Lewis, J. C., 32
Libbey-Owens-Ford, 114
"Little Siberia," 166, 169
"Little Steel," 75 ff., 139, 190, 227-228
Loichot, R. W., 85
Longshoremen and Warehousemen's Union, 156, 157
Lowell, A. Lawrence, 182
Lundberg, Harry, 141

MacDonald, David, 44, 94
Machinists, International Association, 117, 142-143, 201
Magruder, Professor C., 182
Mahoning Valley Citizens' Committee, 83
Management, industrial, 234
Marine and Shipbuilding Workers, 156
Marine Engineers Beneficial Association, 156

Mark, James, 82, 94
Marlin, General William, 88
Martin, Francis C., 80
Martin, Homer, 111, 128, 134, 137-138, 163, 274-275
Mayo, John, 94
McCuskey, E. A., 85
McKeesport Tin Plate Company, 61
McMahon, Thomas F., 37
Mechanics Educational Society, 30
Mees, The Rev. Oscar, 85
"Memorial Day Massacre," 11-14, 91
Metal Trades Association, 198, 200 ff.
Metal Trades Department, 26, 32, 117, 215
Meyers, Carl, 87-88
Mine, Mill, and Smelter Workers, International 32, 37
Mine Workers, United, 16-17, 28, 29, 32, 34, 37, 40, 49, 77, 94, 159, 164, 261
Miners, Western Federation of, 24-25
Mitch, William, 71
Mohawk Valley Formula, 225-227
Molly Maguires, 20
Molyneux, The Rev. P., 53-54
Morgan, "House" of, 73, 75, 100
Morrison, Secretary Frank, 157
Mortimer, Wyndham, 35-36, 137-138, 274-275
Murphy, Governor Frank, 91, 118-119, 122, 125-126, 127-128, 133, 185
Murray, Philip, 34, 39, 40, 44, 68, 70, 77, 94, 138, 163, 166, 170
Myrup, A. A., 32

National Association of Manufacturers, 198
National Erectors' Association, 198
National Founders Association, 198
National income, Ch. VIII, 229-

Index 291

National Income (cont'd)
  230; C.I.O. and secular trends,
  230 ff.; and cyclical trends,
  236 ff.; and economic change,
  245 ff.
National Industrial Conference
  Board 208
National Industrial Council, 198
National Industrial Recovery Act
  (N. R. A.), 28-30, 63-64, 67, 132,
  145, 185, 188, 208, 251
National Labor Relations Board,
  67, 74, 87, 91, 94, 118, 130-133,
  140, 142, 183, 186, 187 ff., 202,
  208 ff., 216 ff., 251, 257
National Maritime Union, 141-142,
  158
National Mediation Board, 187
National Steel Co., 60-61, 71
"New Deal," 62, 63, 109, 185,
  249 ff., 253-256, 259
Nist, Joseph, 86
Non-Partisan League, 254-255

O'Connor, Harvey, 57
Office and Professional Workers,
  United, 151
Office workers, 150-152
Oil Field, Gas Well, and Refinery Workers, 37

Perkins, Secretary, 91, 121, 181
Picketing, 11, 12, 80, 86, 123, 194,
  202
Pinkerton Detectives, 48, 109
Pittsburgh Plate Glass, 114
Political action, 135-137
Political implications of the
  C.I.O., 248 ff.; political objections, 256 ff.; political difficulties, 265 ff.
Porter, Russell B., 116
Postal authorities, and strikes, 90
Powers, Frank, 32
Price policies, 58, 63-64, 245
Professional workers, 148-155

Public ownership, 258
Purnell, President, 76, 91

Quill, Michael, 142-143

Racketeering, 195
Radio Workers, United and Electrical, 39, 40, 158
Railway Act 1926, 187, 188, 190
Railway Adjustment Board, 187-188
Railway Brotherhoods, 172
Rapid Transit Employees Association, 143
"Red-baiting," 214-216, 273-274
Remington Rand case, 216 ff.
Republic Steel Corporation, 11-14,
  61, 71, 75-76, 85, 87, 90, 94
Research, 278-279
Retail Employees, United, 156
Reuther, Walter, 131
Riggs, Mrs. Walter L., 62
Rockefeller, John D., Jr., 197, 207-208
Roosevelt, President, 65, 83, 91,
  92, 93, 111, 120-121, 123-124,
  155, 185-186, 205, 249 ff., 254,
  259-260, 261, 262, 264-265, 276
Rubber industry, 139-140
Rubber Workers, United, 45,
  139-40
Runciman, Walter, 73
Rutledge, George C., 228
Ryan, Joe, 141, 142

Sailors' Union of the Pacific, 141-142
Salaries, steel executives, 61
Savings, national, 235-236
Sayre, Secretary, 201, 203
Schechter case, 67, 145
Schwab, Charles, 61
Securities Exchange Commission, 61
Seniority, 231 ff.
Sewak, Michael J., 80
Sherman Service, 55

292　C. I. O. Industrial Unionism in Action

Shields, Mayor Daniel, 79, 80, 82
Shipping industry, 140-142
Shoe Workers, United, 156
Sit-down, 112, 113, 115, 119, 122-123, 127-129, 140, 175 ff., 186
Slichter, S. H., 237 ff.
Sloan, William, 113, 120-121, 171
Social security, 256
Social Security Act, 202
Socialist Trades and Labor Alliance, 24
Society of Designing Engineers, 109
Sole bargaining right, 115, 124-126, 127, 172
Speed-up, 105-107, 231-232
Sproul, Governor, 54
Stanton, The Rev. John H., 79, 228
Stark, Louis, 44, 71
State, County and Municipal Workers, 155
Steel industry, 19, 51 ff., 56 ff., 59 ff., 63-64, 65 ff., 67, 69, 75 ff.
Steel Labor, 70
Steel Mediation Board, 83, 91
Steel, U. S. Corporation, 19, 51 ff., 56-58, 60, 62, 66-67, 72-74, 97
Steel Workers, Amalgamated Association, 19, 27, 30-31, 41-44, 48, 50 ff., 56, 67, 69
Steel Workers Organizing Committee, 11-15, 43, 44, 68 ff., 73, 74, 76 ff., 81-84, 92-95, 139, 160, 166-171, 185
Stevenson, John, 78
Stolberg, Benjamin, 73, 93
Supreme Court, 189 ff., 257
Suspension of C.I.O. unions, 45-46, 157
Sweeney, Vincent, 44
Switter, Stanley, 87-88

Taxation, 258
Taxi-drivers, 143
Taylor, Myron, 62, 72-74, 91
Teamsters' Union, 143
Textile industry, 144-147

Textile Workers Organizing Committee, 147, 160, 273
Textile Workers, United, 37, 146-147, 273
Third Party, 261 ff.
Thomas, Ray, 83
Tighe, Michael, 30, 31, 41, 43, 52, 56, 65, 67-68
Timko, Joe, 167-169
Tobin, Daniel, 141
Toledo Auto Lite, 110
Toledo Chevrolet, 110
Townsend, Governor, 91
Transport industry, 142-143
Transport Workers' Union, 142-143, 158
Tri-State Metal, Mine, and Smelter Workers Union, 213
Typographical Union, International, 32, 37, 155, 157, 164

Ullman, Carl, 83
Unemployment, steel, 61; autos, 104
Unger, Adolph, 85
Union membership, chart, 156
Unions, craft-industrial, 18-19, 22-23, 26, 29-39, 55; racial antagonism, 94; irresponsibility, 129, 133-134; stewards, 135; labor parties, 135-137; government, 164-165; Tactics, Ch. VI; membership records, 168; literature, 169-170; mass meetings, 170-171; collective bargaining, 171-173; strikes, 173 ff.; sit-down, 175 ff., appeal to law, 184 ff.; incorporation, 191-192; publication of finances, 192; outlawing strikes, 192; English practices, 193-194; racketeering, 195
United Front, 263
Unity in the labor movement, 36
Unthank, Ben, 199

Vadios, Nick, 89
Vandenberg, Senator, 128

Index

Vigilantes, 78 ff., 82 ff., 84 ff., 87 ff., 90, 96, 118, 123, 136-137, 140, 198, 216 ff., 277

Wages, steel workers, 59-62, 69, 71; auto workers, 103-104; national scales, 146
Wages and hours, 256-257
Wages and Hours Bill, 185
Wagner, Robert F., Senator, 50, 128
Wagner Act—*see* National Labor Relations Board
Walsh-Healey Act, 73, 185, 202
War, 260
Ward, George, 199
Watkins, David, 78, 79, 94
Weir, E. T., 61, 63

Welsheimer, The Rev. P. H., 85
Wharton, A. O., 39, 215
Wilson, Woodrow, 52
Wisconsin Federation of Labor, 45
Wolff Packing company cases, 193
Woll, Matthew, 32
Woodworkers Federation, 156
Workers' education, 135, 278

"Yellow-dog" contracts, 194
Young, Arthur, 66, 67
Youngstown Sheet and Tube Corporation, 75

Zaritsky, Max, 37

For Product Safety Concerns and Information please contact our EU representative GPSR@taylorandfrancis.com
Taylor & Francis Verlag GmbH, Kaufingerstraße 24, 80331 München, Germany

www.ingramcontent.com/pod-product-compliance
Lightning Source LLC
Chambersburg PA
CBHW052031300426
44116CB00024B/1236